A MEMOIR (

Fortunate

Isle

RONALD MACKAY

PlashMill Press

Published in 2017 by PlashMill Press, Friockheim, Scotland.

ISBN: 978-0-9572612-8-0

All photographs: Ronald Mackay

Map courtesy http://ontheworldmap.com/spain/islands/tenerife/ map-of-tenerife-island.html

Printed by IngramSpark

Dedication

Lutgarda Méndez Hernández (1902-2001), for providing insight, care and encouragement. The entire Méndez family who ran la Pension Méndez, known simply as 'la fonda' -- especially Pastora, Obdúlia, Angélica, Lula and all their children. The municipality of Buenavista del Norte and its villagers who welcomed me. The island of Tenerife and its sister-islands in the Canaries. All of you contributed to this story.

Pearl Mackay Sword (1913-1998), my mother, for everything.

Viviana Galleno Zolfi, my wife, for suggesting this memoir and for her love.

Acknowledgments to:

Viviana; Euan and Mary; Vivian and John; Denise Morel; Major Donald Howson and Drew Monkman: for reassurance as I wrote.

Diane Taylor whose insightful workshop and book introduced me to memoir.

Rod Fleming: for critical advice after I was so presumptuous as to think I'd finished.

Nayra Segovia, granddaughter of Angélica, great-granddaughter of Doña Lutgarda, for assisting with names.

I blame my memory for any errors or omissions. Please tell me: mackay.ronald@gmail.com

Contents

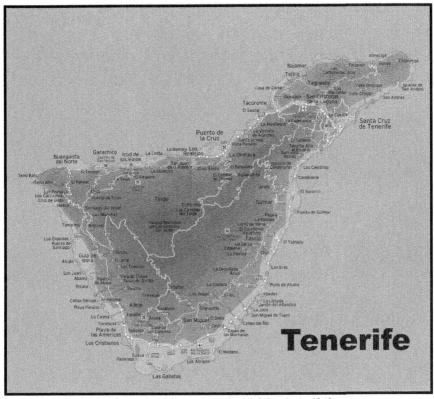

A current map of Tenerife. Many of the roads marked didn't exist in 1960.

1. Arrival in the Canary Islands: Las Palmas

The author on his way to the Canary Islands.

Well before dawn I was up on the lower deck, eager to get my first glimpse of the Canary Islands as the *Ciudad de Cádiz* approached Gran Canaria. Waiting in the slowly fading darkness, two things I knew about the Canaries came to mind. The first was that Las Palmas was always the initial port-of-call after the six-month furlough that my Aunty Lilian and Uncle Fred enjoyed every three years in Dundee. They sailed from Liverpool initially to Nigeria from 1945 to 1947 and after that to Nyasaland in East Africa on one of the Elder Dempster passenger-cargo liners. Uncle Fred's quiet claim, "Gran Canaria is where Lili and I will retire when my time's up in Nyasaland!" was always met by silent, pursed lips on Lilian's part and a sparkling interest by my mother, Pearl. When, once, I found courage enough to ask Uncle Fred "Why?" he answered, "The Canaries are semi-tropical. It never gets really cold there. Besides, it reminds me just enough of Britain to stop us from being homesick." I thought his use of the first-person plural, given Lili's hostile silence, us was overly optimistic. His use of the term 'semi-tropical', however, had captured my imagination, and now I was determined not to miss my first taste of the tantalising vision it held for

1

me just for the sake of a few hours' sleep.

The second thing I remembered was that all the bananas I had ever bought from Mr Grimmond, our green-grocer in Dundee, came from the Canary Islands. Every Saturday morning I did the shopping – until I was 12, that is, and found a paying weekend job and the weekly shopping fell to my brother Euan. Right there in Grimmond's at the top of Graham Street, I would stand in the Saturday-morning queue and wait my turn. The smells varied with the season – feathery, new potatoes from Cyprus or Egypt in early summer; sacks of real, earthy potatoes from Strathmore thereafter. Then the sweet-smelling strawberries followed by pungent rasps and blackcurrants and hairy, purple gooseberries that he called 'grozers', and crisp, aromatic Cox's orange pippins in the autumn, the tastiest apple of all. But always, no matter what the season, the sunshine-filled poster of the port of Las Palmas overprinted with the words Bananas are Fyffe's.

It's four-and-a-half days earlier and I'm handing over the equivalent of £6 in Spanish pesetas, almost a quarter of the entire sum I'd left Scotland with a couple of months earlier. In exchange I'm given a ticket for the cheapest, third-class upper berth in a spartan cabin shared by a dozen others, all Spanish nationals, as poor as myself. The voyage on the cargo-ferry vessel, the *Ciudad de Cádiz*, from the Spanish port of the same name to Las Palmas on Gran Canaria is scheduled to take two-and-a-half days. We're a mere half-day from land however, when a fierce storm hits and reduces my fellow-passengers to helpless, groaning geysers and the claustrophobic cabin to a squalid sewer. Because I find the turbulence of the ocean exhilarating and the brine spray preferable to the din of discharge and the reek of human retch, I seek relief on the windswept deck.

In excruciatingly slow motion, we're clambering up a massive green wave that's doing its best to outrun us but we grind upwards and win. The grumbling ship perches and pauses briefly on the torn crest before being hurtled down into the seething trough. Though it's my first time on the wide Atlantic, I'm more awed than terrified. The combined fury of wind and sea robs me of breath.

Without warning, a hand grabs my shoulder and tugs. Alarmed, I turn to face a uniformed officer and wonder how his peaked white cap manages to stay on his head. He gestures, "Come!" I follow. He opens a door, hurries me urgently inside, and slams it firmly behind him.

In mime, he conveys that the ship is going to turn into the wind. To be out on deck would be catastróphico. I grasp the drama of the gesture and follow him up ladder after ladder until we're finally on the bridge, where all is suddenly and surprisingly calm. He points, "There!" touches his eyes. "Watch!"

For long minutes, none of the officers speak. Then a series of curt instructions. The captain orders the distant engineer to vary the speed of the propeller, directs the helmsman to adjust the rudder so that by degrees and in perfect conjunction with its position on a towering wave, the ship swings in an arc to face bravely into the wind. We're looking back the way we came. I marvel. Now, instead of being driven uncontrollably, we're nuzzling up into the breakers, engines so slow that we're almost standing still.

I panic. We're not returning to Spain?

Reading my concern, the officer, with much gesturing, has me understand. This defensive posture is how the captain chooses to wait out the storm until it's safe to resume our southerly course. I nod.

From the clear view to fore and aft that the bridge offers, our four-and-a-half thousand-ton vessel strikes me as large. I remember the tiny, deep-sea trawlers moored in Aberdeen docks or the even smaller seine-netters in Arbroath and Montrose. But then I recall the immenseness of the SS Mauritania anchored off Greenock on the Clyde. I'd gone to meet my mother, Pearl, after she'd spent a summer with her eldest sister in Boston at a time when it became imperative she escape, even for a few weeks. The Mauritania was twice the length and breadth of our ship and still, Pearl told us, took a fierce battering. Yes indeed, the *Ciudad de Cádiz* was a shrimp by comparison.

"Here? How long?" My hands gesture the query.

The officer shrugs. "All night! Maybe tomorrow too." He casts a look at the torn, black sky and shrugs again. "¡Solo Diós sabe! – God alone knows!"

As suddenly as it came on, the storm abates on our second morning. Black clouds scurry off to the east; the sky reveals itself pale blue; the sun shines and the sea relaxes. On the horizon, a seaman points out the barren Moroccan coast. For two days, we've been forced well off course. Seizing the moment, the captain turns the bow of the *Ciudad de Cádiz* southwest and rings for full speed ahead. The engines take on a purposeful thrum, the sea-bleached deck vibrates underfoot and the propeller spews a heaving white wake, in a determined effort to catch up on lost time. I stand alone in the forepeak and watch smiling dolphins play 'Can't catch us!' with the ship's bow-wave. On either side, slim white flying fish glide from crest to crest, matching our direction. Renewed, we're steaming directly for the semitropical Canary Islands.

The dawn-emerging island of Gran Canaria offered the shapelessness of a sleeping dragon against a velvet sky. Orange sodium lights were the dragon's drowsy wisp of warm breath curling along the esplanade and reaching out onto the pier. In the promising moments before the sun rose out of the sea and our effortless glide towards land, individual lights began to appear in the windows of the pastel-shaded stucco houses that decorated the hillsides overlooking the bay. Beyond the houses were silent, mysterious acres of dark green palm-fronds that one of the seamen identified as banana palms. "Bananas," he explained, "grow on trees in plantations, not in fields." Banana palms, plantations, the promising scents on the breeze seemed to whisper: "Here are your semi-tropical islands in the Atlantic sea-roads between America and Africa, Europe and the East; here lies adventure, the beginning of freedom, of restoration."

Our *Ciudad de Cádiz* cut its engines to a mere murmur a couple of kilometres from the long pier. Seamen took up positions of readiness and a few hardy passengers joined me on deck. The light breeze was comfortably cool and brought the scent of warm wet soil, sweet blossoms and the tingling sharpness of promised rain.

Although I had no clear plan beyond finding work on a ship to take me to South America, I found myself very much in the moment, taking deep breaths, my chest swelling young and easy, green and carefree, without understanding, or even feeling the need to understand why.

We third-class passengers were the last to be permitted to disembark. While we waited, the ship's crew opened the hatches to the hold and the rattling dock-cranes began unloading supplies that the *Ciudad de Cádiz* had brought from the Peninsula. All packages, large and small, were bound neatly within burlap bags sown with twine. Under the watchful eye of a uniformed officer, the stevedores tumbled these, without too much care, into thick rope nets slung from the hoisting-line attached to the swinging boom of the derrick on the dock. Once the stevedores in the hold filled a net with packages, they stepped back smartly. The banksman on deck twirled his hand in the air and the crane-driver raised the load vertically and then swung it clear, onto the stone quay, where a gang rapidly unloaded it onto waiting lorries that drove off to the warehouse with the minimum of fuss.

As my feet hit terra firma, I staggered and had to be righted by a crewmember who stood in position at the end of the gangway for that very purpose. Sea-legs served only at sea! I made my way through noisy, weeping, reuniting families, squeezing past groups of nervous soldiers, each with his own rifle. They hung about without enthusiasm waiting to board a smaller, rustier ship that would ferry them from too

4

short a leave back to Ifni, Spain's tiny province in the south of Morocco. There, they would half-heartedly fight off relentless insurgents intent on driving them into the sea.

Touts for hotels accosted me at every step but I adopted my fail-proof technique of striding as if I knew exactly where I was going. I stopped only when I had passed through the great, wrought-iron gates that separate the seething dock area from the town. A different world waited on the other side of these gates. Here was a wide boulevard lined with tall palm trees and gardens of red and pink geraniums, luminous in the early morning sunlight. Beyond the boulevard were narrow streets crammed with shops whose owners vied for customers from the ships arriving from and bound for all parts of the world.

The touts were of a kind I'd never encountered before. They were dark, insistent young men from the Indian sub-continent. demanding I accompany them into their crowded bazaars: "Bargain! Tax-free! Best price! What you want? Pound Sterling! American dollar!" Cameras, transistor radios, watches, minute portable TVs. All the most modern, technical paraphernalia of the 1960s, none of which I had the need nor the desire nor the money to buy. These traders were used to selling to Europeans from the passenger ships that made Las Palmas their last port-of-call and who had need of last-minute gifts for some forgotten relative at home. I found it vaguely flattering that they mistook an 18-year-old Scot as a potential client – a young man with less than £25 or in his pocket now, and no home or fixed destination.

Having found a room in a pension, as nasty as it was cheap, and learned – to my relief – that they did not serve meals, I left my ruck-sack and went off to explore Las Palmas. Although it was colourful and bright with flowers and smiling, good-looking people, I knew after a single hour there that this bustling, crossroads city was not for me. My vague idea of working my passage to South America resurfaced with increased urgency. Back once more at the dock gates, I asked the capped attendant, grizzled with a three-day growth, where I might find cargo ships bound for South America. After a verbal struggle, I learned that there was América, which included the Americas North and South, Norte América, which meant the USA – Mexico and Canada were not counted – and América Latina, which included every country from the Mexican-American border, through the Magellan Straights and up the Pacific coast to Central America and Mexico.

"I want to go to América Latina."

"Where in América Latina?"

"Anywhere!" It's the travelling that intoxicates me, not the desti-nation.

Demonstrating no surprise whatsoever at such an open-ended request, he disappeared for a moment into his tiny office, came back and pointed to a row of three ships on a dock some distance from the passenger liners and the smart cargo ships that flew one or other of the northern European flags.

All three of the cargo boats were smallish, blemished with flaking rust. Forlorn Spanish flags dangled at their masthead and not a man could I see on board. These boats appeared to be not so much abandoned as utterly forsaken. The gangplank of the first was unattended. Cautiously, I climbed aboard. Silence, except for the gentle putter of a small motor; then a porthole was thrown open and a cloth was flapped, freeing into the oily harbour potato-peelings and carrot-tops that were immediately seized by angry gulls before the cloth was withdrawn and the porthole slammed shut. With every step, I felt more of an intruder. A lit, bare electric bulb just inside an open door suggested there just might be some human presence. Sure enough, a young man with eyes that separately peered in disturbingly different directions was swabbing the passageway. He stood aside to let me pass.

"I'm looking for the captain." I made him understand. Suddenly, realising I was a trespasser, he uttered the words, "Captain, no!" pointed to the gangway and, using his mop as a lance, resolutely marched me down to the dock. Just in case I hadn't got the message, he shook his mop, hooked a chain in place and stood there with angry, misaligned eyes and crossed arms. I shouted my thanks to him, relieved that I wasn't going to have to sit under his crooked glare at breakfast every morning as the ship ploughed its arduous way across the Atlantic. Gratefully, I made for the second ship.

I was stopped at the gangway. "What did I want?"

"To see the captain," I explained.

"About what?"

"Work my passage." He pointed to the bridge and allowed me to climb aboard.

Fortunately, I knew the general layout of a ship from days just spent on the *Ciudad de Cádiz* and soon reached the open door of the bridge where two officers stood just inside, talking. I'd been told that you had to be invited onto the bridge and so I offered a polite "Buenos días" and waited. I was gestured in. "What did I want?" I explained as best I could.

The first mate smiled: "What was the land I came from called?"

"Escocia – Scotland."

"Scotland, England, Ireland, Wales," he chanted in accented English.

"All tied up like monkeys' tails," I added.

"Liverpool, Birkenhead, Greenock."

Afraid that my purpose might be hi-jacked by never-ending rhyming lists, I asked him, "Possible?"

"Possible," he agreed and my spirits rose. "But we make to La Coruña in Galicia. You want we go you La Coruña?" My spirits sank. The north-west of Spain was well out of my way.

I pointed to the third ship, "That one, América Latina?" He turned and his face broke into a mocking smile at the dirty, battered tramp that had lost most of its paint and with it, most of its dignity. His look of contempt told me all I needed to know.

"You want go América Latina? You go Santa Cruz, Tenerife. You speak harbour-master. Much boat go América Latina – Cartagena, Maiquetia, Paramaribo, Montevideo, Puerto Nuevo."

"Puerto Nuevo?" I could place the others. My Bartholomew School Atlas had been well-thumbed.

"Puerto Madera, Buenos Aires!"

"Argentina!" My maternal great-grandfather and my grandfather's two brothers had disappeared into Argentina's vastness in the late 1880s to build the country's railways! Of course! I thanked the mate profusely, shook hands and descended to the dock to find out how to get to Santa Cruz on the neighbouring island of Tenerife.

Santa Cruz de Tenerife

Santa Cruz, the commercial port for the island of Tenerife, was a tranquil city even at noon, entirely without the busy sea-traffic and frenetic passing trade of Gran Canaria. The six-hour crossing had been calm; dolphins plaited the blue-green water inches from the curling bow-wave and flying fish accompanied us, offering an easy welcome. The plantations rose green from the colourful rows of houses that clung like uneven bracelets to the curves of the hills above the port. These gave way to forests of conifers and beyond, dry yellow scrub and cactus and then to bare grey, orange and yellow rock. Above all, grey-blue and sharp even at that great distance, rose the perfect spreading cone of a volcano, topped with a ring of snow. I felt somehow at home with the peace, colour and variety, but since my first priority was to find a berth on a boat, I went in search of the harbour-master's office.

"América Latina?" The uniformed harbour-master eyed me doubtfully, "Try Las Palmas. All boats go América Latina, Las Palmas. No Santa Cruz." I must have looked sceptical for he spoke to his assistant and led me to the docks. The ferry I'd arrived on was loading passengers for the return trip to Gran Canaria. He pointed to another quay where a few tramp steamers were tied up. "That, Cádiz; that, Coruña; that, Santander; that, Bilbao..." His finger ran out of boats. He shrugged, pointed back to the ferry, "Las Palmas!" He turned away.

I wandered back to the quay and the ferry. The harbour attendants were waiting for the order to slip the docklines from the bollards. "Get aboard!" One signalled urgently to me, "the ferry's leaving!" I shook my head. Why not stay and find work right here? I knew the Spanish for work, having used it to my advantage many times in Spain. "Necesito trabajar!"

The attendant, gripping the thick dockline in both hands, shook his head. "No hay trabajo, no work in Santa Cruz", but then his face brightened and he pointed over the hills to the north-west, "Puerto la Cruz. Construction. Many hotels. Much work." He swung an imaginary shovel. Shovels, picks, crowbars and cement mixers, I was well familiar with and I enjoyed hard work. Spanish lorry drivers who had given me lifts simply in order to help keep them awake at the wheel, had often paid me to help unload their merchandise when we'd arrived at a depot after the workers had gone home for the day. These drivers, owner-operators desperate to pay off their bank loans on their Spanish-made Pegaso and Ebro vehicles, relied on shedding one paid load and picking up another with the minimum of delay. They respected no regular hours, smoked continuously, travelled with falsified logs. These regular windfalls, and my native frugality, had made it unnecessary for me to spend much of my carefully-hoarded capital.

And so, since it was still very early afternoon, I first went in search of lunch – a delicious steaming plate of lentils well-seasoned with garlic and herbs. Well-fortified, I inquired about a bus to Puerto La Cruz. It seemed that there was no bus at all but there was a vehicle that sounded like 'wawa'. I bought the ticket anyway and lo and behold I was directed to – a bus! In Spain, they say autobús but in the Canary Islands they call the same vehicle, guagua. Being a Scot from rural Angus and then urban Dundee who had from childhood delighted in the rich, varied speech around him, I reflected on how much more at home I felt in the Canaries than I had in Peninsular Spain, as the crowded guagua climbed into the steep hills above Santa Cruz leaving the coast and the blue sea behind.

From my aisle seat, I had to crane my neck to catch glimpses of the villages and the countryside we were passing. There were massive patches of coloured flowers everywhere. We passed fields of crops I was unable to recognize despite all the weekends and summers I'd worked on arable farms in Angus and Perthshire. My evident curiosity and frequent puzzlement over the countryside attracted the attention of other passengers. Since the bulk of them, except for my immediate neighbour, seemed to alight at every stop to be replaced with new faces, my antics had a continuously fresh audience.

For the locals, it was an amusing novelty to have a naïve foreigner, un extranjero, aboard. At first, they smiled at the simple things that attracted my attention and then they chuckled to one another. At one stop, the bus conductor had a passenger up front exchange seats with me. The advantage was that now I could see more easily without craning my neck; the downside was that I had to listen to his running commentary on every single thing we passed. "That's a large tree! That's a prickly cactus! Look! A dog!" They seemed to equate an inability to speak Spanish with mental deficiency and made me feel like an idiot. However, I was able to keep a smile on my face and offer the occasional nod to satisfy him that I was still paying attention. Not to be outdone, the driver too, started pointing things out to me. I began to feel like a nodding doll, now acknowledging the driver, now the conductor.

Abruptly, we crested a hill and there to our right was the bright green Atlantic stretching away as far as they eye could see, a cuff of lacy, white waves crashing along the rocky shore. And then, as we swung off the main road and began descending towards the coast, lay the tight little town of Puerto la Cruz, crouched by the sea as if it had been there forever. It was ochre and elegant, compact and tidy, with church spires, treed parks, a harbour and a sweeping bay lined by tall palm trees and small, pastel-painted fishing cobles drawn up on the beach.

By the time the guagua zigzagged its way down the hillside using first gear as its brake, my head was reeling from my care-givers' non-stop commentary. Despite their well-intended kindness, I was relieved to wave them goodbye and set out, in blissful, solitary silence, to search for construction work.

Puerta La Cruz

This is the view I had of Puerto la Cruz after unsuccessfully seeking work there in 1960 and just before meeting the plantation manager who offered the inspired suggestion that I take the guagua to Buenavista del Norte.

There were indeed hotels being built, many along the boulevard facing the sea, but there wasn't a single worker on any of the sites I visited, just the smell of damp concrete and crushed stone. It was well into the afternoon before I found the explanation. "Paro!" I was told by a watchman, "there's a strike and everything is closed down!"

"For how long?" Open hands and a shrug. "God alone knows!"

"Other work?" Again he opened his hands and shrugged.

"A cheap pension for the night?"

"Cheap? Here?" A shrug. "Expensive! Muy caro! Very expensive! No cheap!"

I began to feel demoralised. "The guagua back to Santa Cruz?"

Once more the eloquent gesture. "Not from Puerto la Cruz." I must go back up the hill to the main road and catch the bus from the town of Orotava on its way to Santa Cruz. I hesitated. "The guagua," he assured me, "will stop on request." He raised and lowered his right arm as if spinning a yoyo, to show me how to have the guagua stop for me.

Thanking him, but with an inner feeling of exasperation and defeat, I hoisted my rucksack, stuck my thumbs into the webbing straps to ease the weight off my shoulders, and began plodding back up the steep hill with plantations of leafy green fronds on either side of me. I wondered if it might be safe to sleep the night or if hairy spiders or slithering reptiles might be lying in wait in the dark groves. It wouldn't be my first sleepless night in alien undergrowth.

A fortunate encounter

When I reached the main road at the top of the hill, I sat down on a wall that separated the side of the road from a plantation. It was now late afternoon and no traffic passed save for the odd tired worker on his bicycle. Things didn't look great. I'd have given anything to be back in the warm camaraderie of the Casa Campello.

Casa Campello was a private hostel run by three laid-back New Zealanders, a few miles north of Alicante on Spain's Mediterranean coast, a favourite place with travellers in their mid-twenties from English-speaking Commonwealth countries. The New Zealanders spotted the readiness with which I undertook extra chores and my aptness at preparing simple meals in the kitchen. They offered me a job as a factotum in return for a bed in a dormitory and a small share in the evening meal that I prepared for them. There, I'd found a temporary refuge from whatever it was that was driving me on.

What had induced me to leave Casa Campello's ease and stability? I heard a noise behind me and turned to see come out of the dark shadows of the plantation a man, taller and heavier than I. In his right hand he carried a machete, its wide blade at least two feet long. The front of his khaki shirt and trousers stained with something much darker than sweat. He looked surprised when I leapt to my feet but offered a friendly nod and a "¡Buenas tardes!" To my relief, he slipped the blade of the machete into a sheath attached to his belt before approaching me with his hand outstretched.

I was suddenly flooded by a wave of envy at the evidence of his belonging. His stained clothes signalled gainful employment; he commanded the leisure to exchange a few words with a stranger. Most of all, I envied him his machete. I couldn't imagine what kind of work, other than buccaneer, that demanded such an over-sized cutting tool, but whatever his work was, I knew there was nothing more I would rather do.

It didn't faze him, as it had the bus conductor, that my Spanish was rudimentary. He sat down on the wall beside me, took his hat off and wiped sweat off his face. His comfortable gestures announced, "My workday is done; now I'm taking my ease." I managed to have him explain that he worked as a foreman of the plantation he had just emerged from. He'd been checking on the health of the plants, the moisture in the soil and the development of the piñas. Piña I knew from the Peninsula as the word for pineapple.

"Pineapples!" I said, surprised, and pointed to the green grove he'd just emerged from, "not plátanos, not bananas?"

He laughed and led me down into the plantation. The green, fronded leaves all grew out of the top of a round trunk about six or seven feet high. Behind him, hundreds of perfectly spaced stems disappeared into the gloom caused by the wide, arching leaves meeting overhead and cutting off the light from the sky.

He tapped one of the stems with the flat of his machete blade: "¡Planta de plátano!" I could still see neither bananas nor pineapples, just a thick green stem that grew out of the plant just above my head and bent down towards me with a large dark reddish-brown leafy growth on the end. He tapped it: "¡La flor del plátano!" I listened sceptically; a banana flower? Was he taking the mickey? Giving me the equivalent of the wild haggis story? He could see my disbelief and led me to another plant. This time, the short green stalk that bent down towards me had rows of miniature banana hands clustered neatly around it, from top to bottom. At the extremity, the purple petals of the flower still clung. He smiled, seeing that I was getting the picture.

Then we moved to another plant. Here, right above my head, was an enormous stem entirely circled by fully developed, bright green hands of bananas. He gestured to the entire stem. "¡Piña!" Then to the individual fruit on each hand. "¡Plátano!" The penny dropped; I nodded. Now I pointed to a whole round stem replete with bananas: "¡Piña!" Now to a single hand of curved bananas: "¡Mano!" The foreman laughed, delighted that his lesson had succeeded.

So, that's how bananas grow! Not on a tree as such but on a kind of trunk formed from the protective covering of multiple leaves. Nor did they grow separately in ones or twos! They grew in hands of seven or eight around a central core of thick, green stem. They were the fruit of a flower and developed only once the flower had been pollinated!

"How do I find myself a job in a banana plantation?"

"Not here." He looked apologetic as if disappointed not to be able to offer me a job there and then.

"Then where?"

He pointed in the opposite direction from that leading back to Santa Cruz and repeatedly shook his extended hand to indicate I had to keep going and going and going until the road came to its very end. "Buenavista del Norte! They're constructing plantations. That's where there is work!"

"Can I walk there? Tonight?"

He laughed. "Much too far!" But a guagua would take me. Soon! "The guagua's on its way!" He growled like a diesel engine to emphasize the truth of his assertion. As if to further guarantee his confidence in the imminent appearance of the guagua, he sat down beside me on the wall. In less than 20 minutes, we could hear the gears of a diesel engine grinding round steep, tight corners. He stepped confidently out into the road and flagged it down using the yoyo gesture I'd been shown.

"This young man," he told first the conductor and then the driver and then repeated the same message to all of the passengers who crowded to the door to listen. "This young man must get to Buenavista del Norte!"

The driver shut off the engine, emerged from the guagua and shook my hand. "¡Manolo!" His conductor did likewise, "¡Santiago!" They proudly pointed to their uniforms – grey shirt, matching trousers and numbered badges – that identified them as genuine bus-line employees.

They grinned delightedly at the news I was heading for Buenavista del Norte. So did the score of passengers all of whom insisted on alighting and introducing themselves. Buenavista would welcome me! Sober nods of agreement all round. Their confidence bolstered mine.

"How long will it take to get to Buenavista?"

"Not long! An hour, an hour and a half. It all depends!" Manolo, climbed back into his seat behind the wheel and started the engine. Heads nodded, "Not long!"

"¡Vámonos!" called Santiago without much urgency, and the passengers climbed back on the bus and took their seats. Santiago grabbed my rucksack and swung it up onto a flat space behind the gear-change. He dismissed my efforts to pay for the trip. "It's our pleasure!" He and Manolo beamed and looked at their passengers for confirmation. "¡Sí!" It was their pleasure too!

My saviour, the buccaneer foreman, shook my hand, "¡Suerte!" Good luck! And before the guagua took off, he turned, unsheathed his machete, swaggered back into the planation and was immediately swallowed up by its mysterious, sunless depths. Manolo revved the engine noisily. Santiago gestured all the curious passengers to sit down and hold tight. With a gracious gesture, he offered me the preferential seat beside him within talking distance of the voluble Manolo and with another "¡Vámonos!" we were off. Off as far as this road could take us. Off to Buenavista del Norte. At the farthest end of the island.

I had the distinct feeling I was on my way home.

2. Getting there: By guagua to Buenavista del Norte

By comparison with my desperately lonely walk up the hill from Puerto La Cruz, the warm, unabashed curiosity of the busload of homeward-bound passengers was heart-warming. Driver, conductor and passengers young and old all wanted to know everything about me right away, starting with my age. Everybody on the guagua appeared to know each other intimately but now a total stranger had been thrust unexpectedly into their midst. The unusual character of this event clearly excited their unbridled curiosity. Not only was I a stranger, I was a foreign stranger and so as exotic as a penguin in the Edinburgh Zoo. Such was my status as a novelty that the passengers were incapable of addressing me. They directed their overflowing questions not to me, but to Manolo and Sebastian. By virtue of their superior rank, they now enjoyed the status of 'Keepers-of-the-Exotic-Animal-on-Display'.

Even before I was seated, the questions began.

"How old is the foreigner?"

"Ask him where he's from."

"Why is he coming with us to Buenavista?"

"Who does he know there?"

"Ask him if he's married." Laughter!

"Ask him if his mama knows that he's away from home alone." More laughter!

"Ask him if he shaves yet."

"Would he like a drink of water?"

"Is that smell coming from him?" "Not him, just his feet!" General hilarity!

"Ask him what he has in that funny-coloured canvas bag he brought onto the bus."

"Ask him if he's a deserter from the army."

"What's his native language?"

"Ask him if he's from a Christian country!"

"Why can't he speak Spanish?"

"Maybe he's feeble-minded!" Delighted laughter!

"Ask him if he's a millionaire."

"All foreigners are millionaires!" Sober nods. Of course they are!

Now that I was on my way to Buenavista with real, live local villagers, I couldn't bring myself to tell them that I was looking for work. The idea seemed presumptuous. I didn't speak the language; I didn't know anything about bananas or building the plantations to grow them in; most obviously, I didn't have the muscular build of the men on the bus or the huge calloused hands that they waved about so spiritedly, as if their gestures spoke more eloquently than their tongues.

Santiago stood up, making a sudden grab for the overhead rail as Manolo swung the guagua round a hairpin bend in the narrow road. He faced the excited passengers. Despite the risk presented by the lurching bus, he held up one hand. "Quiet now! Calm down, all of you! I'll take questions one at a time!" I was the central figure in a mobile press conference on the Queen's Flight. Santiago was my press secretary. Given that I was catching only a fraction of what was being said, I was glad to have this tall, genial man on my side.

And so, by degrees, I became known – at least in parts – by all those on the guagua, and their curiosity was minimally satisfied. The single question that I fudged was the one about my age. I'd discovered in Spain that if they grew up at all, it took young men until they left home to get married in their mid, even late, twenties. Until that happened, they remained little boys who had everything done for them by their mamás and everything paid for by their papás. They even enjoyed a status superior to their sisters, who were taught to revere them and show them deference. They, at 18, were more often than not still happy to be treated as children, and what was worse, to act helpless. I was adamant about being seen as an independent adult. And so, when asked the inevitable question: "How old?" I'd learned to respond with a further question: "How old do you think I am?" For some reason, they didn't find this evasive. Instead, they responded to the challenge enthusiastically, roaring out estimates from 15 to 27. My strategy was to grimace at any number lower than 21 and nod benignly at the higher numbers. By this subterfuge, I managed to have them believe I was in my early twenties.

Their curiosity satisfied, the passengers soon settled down to more mundane conversations and left Santiago and Manolo to squeeze out of me whatever remaining information I possessed – or at least was willing to divulge. They showed surprise and sad-eyed disappointment that I carried no photographs of my mamá, papá, brothers and sisters, wife, children, grandchildren, or the football team I supported. Their accusing eyes told me that all men should carry at least a well-thumbed, black and white photograph of their mother! As if to fill my breach, Manolo took out his wallet and, with a single hand on the wheel and a single eye on the empty road, showed me photographs and gave me the detailed history of each and every member of his extended family. When Manolo finished, Santiago took over. They did this with pride but also with the occasional meaningful look that said: "This is how we introduce ourselves in our country. We don't keep our lives secreted away in faded, second-hand rucksacks. We're an open, straightforward, nothing-to-hide kind of people." I felt appropriately guilty; deficient and socially inadequate by comparison with my protectors at not being able to share. How to disclose what I barely understood myself?

At my grandmother's home in Coupar Angus, I'd been born into middle of the Second World War. These early years with my elder sister Vivian and then my younger brother Euan had been both happy and puzzling. Happy, because we played unsupervised from dawn till dusk in the fields and woods and barns of the surrounding farms and returned hungry to meals of potatoes and carrots and the tiny portions of meat that our mother Pearl and her sisters gave us children because they had no appetite. Puzzling, because of the visits of unfamiliar uncles and father George who arrived in uniform and spent their leave with their ears glued to the wet-battery radio for recall to their regiments.

Once the War was over and troops began the slow process of return, we lived in Dundee in permanent tension. George had come back pitiless and uncaring of the unhappiness he wrought around him. Though he lived in the house, he never sought to be part of the family. Against his barren, self-isolation that erupted unpredictably into assault, Pearl, Vivian, Euan and I wove ourselves into a warm togetherness of mutual protection. Our several unsuccessful efforts to desert grew into the firm understanding that once Euan, the youngest of us three, had completed school at 17, Pearl and Vivian would create a new home in distant London. Euan and I would visit regularly from wherever our university studies or careers might take us.

3. *Arrival in Buenavista del Norte*

The battered bus shuddered to a halt alongside a simple red and ochre stucco building on one side of a timeless village square dazzling with marigolds and geraniums and shaded by trees bearing bright oranges. Children played on a small, roofed bandstand in the centre of the plaza; mothers talked under rustling palms. Manolo turned off the engine and stretched. Blessed stillness reigned.

Signalling to me, "Wait in your seat!", Santiago called out a genial, "Here we are, friends! Buenavista del Norte. End of the line. Everybody off!" Then passengers were on their feet, gently waking children, tugging parcels from the overhead rack, ending conversations. He tugged open the folding doors, ducked, and descended to the pavement, ready to assist any passenger needing help. Each, however, from oldest to the very youngest, found it necessary to shake my hand and smile; only then did they step down to exchange banter with Santiago or hold their children up for a kiss, an easy intimacy born of long familiarity, neighbourly trust and caring.

When they'd all alighted, Manolo signalled me to precede him. "Come and meet Doña Lutgarda! She's the cherished owner of this fonda. Doña Lutgarda will feed you and find you a room." To make sure I understood, he united the fingertips and thumb of one hand and gestured back and forth towards his mouth, "Eat!" He then placed both palms together as if about to pray, inclined his head to one side and laid his hands alongside his face, "Sleep!" While I couldn't fail to understand, I promised myself that I would free myself from the absurd tyranny of comic mime by learning the language right away.

Hoisting my ex-army rucksack onto one shoulder, I stepped down onto the concrete pavement and was prodded into a position between Manolo and Santiago, both of whom towered over me. I was the precious surprise whose unexpected appearance on the road had added novelty to their repetitive journey. They were determined to hang onto the prestige their prize awarded them for as long as possible. Facing us was a double wooden door set in a ochre plaster wall still warm from afternoon sun. This double door stood wide open in welcome, like a broad, toothless smile. Inside, the lights had been turned on against

17

the dusk so that beyond the door I could make out tables and chairs on a tiled patio lined with leafy plants in terra-cotta tubs. A middle-aged

A view of El Rincón from the sea. These are the mountains that partially surround Buenavista and, at that time, cut it off from the southern part of the islands.

woman, almost as broad as she was tall, stood smiling on the threshold between the doors drying her hands on her apron. Everything about her seemed to stretch horizontally – grey, spreading hair, alert narrowed eyes, her ruddy cheeks and generous mouth, even her homely girth: Doña Lutgarda.

Manolo and Santiago stepped forward and up onto the threshold to greet her. Their respect and affection were evident. While Manolo exchanged banter with three of the four young women who clustered around Doña Lutgarda, Santiago dragged some small parcels from the bus's locker and passed them to the fourth young woman. She took them into the venta – a large antechamber within the pension, fitted out as a shop. The venta was directly accessible from the pavement and doubled as the distribution point for parcels brought by bus from the island's capital, Santa Cruz.

Once he'd closed the locker, Santiago, a good head-and-a-bit taller than my compact five-foot-seven inches, took me by the arm and presented me to Doña Lutgarda. "This young man needs something to eat and a place to stay. "Es extranjero de la Suecia – He's a foreigner from Sweden." My geography lesson on the bus had gone astray!

Doña Lutgarda looked at me severely but, I trusted, not unkindly. Her eyes narrowed as she summed up, first my face, then my general appearance, and finally my shabby rucksack.

18

"Your baggage?" She looked at Santiago and Manolo. Both nod-ded.

"That's all he's got!"

Doña Lutgarda raised her eyebrows and turned back to me. "How long do you plan to stay?"

I held up my right hand and showed thumb and fingers. Five days. Admitting my need to work would expose my impending penu-ry. Moreover, how could I possibly find work when, even to answer a simple question I was reduced to holding up the fingers of one hand? My confidence was seeping away like water into sand. Maybe I would just stay for four or five days, take the guagua back to Santa Cruz, catch the cargo-ferry back to Cadiz and hitch-hike back to Scotland. Despite having suffered the ignominy of failing to gain entry to Aberdeen Uni-versity to study agriculture, I could find something to keep me occupied there until I decided on a permanent career. Feeling embarrassed and slightly foolish, I dropped my hand to my side.

There was a pause. Doña Lutgarda was in no hurry. In her world as inn-keeper, much depended on her accurate assessment of the suita-

Roads in Buenavista were made for walking -- and for flowers.

bility of potential guests. The four girls stood awaiting a decision that was hers and hers alone. They were neither for me nor against me. I held my breath. She offered a curt nod. "You're welcome. We can give you a room. We can feed you. Five nights, meals included – 42 pesetas a day."

About 5 shillings, a good deal, I reckoned. My daily budget was 60 pesetas. I smiled, nodding willing acceptance. If need be, I could last out for another month, at this daily rate. A little confidence seeped back into me warming my body. I liked this stern woman, this pension, this village at the end of the road. I would see what it brought.

19

For a moment or two longer her eyes continued to scrutinise me. She sniffed, raised her eyebrows once more and declared, "Laundry is included!" Then to Manolo and Santiago: "Your meal is ready. Fish and potatoes. Pudding! The youngster must be hungry too." And because she recognized my hunger, I forgave her the youngster.

Doña Lutgarda led the way inside. An appetising aroma coming from the kitchen was already tantalising me. Manolo, Santiago and I were shown to one of the tables together. Pots clanged in the kitchen, cutlery rattled on the table. We were served. While they chatted comfortably with Doña Lutgarda and her girls who glided back and forth from kitchen to table, I reflected. Thanks to a chance encounter with a plantation worker at the side of the road and to the conductor and the driver of the guagua, and now to Doña Lutgarda, I'd found a home – at least for five nights.

Buenavista del Norte nestles comfortably on the edge of the arid plane, surrounded by cliffs, mountains, and the ocean.

4. Don Eduardo, Judge

My five nights extended into a fortnight. I was learning Spanish, getting to know the village and its surroundings. My confidence had grown to the point where I was dropping hints that I would like to stay longer if only I could find work. Initially, Doña Lutgarda had listened to these hints in silence but then began asking about my previous work experience. I told her all about working on farms in Scotland during my Easter and summer holidays from the Morgan Academy: pricking out cabbage and cauliflower seedlings for a market garden, harvesting vines of peas and feeding them into a viner that separated the green peas from the aftermath, managing a raspberry field where the pickers were rough families dominated by women who thought nothing of blatantly sitting astride the buckets of fruit to add unsanitary weight to the juice – though I didn't confide that detail to Doña Lutgarda!

I was making progress learning Spanish and also getting to know the other long-term guests living in the fonda. There were three, a middle-aged couple and a single man. The couple, Don Eduardo the municipal judge, accompanied by his wife Doña Juana, he in middle age, she younger. The single man, Don Juan-Pedro, was in his late twenties.

Don Eduardo, conscious of his importance and heavily overweight, was the Spanish government's legal representative and arbiter in the municipality of Buenavista del Norte. He was addressed respectfully as 'Don Eduardo', or simply 'Señor Juez'. He was referred to with equal respect as el Juez – the Judge. His wife, Doña Juana, good-looking and well-dressed, was referred to as la Señora Juez – The Judge's Lady. She matched him in splendour though not in girth.

They resided in the fonda's most elegant quarters. Their large chamber, complete with private bathroom, was on the upper floor. However, instead of overlooking the internal court-yard that served as the dining room, theirs had been built as more private quarters at the end of the terrace on the flat roof, the azotea overlooking the plaza, with access to the internal stairs. It was the most luxurious accommodation in the fonda – no doubt in the entire village. Their windows must have offered a panoramic view of the Plaza de los Remedios, as well as the dark stone and white-washed church, Nuestra Señora de Los Remedios. Perhaps they even offered a glimpse of the Atlantic Ocean beyond.

Don Juan-Pedro was one of two teachers at the only school in a tiny village of a hundred or two, perched on the side of the mountains four or five kilometres above Buenavista. Every morning, Don Juan-Pedro rode the steep zig-zag road up to the school in El Palmar in the morning and returned every afternoon at 2.30 sharp.

My path often crossed with that of Don Eduardo. I'd found that the open-air upper terrace was the most pleasant, and private, place to sit and assiduously study Spanish, to read, or write letters home. Don Eduardo would open his front door, step out onto the terrace and greet me with a formal but friendly, "Buenos Días, Orlando!" And I would return his greeting, "Buenos Días, Don Eduardo!" Pause. "Ah, studying your Spanish!" he would say, or "Ah, writing another letter to your mamá!" or "What are you reading today?" For some reason, my Christian name had been Hispanicised to 'Orlando' and I had no alternative but to accept it. 'Ronald' was alien to Spanish phonology and 'Ron' caused hilarity because it meant rum – as sold in the light and dark bottles in the bar on the plaza.

At first, Don Eduardo's attempts to engage me in conversation ended in mutual frustration. However, he possessed dogged patience, was never in a hurry and seemed genuinely curious about me. I, for my part, applied myself continuously to a second-hand copy Spanish in Three Months. The fact that I'd studied Latin at school was of enormous help. After only a few days I was able to understand and respond to most of his simple, basic questions: "Who was I? Where did I come from? How old was I? Did my mamá know where I was? Was Scotland a Christian country? Did the people there speak a Christian language? Did I have a profession? Was I a man of private means? How long did I plan to stay? Why?"

I answered his questions frankly. I still played the guessing game when asked about my age and it continued to serve me well. The question I had greatest difficulty with was, "Who was I?"

On the face of it, it was a straightforward question that could be answered in many ways, all of them as simple as the three words themselves. I could answer with my name: Ronald Mackay; my nationality: Scots; the school I'd gone to: the Morgan Academy; how I'd managed to save enough money to get to Tenerife: by working incredibly long hours over the summer in Lockwoods canning factory in Monifieth. Although my answers seemed to satisfy the curiosity of the questioner, the question "Who am I?" merely kindled mine. Often, before I fell asleep in my single room in the fonda, I'd grappled with it. Who was I indeed? I looked at this tantalising question from as many angles as I could imagine, but could get traction neither on the question itself nor on any answer that I found convincing. The best I could come up with was, I don't really know! At night, I'd wrestle with it but during the day I just absorbed life in and around the village hoping that, in time, an answer might come.

Don Eduardo, like any competent lawyer, evolved the scope of his gentle cross-examination. One morning I was reading my school copy of Palgrave's Golden Treasury when he opened his door. We exchanged greetings and then, "What are you reading?" I showed him the compact little book. He glanced at it. "Shouldn't you be reading Spanish poetry?" In Spain, I'd bought a slim copy of Federico García Lorca's Romancero Gitano, his Gipsy Ballads. Using a small bilingual dictionary, I'd found abandoned in Casa Campello, I deciphered the poem that intrigued me most. It was 'The Arrest of Antoñito el Camborrio'. I was learning its lines by heart to help improve my fluency.

"But I do!" I protested. From memory, I began to recite the dramatic story of Antoñito, a proud Andalusian gipsy, on his happy way to Seville, on a care-free public holiday, to watch a bullfight. On the way, no fewer than five Civil Guards violently apprehend him, without clear cause.

I was in full flight and had reached the most dramatic point where the ghost of one of Antoñito's ancestors taunts the young gipsy, saying, "If you truly deserve the name Camborrio, you would whip out your blade and decapitate all five Civil Guards, one after the other!"

Don Eduardo held up his authoritative hand, palm towards me. I was irked to have had my dramatic prowess interrupted.

"Orlando, what do you know about Federico García Lorca?"

I paused and considered. "Not much," I admitted.

"I thought so! Listen to me, Orlando, Federico García Lorca was a communist and also sexual pervert! He was executed by the Civil Guard."

"I'd no idea!"

"With respect, there is a great deal you don't know!" I couldn't deny it.

"Listen to me, Don Orlando." For Don Eduardo to suddenly address me with the formal 'Don', I judged that he was either angry or dissociating himself from me for a good reason and so I listened to him carefully. "Federico García Lorca got what was coming to him. Federico García Lorca got precisely what all communists and sexual perverts should get. What vagabonds, Masons and all those who have no respect for law and order, no appreciation for Christian values, no esteem for the honour of our great fatherland, Spain, deserve!"

23

He paused dramatically. Gravely, his eyes on mine, he drew the side of his pudgy hand across the turkey wattle that hung from his throat. I could think of nothing useful to add.

Don Eduardo drew himself up to his full 5'8" – a proud inch taller over my personal best. "Listen to me, Don Orlando, I studied law. I have my diploma. I studied for the State competitive examinations and classified among the top ten in the whole of Spain. That guaranteed me a senior post in the public service of our great nation. Here in Buenavista del Norte, I, Don Eduardo Champín Zamorano, represent the Most Supreme General, none other than our great national leader, Francisco Franco Bahamonde, whose hand I have had the personal honour to shake. I know!"

I said I was sure he did know. That visibly pleased him. He looked at me as if making a decision of great importance. "One of these days, very soon, I am going to invite you to my office. It's just up here past the plaza on Calle de la Alhóndiga. There, in my office, I am going to show you a Spanish Encyclopaedia that contains all the information about our fatherland. I'm going to show you my diploma as well; it hangs in a frame above my desk beneath the portrait of El Caudillo – our supreme leader."

"Thank you, Don Eduardo!" I couldn't think of anything else to say. He acknowledged my apparent gratitude and took his leave, heading to his municipal office.

That evening, after dinner, he sent Lula to find me. "Don Eduardo's waiting for you on the azotea. Right now!" Her usually smiling face was serious.

I walked the twenty paces from my room and passed through the door onto the open terrace. Don Eduardo gestured for me to close the door behind me. "I have something to show you!" His voice was genial. He held a small beautifully-bound book in his hand. "You love poetry?" I nodded. "I too, love poetry and this, this is real Spanish poetry." He raised the volume. "Gustavo Adolfo Bécquer. This, I read to my wife, Doña Juana." He opened his Béquer and began to enunciate the Spanish in cumbrous tones:

"What is poetry? You direct the gaze of your blue eyes into mine.
What is poetry?
Do you really want to know?
You are!"

He lowered the volume and looked at me expectantly. My first thought was: "Only four short lines and you haven't yet memorized them?" But I kept that unkind observation to myself.

"Beautiful!" I said. "Your wife must feel admired."

"Admired, treasured and cherished! Listen to me, Don Orlando, this," he raised Gustavo Adolfo Bécquer above his head. "This! This is how to love a woman!" Alas, all too conscious that I lacked first-hand experience, I could only remain silent.

"Listen to me, Don Orlando, love is not about the 'me', it's about the 'you'. It's about the 'you' that I, the 'me', loves. "¡Tú!" Just as Béquer says in the last line: "¡Tú!" The sunlight caught the tiny, twin comets of spittle that accompanied the explosive 'tus'.

My heart went out to Don Eduardo. I'd cherished uncharitable thoughts about him and his relationship with his wife. She appeared to be a good decade younger and was beautiful in a helplessly appealing sort of way. She seldom seemed to leave their suite and their meals were carried up on a tray by one of the girls so they could eat in private. "He probably doesn't want any of the male diners – even me – admiring her," I'd unkindly guessed. He was twice my age and barely an inch taller, but double my 125 pounds. His face carried so much flesh that his cheeks pulsed like gills when he spoke and wet spittle flew from flabby lips.

"Thank you, Don Eduardo, there's much I can learn from you. Thank you very much!" I felt both chastened and the need to show contrition.

At the end of that week, Don Eduardo issued me a formal invitation to visit his office the following Tuesday. From ten in the morning until noon! I was slightly puzzled by the precision indicated in the 'ten until noon', but thought little more about it. When Tuesday arrived, I showered and dressed in my clean shirt and trousers. Shoes polished, I made my way up Calle de la Alhóndiga to the modest municipal building where Don Eduardo toiled on behalf of his beloved state.

"Don Orlando!" He greeted me fulsomely, with open arms and a smile. I followed him into his spacious office smelling of furniture polish, ancient paper and fatigued bureaucracy. Green box files lined two walls. A dark bookcase full of bound tomes took up all of the third. His massive, dark-grained desk was placed so that he sat with his back to the two tall windows. On the wall in a gilt frame in the space between the windows hung a coloured, head-and-shoulders portrait of General Franco, the Spanish Caudillo, in a khaki uniform buttoned to the neck, a medal pinned above his heart and a wine-coloured sash over his left shoulder. At a discreet distance below the Caudillo hung a plain-framed diploma attesting, in Spanish, to the Graduation in Law of Don Eduardo Champín Zamorano from the Faculty of the Universidad de Madrid in 1942, 18 years earlier. The year I was born, right in the middle of the War.

"These, he nodded emphatically several times to highlight his sincerity, are my two most treasured possessions!" Then his pudgy face broke into a simper. "I don't include my wife, you understand, because she is not a possession, she is my beloved partner on the rocky road of life."

He wiped what might have been a tear from his eye. Again, my heart went out to him. Eighteen years after graduation and here he was, the legal authority for the Spanish government in a village and municipal hinterland of perhaps a thousand souls, living with his beautiful, bored wife in a furnished room where they slept, took their meals and carried out their daily ablutions. All in excess of 2000 kilometres from home, among people who didn't refer to themselves as Spanish but as Canarios and for whom he and his partner on life's rocky road would always be forasteros – people from away, aliens, strangers – from the far-distant Peninsula.

To assuage the heartache I felt for Don Eduardo, I decided to admire his possessions in detail and with enthusiasm. When conversation faltered after about ten minutes, he pointed to a collection of heavy, leather-bound encyclopaedias. Select one, Don Orlando, sit in the armchair! Read!" He enthroned himself behind his desk, shuffled documents, from time to time looking up and smiling at me. If I closed the volume I was perusing and appeared to be on the point of leaving, he would solicitously rise, walk round his desk, take it from me, replace it on the shelf, and bring down another. He'd open it at random and point out an entry.

"You would do well, Don Orlando, to read this in close detail!" It was clear that I was being held captive in his office 'from 10 until noon' whether I liked it or not. The text of the articles being far beyond my reading level in Spanish and the detail beyond my interest, I contented myself with examining the many colourful illustrations.

At noon precisely – the church bells were ringing Angelus – Don Eduardo stood up, thanked me for my visit, formally shook my hand and told me that I was welcome to return to his office at any time to read any volume of his set of encyclopaedias that I felt the need to consult for my edification.

Immediately I re-entered my room back in the fonda to change out of my good clothes, I noticed that everything was slightly out of place. I owned very little, but knew exactly what I kept in the small chest of drawers and what I preferred to keep buckled into my rucksack. Even the bed and the chair had been moved. A spring cleaning? When I went downstairs to the patio for lunch, I asked Pastora if she thought I was an untidy person.

"Untidy? No, you're very tidy!" Her dark eyes regarded me with caution. "Why?"

"Because somebody has moved everything around in my room." Her look transformed into unhappiness. "I don't mind in the least," I was quick to reassure her, "I can keep my things the way you've left them if it's easier for you and your sisters that way when you clean." Eyes downcast, she fled to the kitchen. I'd done, or said, something to offend her but what?

The fact that not Pastora but Doña Lutgarda brought the plate of lentils from the kitchen to my table confirmed my guilt but still left me puzzled. Pastora remained in the kitchen; Obdúlia and Lula, while glancing covertly over at my table from time to time, were avoiding my eyes.

"Have I done something wrong, Doña Lutgarda?" She hesitated, frowned. Her evident discomfort increased my unease.

I looked into her knowing eyes, pleading enlightenment. I was happy living in her homely fonda and prepared to apologize for any unintentional breach of manners that I might have committed.

"Don Orlando!" She was close to tears and apparently felt the need to address me in the most formal way she knew how. "¡Chicas!" She gestured to Pastora, Obdúlia and their cousin Lula to approach my table. On tenterhooks, I looked from one to the other to glean any inkling of who or how I'd offended.

"Don Orlando!" Doña Lutgarda had pulled herself together. "This fonda is our family business." The three young women nodded in agreement. "Together, my three daughters, my niece Lula and I, run it for the pleasure and satisfaction of our guests. We try to make you all comfortable and happy." I nodded to indicate I more than appreciated all she and her family did, that I was indeed both comfortable and happy. "But there are forces beyond my control." She paused, swallowed and then forced herself to go on. "After you left this morning just before ten o'clock, the two Civil Guards arrived. They asked which room was yours. Why? I asked them, but they told me to show them your room. They had to search it. They had a paper." She looked at me to see that I was following. I nodded my understanding. "There was nothing I could do. They turned your room upside down, went through everything.

There was nothing I could do!" Her breaking voice told me she was unused to being stripped of authority in her own home. "After they left, Pastora put everything back in its place again. I am sorry."

I felt a huge wave of relief. The breach wasn't mine! Doña Lutgarda thought it was hers. Against the Civil Guard, however, no opposition was tolerated! "No apology is needed, Doña Lutgarda!"

The Civil Guard were ubiquitous throughout Spain. They carried out all national police duties in the rural areas and on the roads and highways that I'd walked, for weeks, with my thumb out. They invariably worked in pairs and served for two-year periods in regions far from their homes so as to prevent loyalties forming and to curb friendships. They stood out in their drab, ill-fitting, olive-green uniforms, three-cornered patent-leather hats, packed bandoliers and prominent weapons. One carried a bolt-action rifle, the other a machine gun. Not known for their acumen, they relied on their threatening demeanour and the freedom of action they were accorded by the state. It was quietly whispered, well out of their earshot, that they patrolled in twos and sometimes threes because one was able only to read, a second only to write and, if there was a third, he was serving his apprenticeship under these model officers.

Instantly, I knew I didn't want to begin to imagine what might have happened. It didn't in the least offend me that the Civil Guard had decided on their own initiative that they needed to find out if I was a subversive, if I planned to distribute underground literature or sow disruption. They simply couldn't, I knew, fathom a young man from a foreign country arriving in a tiny village and establishing himself there without any visible means of support and for no obvious purpose, far from his own. But what I didn't want to do was to speculate on any part that Don Eduardo might have played in spawning suspicion or collaborating in their intrusion within the fonda.

"Don't worry!" I looked at Doña Lutgarda and then at the despondent girls. "Everything's fine. I don't possess anything incriminating and I'm not doing anything amiss, so there's nothing at all to worry about!"

My clumsy justification brought little comfort to their eyes. Even a limited experience of Spain had taught me that the Spanish tended to deal in persuasive assertions rather than in rational explanations and so I added, as sincerely as I could, "I'm a good person!" With these words, I saw the tension visibly drain from the faces of the women. They believed me quite simply because I had said it – that I was a good person – but they still believed they needed forgiveness for the breach of privacy I had suffered while in their care.

"We couldn't do anything to stop them!"

"I understand."

"You're not angry?"

"I'm not angry!" The truth was that I was so relieved at discovering I wasn't the cause of their wretchedness that nothing else really concerned me.

After enjoying my lentils – the exciting events had done nothing to curb my appetite – I thanked them all for my lunch, then climbed the cool marble stairs to the terrace. I needed to think. There was no way I could discover whether the Civil Guard or Don Eduardo had initiated the search order. I hoped that Don Eduardo had merely supplied the legal warrant and agreed to keep me out of the fonda for two critical hours. Even if playing only a minor, supportive role, Don Eduardo would have been carrying out the inescapable orders delegated by functionaries who served his beloved Caudillo in the distant Peninsula. He no doubt aspired to serve in that Peninsula and return to it with his wife one fine day before he decomposed entirely, along with his musty files and his leather-bound encyclopaedias, two thousand kilometres from home.

Franco had waged, and won, a brutal civil war only to form a repressive, authoritarian system to guarantee that Spain and the Spanish were not overwhelmed by a coercive, Godless, communist ideology. The rights and wrongs, the pros and the cons, were beyond the grasp of my school-taught history.

The best thing I can do, I decided, is to live without needing an answer! And so, when I passed Don Eduardo and his wife walking fondly arm-in-arm among the villagers in the happy plaza that evening, I smiled, greeted them with due courtesy. Our formal, even friendly, relationship continued just as before. The Civil Guard – the Beneméritos, the Merciful as they were called – awkwardly clad and ferociously armed, didn't appear to glower at me with any greater unpleasantness than at the others, and so I didn't in the least feel singled out. Indeed, I felt as though I had undergone an unexpected and inevitable test, and had passed with flying colours.

5. *Learn early, learn easy*

My good fortune at having been accepted as a guest in the fonda, as the Pension Méndez was known to everybody in the village, was assuredly the foundation of my rewarding reception in the village. Doña Lutgarda and her daughters had been born and bred in Buenavista and both she and her fonda were cherished institutions. By virtue of the fact that I'd extended my original five nights by a week followed by yet another, I was continuously coming into contact with villagers young and old.

The plaza and the buildings that surrounded it with a fitting harmony formed the beating heart of Buenavista. The church bells announced the liturgy of the hours; the church's doors stood permanently open. Unhurried villagers criss-crossed the square all day, stopping to exchange gossip in the shade of the trees or the central decorative bandstand. In the evenings after work, it became an oasis of relaxation. Couples and entire families circled, chatting, laughing and enjoying the warmth radiating from the tiles that had absorbed the sun's heat all day. It smelled of flowers and leaf-mould, of the rest from work and gracious human contentment. The smooth, pastel-painted, stucco walls of the simple but dignified, two-story buildings looked as though they had survived unchanged from time immemorial. They were built to fit in, not to stand out. They housed a couple of cafes where players clattered dominoes, quiet surgeries belonging to the veterinarian and the doctor, the more important homes and an office or two.

The compact central square offered the secure, timeless warmth and security of a walled garden. It whispered of decorum, propriety and community. The narrow streets that led off it had been built at a time when villagers walked or rode on mules. Four times a day the guagua would arrive and disgorge those happy to be home again. Later, it would depart with a handful of passengers seen off by family members. There wasn't a sound, a sight or a smell out of place. Everything and everyone fit, matched, related and neatly dovetailed. The Plaza de los Remedios offered both a focus and a mature dignity to the modest, daily life of Buenavista del Norte.

The Pension Méndez, referred to simply as the fonda, added hospitality and character to the north side of the plaza, fitting in as much as standing out. If the ayuntamiento – the municipal office on the adjacent

Calle la Alhóndiga – was the sleepy administrative centre of the village, the fonda was the focal point for quiet enterprise, conversation and companionship. Its faded elegance occupied one half of one side of one of the quartet of streets that bounded the plaza. Its symmetry and balance, its thoughtful decorative features and its worn dignity were more comforting than distinguished. The buff and pink plaster façade rose three or four meters to a decorative painted balustrade that concealed the promise of a wide, empty terrace directly overlooking the plaza. The single large room that rose from one end of that terrace offered the elegance of a dignified tower with a pair of high, narrow windows and shutters that could be closed against the sun. Set back from the ample terrace, the upper story, equally decorative, could just be seen promising the traveller refuge and privacy.

Massive, time-worn, wooden doors two meters tall, and graciously folded back from early morning until after dinner, extended as boundless a welcome as an open smile. "Step inside, Señores! Rest! Eat! In Buenavista del Norte all is well!"

An identical double door was set at the far-right end of the façade and opened into the venta, the store that was run as part of the services the fonda offered. As far as I could make out, it boasted little more than cans of sardines, tuna fish and sacks of lentils and garbanzos that were sold by the kilo. Its principal function seemed to be the soothing meeting place for those women and men who sought company and conversation without feeling pressure to purchase.

The interior of the venta was divided by a wide, worn, wooden counter extending from wall to wall. Doña Lutgarda or one of the girls – whoever could be spared from the kitchen depending on the time of day and the press of patrons in the dining room – would stand behind the counter facing the open door, resting her elbows on the countertop, and a local or two would stand back to the door, elbows on the counter facing her. This was where local news, private joys and heartbreaks, rumours and gossip could be exchanged under the reasonable guise of hunting for something that a villager had run out of at home. All were welcome, listened to, shown sympathy. If I happened to pass still too early for lunch, and the venta were without a customer, even I, the Foreigner, might be invited in as a passable substitute for real company. It comforted me to feel acknowledged, even vaguely interesting.

Once you stepped through the tall, open main doors into the fonda itself and were invited deeper into the interior, you found yourself in a different world, one of cool shade, alluring alcoves, seductive Andalusian tiles and leafy plants in ceramic tubs whose scent immediately stirred memories of warm, rich, organic humus recently drenched.

31

You were in the large tiled courtyard, open to the sky, that served as the dining room. Tall, slim, wrought-iron pillars, twice the height of a man, supported a balcony on the floor above. Over the stone balustrade that surrounded the gallery spilled lush ferns and the long, variegated tendrils of air plants. The balcony's underside formed a protective covering sufficiently wide to allow the small wooden tables and chairs in the courtyard to be hastily drawn in beneath it so that patrons would be sheltered from frequent, light showers from the Atlantic.

In a very large recess within the inner wall was the archaic kitchen where Doña Lutgarda reigned supreme. Over glowing charcoal and popping gas, she prepared delicious meals of whole fish fried fast and crisp or gently poached in broth; dark rabbit stews made fragrant with whole heads of garlic, aromatic herbs and a splash of red wine; lentils or chickpeas boiled with onions and carrots and served fresh, sprinkled with coriander; and salty papas arrugadas – wrinkled potatoes allowed to boil dry in sea water. Gas arrived in small, round cylinders; charcoal was delivered every few weeks in sacks, tied two or three at a time, to the back of a donkey led by a reserved man whose skin and clothes were almost as black as the charcoal itself.

Doña Lutgarda's fragrant sauces perfumed with spices and fresh herbs never failed to set my mouth watering. The homely, flavoursome meals I'd grown accustomed to at home in Scotland had been almost entirely replaced by a range of equally simple and equally delicious, though very different, dishes. My invariable praise for everything, from hen's feet roasted over charcoal; chicken gizzards, pork or chicken liver tossed in olive oil; pungent goat kidney and delectable soup made from the same goat's grinning jaw-bone, gratified the girls and endeared me to the cook.

Just inside the foyer close to the main doors, wide marble stairs led up to the first-floor gallery and there you could appreciate the plants in all their glory. Many I'd never seen before, like night-scented jasmine, red glossy-petalled anthurium – I had to touch it to be convinced it wasn't plastic – and exotic lizbona. But there were others whose names, to the girls' surprise, I knew. There was croton, euphorbia – they knew it as La Corona de Cristo, Christ's Crown. There was unobtrusive hoya that suddenly burst into tight disks of tiny, white, sweet-smelling blooms that dripped nectar.

I knew these because the husband of one of my aunts on my father's side had been the gardener on various estates – Balcaskie in Fife, Airlie in Angus and Ravenscraig on the Firth of Tay. All had their heated glasshouses where exotic, scented houseplants were propagated. As a country-lover from childhood, I engineered grudging invitations from my Aunty Bunt to visit. The vast walled garden at Airlie Castle had an enormous glass-house on its interior north wall that absorbed heat from the reluctant Scottish sun. Within its pungent humidity, Jimmy Ramsay grew decorative houseplants for the appreciative Dowager Countess as well as musk-melons, table-grapes, figs and lemons. He'd been an engine-shunter in Kenya before being made redundant in the early fifties, and turned to estate work and gardening. He knew what it was like to begin a new vocation. He was as patient a teacher as I was an avid learner. His unhurried explanations and hands-on demonstrations came with botanical names. Intrigued, I absorbed and remembered.

The columns that supported the balcony rose all the way to the roof. Because the rooms on both the ground floor and the upper floor were high-ceilinged to conserve cool air, these slim columns must have risen to a height of over 30 feet. The balcony formed a protective roof around the entire perimeter of the courtyard below and, on the first floor, gave access to each of the 10 or 12 large rooms in the fonda. Each of these chambers, in addition to having a tall, wooden door, also had a 'window' entirely without glass, that gave directly onto the gallery. Each 'window' could be closed from inside by a set of louvered shutters and so provide privacy if needed.

This conservatively elegant interior of the fonda – charm that couldn't be guessed at from outside – gave the impression of space, dignity and the kind of respectful peace and serenity I'd experienced previously only in old stone churches or at Sunday school when I was a child. I felt a sense of timeless protection that took the edge off my occasional loneliness.

Some of the status and respect that Pension Méndez enjoyed as a central institution in the life of the village rubbed off on me, to my good fortune. I could stand at the main double door of the fonda and watch as the guagua from the capital drew up and disgorged its clucking passengers. I could greet and banter with Manolo and Santiago as they noisily passed parcels and paper-work to the girls for safekeeping on the dedicated shelf in the venta until such time as their owners chose to collect them. Haste was almost entirely unknown in the village. Hustle and bustle were looked upon as vulgar.

By looking to my right from the doorway, I could see who was entering the church to recite the Angelus or perform private devotions. By looking left, I was able to see who was drinking coffee or sipping liqueurs at one of the two bars. All I had to do was cross the street and I was in the plaza itself, in the shade of trees and surrounded by flowers.

At any time of the day, there would be older couples enjoying the fresh air, even older men sitting on the benches telling tales of their shared experiences in Cuba, young mothers whose babies smiled at admirers to be spoiled with compliments, chucks under the chin and little coos at how chubby they'd become or how well they were striving to walk or talk.

Shortly after my initial arrival, I'd taken stock of my situation. Here I am, I pondered, I've found a comfortable, homely pension in the heart of the village where I can eat and sleep in comfort. From my hosts and from the villagers, I attract curiosity tinged with respect. However, without Spanish I can neither relate closely nor find a job! And so, eager to reduce that disadvantage, I'd earnestly set about learning the language.

And that's where Doña Lutgarda and her family came to play a supporting role.

Twice a day, at lunch and dinner in the fonda, I'd be asked questions by Doña Lutgarda or the girls either singly or in an eager group. I was grateful for being left alone at breakfast. At that early hour, Doña Lutgarda was fully occupied getting the kitchen fires going, taking receipt of the morning bread and milk and laying out the ingredients and the utensils she'd need for the day's menu. Her eldest daughter, Angélica, and her cousin Lula, each had small children to dress and get ready for school. The younger daughters, Obdúlia and Pastora, were sleepy-heads who found it arduous to serve breakfast and when they did, neither was in any mood to engage in conversation.

The fonda had never before hosted an Extranjero and this was their chance to find out if Extranjeros were normal people like Canarios, slightly odd like Peninsulares, or entirely different from both, and if so, in which ways. When there were few diners, all five women would congregate around my table and ply me with questions. Initially the questions were personal like: "What country do you come from?" "Do you speak Christian?" "Does your mamá know where you are?" That they would rephrase these questions in multiple ways, suggested that they found my answers somehow unsatisfactory – were they perhaps hoping to catch me out in an inconsistency? – but they gave me lots of varied practice.

As soon as I began to go out and explore the village and its surroundings, the nature of the questions expanded: "What are you going to do today?" "Will you go walking again?" "Where to – the cliffs, the shoreline, the plantations, the arid plain, the mountains?" Any hesitation on my part would elicit detailed suggestions. "If you cross the bridge over the barranco – an ancient dry creek-bed – bear south and keep going for half-an-hour, you'll come to la Casa Blanca, it's the last farm on the track. If you go a little bit further, you'll come to the biggest cactus tree in the entire island, El Cardón." Or: "Go out of the village and head downhill towards the sea. Go past the graveyard and then bear south. In 40 minutes or so you'll come to the beach that we villagers use in the summer time. It's just pebbles now, but every year in the spring, great waves wash the sand back in. It's the loveliest black beach you'll ever see." Or: "Take the path that leads towards the mountains but bear right. In four or five kilometres you'll see the Barranco Negro – but don't get too close to it because it's haunted! You may never come back!" And they'd shriek with laughter at the look of horror I'd assume to amuse them. Not only did I have to learn to speak and answer questions, I also had to listen and understand what was being asked of me and the sometimes-complex instructions I was being given. It was clear that I needed a strategy to learn Spanish quickly so that I could find paying work.

To master the language rapidly, I adopted two complementary strategies. The first was to work my way systematically through each lesson in Hugo's *Spanish in Three Months*, a slim volume I'd bought in Menzies' before I left Dundee. At the Morgan Academy, I'd thoroughly enjoyed English grammar and had been intrigued by Latin noun declensions and verb conjugations, so learning from the traditional grammar-based approach adopted by Hugo suited me just fine. Mastering the sound-system, conjugating verbs, declining nouns, grasping syntax and grammar, acquiring essential vocabulary, all gave me the big picture of how the Spanish language was constructed. With those schemas under my belt, I could then compare my efforts at pronunciation, sentence formation and meaning-making with the native-speakers around me. When I noticed I was deficient or fell short, or when I was met with open-eyed puzzlement, I would go back to the drawing board and come back with a new attempt; and usually succeed.

Going through *Spanish in Three Months* – it took me about 10 days – to capture the essentials helped me build, inside my head, a kind of schema that reflected how the language worked, the order in which clauses were put together, and how what bits of what words changed depending on gender or number or mood or tense. Getting these details right, I discovered, made all the difference to being understood easily and with precision.

On my travels, I'd picked up a small, paperback Spanish-English/English-Spanish dictionary. Now I used it constantly to find words I heard but couldn't understand. I also used it to find the Spanish equivalent for English words I needed to use when I wanted to explain something in Spanish. I carried a small notebook and pencil in my pocket. Every day, I'd make note of the difficulties I encountered both understanding and expressing myself. Every evening without fail, I'd draft out short answers to questions I'd been asked, and had understood, during the day but found myself at a loss to answer clearly because I lacked the vocabulary or the correct tense or the appropriate conjunction. I'd also translate into Spanish, questions that I wanted to ask others and also details about my life or work experiences that I felt necessary to convey but my interrogators hadn't yet thought to ask.

Every day, I'd have all five women of the fonda gather round my table and remind them of any question I'd failed to understand or to answer clearly. Once they remembered and we were all focused, I'd offer them a fuller answer in greater detail. They'd listen and then invariably nod. "Ah, now we understand!" And often they'd correct my grammar, supply a better word or a better, more socially polite, way of expressing myself.

On one of my long treks, I'd stopped to talk to a horseman. As we talked, his horse urinated, splashing me unmercifully. The rider had laughed but I'd left having mastered a new word, mear – to urinate. One evening after dinner in the fonda when I was being plied with questions, I excused myself explaining I really had to 'mear'. The women went off into shrieks of laughter. When they caught their breaths, they asked me to repeat what I'd said and when I did, they shrieked some more. Doña Lutgarda had later explained to me that the word mear was used only of animals; the equivalent, more polite form for the human need was orinar. The difference between: "I gotta go and take a pish!" and "Excuse me, I have to empty my bladder."

Within a couple of weeks, these two techniques I was using to learn Spanish, coupled with enthusiastic encouragement from my hostesses who found my mistakes hilarious, I was able to handle myself passably well. Being able to converse in even rudimentary terms raised my status enormously in the fonda. It was as if they'd believed that because, when I'd newly arrived, I spoke almost no Spanish at all, it must therefore follow that I was also deficient in most other ways!

Now that I was mastering their language, I was relieved to see they stopped glancing at me pityingly. I was glad too, that they felt they could reduce, by several hundred decibels, the volume of their voices when addressing me. They seemed to be saying, much to their own surprise: "Maybe extranjeros aren't, after all, inherently feeble-minded! Orlando's not as different from us as we had imagined when he first turned up like a stray puppy on the guagua a couple of weeks ago!"

The Spanish language, however, wasn't all that Doña Lutgarda and her family were teaching me. They were also my mentors in how to best conduct myself in the village; how to act in ways that would cause no offence or inadvertently embroil me in socially awkward or compromising situations.

Simply courting

In 1960, Sundays were the day of rest in Catholic Spain, as they were in Scotland. In the village, nobody worked unless they were unavoidably obliged to, as in the fonda. Most, even those who worked, discarded their everyday clothes for their Sunday best and polished shoes. The church bells rang for those who would attend mass. Those who preferred leisure pursuits took a long cane, a line and some worms to the rocky shore. Others played football, took their toddlers for a walk or visited with friends in the quiet, narrow streets. After mass, however, it was a tradition that the unattached teenagers would walk around the circumference of the plaza. In groups of four or five, well-groomed young women promenaded clockwise and young men, also in groups and equally well-groomed, promenaded counter-clockwise.

The third Sunday after I'd arrived in Buenavista, I was sitting alone on one of the benches watching this ritual. The boys wore smart slacks and starched shirts neatly pressed and ironed by their mothers. The girls were dressed in colourful skirts and flattering blouses – not that they needed flattering since, to a woman, they were glowingly pretty, blossom-fresh, hair immaculate. When a small group of youths beckoned me to join them, I did. It seemed contrary on my part to refuse, and besides, I wanted to join in, to be less of a solitary outsider.

Now that I was circulating with the boys in the outer of the two concentric circles, I could appreciate in greater detail what was happening. Girls and boys would scan one another's faces as they casually passed one another. Eyes would meet eyes and if the admiration were mutual, the briefest, tiniest of smiles would be offered. If accepted, it would be equally briefly returned before the progress of the circles broke the fleeting contact. The young of both sexes were highly skilled at catching these tiny signals between one or other of their companions and a boy or a girl in the other group. Girls would giggle and nudge; the boys would elbow their friend if his smile had been reciprocated. And then on the next passing, the flirtatious glances and the smiles would grow in confidence and last just that fraction of a second longer.

Villagers walking in la Plaza de los Remedios after Sunday mass.

This innocent and gentle flirting between the sexes fascinated me with its artless honesty. I'd known its less charming Scottish equivalent at school dances where the hall was divided into sides by gender. When a boy on the boys' side of the hall would catch the eye of a girl on the girls' side, she might maintain the contact for a mere fraction of a second longer than necessary. This nanosecond offered the boy just enough confidence to make a bid. But to do so, he had to cross the floor, as wide as the very ocean, and invite her to dance just as the music started up. He carried with him the slender trusting hope that she wouldn't reply to his, "May I have this dance?" with a devastating "No thanks!" or worse, a disdainful snub delivered by a flick of the head and averted eyes. And there was the additional fear that another young man, walking more swiftly, might claim the prize and leave you foolish, alone and startled under the beseeching eyes of the wallflowers.

As the exotic Extranjero, I received and returned several brief, harmless looks, perhaps even with one young woman in particular, and felt flattered and flushed with the freshness of youth for the first time since leaving Scotland. When the two circles finally broke up so that everybody could go home for lunch, small groups of boys shyly spoke directly to small groups of equally shy girls, allowing those who had exchanged flirtatious glances to spend a few moments in each other's company before all departed. The group of boys who'd welcomed me wanted to take me to the group of girls in which the one who had most courageously returned my smiles was lingering at the side of the plaza. Self-conscious of my deficient Spanish, I resisted. They teased me for my timidity and everybody simply dispersed each to his or her home.

When I sat down for lunch at my table in the tiled courtyard that midday, none of the four girls who usually waited on me approached. They appeared to be busy with other guests. Sunday being the day when the more affluent couples or families decided to lunch out, I thought nothing of it, but when Doña Lutgarda emerged from the kitchen wiping her hands on her apron and looking severe, I suspected something was amiss. Having declared, shortly after I arrived, that I was a Protestant in order to explain why I didn't enter the church on the plaza, I guessed that I'd perhaps offended by joining the flirtatious circles under false pretences. All of the others, as far as I could see, had arrived at the plaza directly from mass. They had paid their dues; I was delinquent.

Doña Lutgarda drew up a chair. "Don Orlando, you're an Extranjero. A person from another country." I nodded. "You're new to the village and you don't know our ways." Again, I nodded. "Here in Tenerife, here in Buenavista del Norte, girls marry young, when they're even 16 or 17." I began to say that in Scotland the age of permissible marriage was 16 but she silenced me. "Please listen! Usually, the young man is several years older, has a job, prospects, and may court the young woman from the time she's 15 or so."

I couldn't see where this was going but I nodded and remained silent. She continued. "In villages like ours, young people meet each other in the public plaza, usually on Sundays after mass, right where all can see them, and that's where they form a noviazgo." She enunciated each syllable of noviazgo and looked at me earnestly, apparently to make sure I'd captured the import.

"¿Noviazgo?" I was at a loss. "No comprendo, Doña Lutgarda."

With great patience and equal seriousness, Doña Lutgarda explained 'noviazgo' as a sacred relationship between a young man and a young woman that implied eventual marriage. It meant that the couple had exchanged glances, talked together, albeit still in the company of their giggling friends on a Sunday after mass and on subsequent Sundays. By the fourth or fifth Sunday, without ever having left the public square filled with villagers, they were considered to be novios, to have begun to contract a noviazgo.

Doña Lutgarda paused. I shook my head in disbelief. "I don't think I've understood correctly." I summarized. "They have entered a noviazgo that leads to marriage merely by flirting and exchanging a few words within a group of friends?"

"Yes!"

"Because they've spoken together? The plaza is a public place where anybody can attest to the innocence of the exchange!" Incredulous, I was groping for understanding, enlightenment.

"In the plaza, in public, Don Orlando, that's the point! The young man has expressed his interest and the young woman has confirmed hers in these glances and with just a few words of innocent conversation. Everybody knows about it. Unless their families disapprove, and that's unlikely, the noviazgo becomes formalised. The young woman and the young man now have expectations. So do their parents and so does the rest of the village. They are novios; they have a publicly witnessed contract of noviazgo. If the young man chooses to break that contract, it won't be the end of the world for him. He'll be harshly thought of for a year or two. But the young woman! She may never marry! No other young man may want her. She may be condemned to live the rest of her life as a spinster, without children. Her life will be caring for her parents, loving her nephews and nieces."

Doña Lutgarda regarded me soberly, intent on making me understand. I strove to take her words in. She was cautioning me that what might appear to me as harmless flirtation, could have ruinous consequences for a young woman, consequences that could determine the rest of her life. To be absolutely certain I'd understood correctly, I repeated the bare details of her warning. When I finished, she nodded. "That's it! Now you understand!" The appeal in her eyes signalled: "Behave accordingly!"

That afternoon I stood on the terrace, alone once more, and looked out on the plaza. It was quiet, wouldn't begin to attract casual strollers until the sun began to set after 6 o'clock. I reflected on the critical lesson that Doña Lutgarda about local custom, one that I needed to learn, if I intended to live harmoniously in this cohesive village, a village about the same size as Coupar Angus, where I'd spent my earliest and happiest years. Actions that truly mattered, conduct that protected the integrity of small communities could not be treated with careless disregard. Now I knew that a precious aura surrounded the after-mass Sunday ritual.

How fortunate, I thought, that I have never had a serious girlfriend, or even a close-to-serious relationship for that matter. I'd been one of those young man who had, more often than not, received the dismissive shake of the head at school dances. These crushing experiences at 15 and 16 had so discouraged me that I'd turned to less humiliating pursuits like cycling the Angus glens. I'd used my weekend evenings to cram for all-important school examinations and had done so somewhat forlornly but without feeling particularly deprived.

Respect for girls, in the 1950s, was something that we learned early and accepted as normal, a duty and so Doña Lutgarda's lesson wasn't too difficult for me to digest.

Never again did I join the circles of young people rotating in different directions round the plaza on Sundays after mass. Moreover, I was careful to greet young women formally and with not even the slightest hint of coquetry. I wondered if it were my destiny to feel apart.

Worshippers gather outside Nuestra Señora de los Remedios to celebrate the festival of San Antonio Abad.

6. Settling into Buenavista del Norte

I didn't intentionally go out to 'make friends' in the village. From past experience, I'd learned that any friendship has a way of simply 'forming' if an offer is made, accepted and there's time available for cultivation and nurture. While I'd been travelling through France, I'd typically spend no more than a day or two in any one place. Each morning I'd consult my map and plan to reach a particular youth hostel, the only accommodation I could afford, by early evening. The overnight charge for a bunk in a common dormitory was modest. There was always access to a kitchen, so I'd prepare my simple evening meal and eat it in the company of other young hitch-hikers, usually couples or small groups in their early twenties from Canada, Australia, New Zealand or South Africa.

In peninsular Spain, it wasn't essential to reach a youth hostel – there were, in fact, very few. But even the tiniest village offered a pension with a cheap, clean bed. A filling meal of soup or tomatoes chopped in olive oil with raw onions and crisp bread was always on offer no matter the hour. Urban Spaniards, including children, seemed to stay up half the night, talking noisily. Villages were quieter.

My only two experiences of youth hostels in Spain were discouraging. In the first, I'd had to search out the warden. When I found him, he looked at me cautiously, shook his head and declared that the hostel was for Españoles only! Indignant, I showed him my Scottish Youth Hostel Association lifetime membership card bearing the affiliation logo that allowed members to use their Spanish counterpart, Albuerges Juveniles. He eventually backed down but with bad grace. Printed documents always impressed in Spain. Sullen, he assigned me a lower bunk in the men's dormitory. His initial opposition soon became apparent. In flagrant violation of hostel rules but doubtless to his personal financial advantage, he was renting beds for migratory agricultural workers until the grape harvest ended and they returned to their homes in and around Barcelona.

In my second Spanish youth hostel, a contingent of uniformed Falangist Youth were holding some sort of rally. The Falange was the only authorised political party in the country. These school-age youngsters, all dressed in identical blue shirts and shorts, were being introduced to Francoist ideology to help them fulfil their potential as future protectors of the dictatorship. Indistinguishable to my eyes, one from the other, they regarded me with open-mouthed wonder as something totally alien and strange. Spain had been virtually isolated from the rest of Europe since the Civil War ended in 1939. Their teacher-supervisors frowned and made it clear that my presence was unwelcome. Irritated by their open hostility and to save myself embarrassment, I checked out of that hostel and found a bed in a cheap, welcoming pension nearby.

This pattern of constant movement, one night here and the next a hundred kilometres further on, prevented me from forming any relationships save those captured in cursory conversations with the lonely, chain-smoking truck-drivers who took me from crossroads to crossroads or whose trailers I unloaded when we arrived at a destination and no willing labour was available.

In contrast, here and now in Buenavista del Norte, I was no longer on the move. I had settled, established myself, put down roots in the final village at the end of the serpentine road, at the terminus of the guagua, the most distant, isolated point on the island from the capital, Santa Cruz. Being at the point where the asphalt ran out and gave way to earthen tracks, there was nowhere to go except, of course, 'back', and at that particular point in time, the idea of going back held no appeal for me. Back where? Back to what? I'd taken hard, the blow of not having won a place to study agriculture at Aberdeen University, especially after staying on at the Morgan Academy for those extra three years to gain the entry requirements for that very purpose. My father had belittled my aspirations. "I left school at 14. Think you're any better than me, do you?" Ambition meant nothing to him and my not succeeding turned me, in his eyes, from a moocher into a failure. "See?" Triumph glinted in his eyes. "See where pretension gets you? Now get out and find yourself an honest job!" For that triumphant glint and other reasons, remaining at home was out of the question.

I wanted, needed, to go forward, to advance, even though my mind wasn't at all clear what that might entail. Having decided, at least for the moment, to shelve my plans to reach South America and stay put in Buenavista as well as master Spanish, I immediately began to explore first the narrow, walled streets of the village itself and then the more open, more interesting surrounding countryside. As a consequence, I repeatedly bumped into and recognized the same people and, by dint of familiarity, started to make acquaintances who became friends.

Juan José

One morning, a few moments after I'd stepped out of the fonda to take a look around, a thin young man, aspiring to grow a moustache, approached me with a smile and his hand extended: "I am Juan José." I'd occasionally seen him striding purposefully across the plaza but despite appearing pressed for time, he always smiled and nodded. I shook his hand: "I am Orlando." By now I realised it was futile to insist on Ronald or even Ron. They pronounced it 'Wrong', screwed up their eyes and laughed: "Cuba-libre!" – their preferred drink apparently, made with rum (ron as in wrong) and Coca Cola on ice.

"Ai waanteen elearn eenglees!" He wanted to learn English!

We sat down on one of the benches in the fresh morning air, immediately attracting a host of canaries, the sparrows of Tenerife, looking for crumbs. We had none to give and they flew away. Juan José, his face thin and serious, explained his request. He'd completed school a couple of years earlier. Wanting to study a profession but, lacking the funds to leave home and study at university, he'd begun taking correspondence courses in electrical engineering as applied to radio communications. He was in the process of building his own short-wave receiver and intended, eventually, to build a transmitter. He could read Morse code signals but much of the traffic he managed to pick up was in English putting him at a disadvantage. Once he'd finished his certificate, he planned to use his qualifications and his English to enter the Spanish Navy as a communications officer. Could I help him?

He was a likeable lad, two years my senior. His sense of ambition and the effort he was willing to make to achieve it appealed to me. Our school teachers in Scotland had urged us to have ambition and, like all born without silver spoons in our mouths, we were admonished to work hard to accomplish that ambition! "Ambition and hard work! There's no other way!" Having failed to achieve mine by not winning a place to study agriculture in Aberdeen University – entry was highly competitive – I was all the more conscious that I'd lost my way and, for time being at least, was unable to find it again.

"I'd like to help you," I told him sincerely, "but there's a problem." He raised his eyebrows. I told him about a disturbing event that had befallen me at the docks in El Ferrol del Caudillo in Galicia a couple of months earlier.

Coming from a fishing nation and having occasionally spent our two weeks' holidays in ports on the North-East coast of Scotland like Arbroath and Montrose, I'd become intrigued by the romance of fishing boats and visited the harbour in any coastal French or Spanish village that I happened to be in. One night, I'd wandered along the quay in El Ferrol looking at the trawlers tied up. By their battered appearance, they fished in distant, cruel waters. There was nobody about. All was quiet except for the gentle stutter of the odd auxiliary motor that ran a generator to give light to or pump bilge-water from one or other of the fishing boats. Suddenly, a hatch opened on the trawler immediately in front of me and a crew-necked fisherman emerged on deck. "¡Buenas noches!" He lit a cigarette and offered me one. I shook my head but returned his "¡Buenas noches!", glad of the companionship.

"You're not from here." His statement was in Spanish.

"I'm Scottish. I come from Scotland." I made him understand.

"Greenock, Oban, Stornoway!" He looked pleased and I surprised. He told me that his skipper would shoot their nets in the Atlantic off the west coast of Scotland and they'd put in at Scottish ports for supplies or spare parts. He was the radio operator and doubled as a winch-operator.

"How long have you been away from Scotland?"

"About six weeks"

"Come aboard. I'll find a Scottish trawler for you to talk to." I followed him into the wheelhouse where he began to adjust knobs on the radio. No sooner had he isolated a Scottish voice from the confusing stream of staccato Morse and swelling interference, than the door burst open and a Civil Guard, bearing the rifle, whose butt he'd used to gain entry, stood in the cramped space. His partner with the machine gun was right behind him.

"You two! What are you doing?"

The radio operator was more alarmed than I was. Two or three times I'd been accosted by the Civil Guard, always in pairs, on lonely roads and had had coarse questions barked at me: "Who are you?" "What are you doing here?" When I explained that I was hitchhiking round their beautiful country to get to know their delightful customs and enjoy their world-famous hospitality, they'd pause, unsmiling, one would thrust out a hand and demand: "¡Pasaporte!" Then they'd scan each page as if there might be secret codes to be found if they stared long and hard enough. Eventually they'd hand it back to me, and, jerking the loaded barrel of rifle or machine gun, order "Get going!" Used to these intrusive experiences, I wasn't overly concerned, but I could see that the radio operator was, and they, sensing his fear, directed their bullying tactics at him.

"What's that?" One Guard jerked his rifle at the squawking radio.
"It's the trawler's radio."

"What's it for?" They had a habit of asking the obvious.

"It's how we get weather reports."

"But you're in harbour, tied up!"

Alarmed, he gestured at me. "This tourist is from Scotland. He's been away from home for a couple of months. I'm trying to find a Scottish trawler so he can listen to his own language spoken."

The Guard tried to raise his rifle but found it impossible in such a small space. "You're trying to communicate with foreigners!" The radio operator's face tightened. This wasn't good!

Civil Guards were, on the whole, brutish, poorly-trained, unclear about their function beyond intimidation, and possessed a short attention span. Knowing this, I dared to take control of the situation using distraction as my tactic.

"My passport!" I tried to give my voice the kind of authority that Captain Bentley of Balmuir Estate where I'd worked during summer holidays might have used with one of his errant farm-labourers. With both my hands in clear view, I slowly extracted my passport from the money belt inside my shirt. Swaggering functionaries were intrigued by documents of any kind, I'd discovered, and in proportion to the number of mysterious signatures and smudged stamps they bore. My distraction worked. Since there was too little space for them to examine the passport and keep their weapons in check they ordered us both back onto the quayside. One after the other, the Guards turned scrutinized every entry and exit stamp.

"You've been in Morocco!" They peered at me with suspicion.

"Of course," I said confidently. I'd hitch-hiked to Zagora on the Saharan border of Morocco and Algeria in 21 days just before my final year at school. "I wanted to see Tétuan where your Maximo Caudillo started his glorious campaign to liberate Spain from the republicans and the communists."

"Are you a republican?"

"No!"

"Are you a communist?"

"No!"

"Are you a Mason?"

"No!" I decided against admitting that my Uncle Willy Harvey had initiated King George VI into Scottish Rights.

They paused, looked at each other for inspiration but failed to discover even the slightest glimmer. Then the Guard with the machine gun looked at me slyly, caught his colleague's eye as if to boast: "This brilliant question will flush this devious foreigner out!"

"You say you're not a republican, you're not a communist, and you're not a Mason." I shook my head to deny any such perfidy. The Benemérito paused as if for dramatic effect before coming out with his most incisive question: "Are you a good person?"

The radio operator caught my eye and I was terrified that we would both burst out laughing, so I paused, adopted a serious expression to mimic religious piety and admitted with all the dramatic humility and simple Spanish I could muster: "Señores, I do my best, my very, very best. I go to confession and ask the Blessed Virgin Mary's boundless help to be a good person." I was glad that I'd got over my Protestant prejudice enough to spend hours in cool cathedrals and quiet, candle-lit chapels where the windows created puddles of fractured colour on the stone floors.

Both Beneméritos searched my face to be certain of my sincerity, looked at each other for confirmation, appeared to find it. Satisfied, they nodded. "Fine! Good! But you should not be on the quay at night. It is forbidden!" I'd learned that the Civil Guard could say that anything was forbidden and simply by saying so, make it so. "Now we will escort you back to town." And to the radio-operator: "You! Back on board! But don't go trying to speak to foreign trawlers again, not for anybody. Not even for good tourists like this one. There is evil everywhere and it's our job to protect our glorious country from bad people!"

I resisted the temptation to stand to attention, raise my voice and shout: "¡Arriba España! ¡Viva Franco!" These were the assertions cried out on the Spanish radio every hour following the national anthem and preceding the news. The radio operator nodded contritely to show his intention to obey, and without daring to look at me, stepped aboard and locked the hatch noisily. The pair of self-satisfied Beneméritos walked me back to the dim lights of the main street and dismissed me with the hauteur of those who know they wield undisputable power.

After I'd told Juan José my tale, adding that I wouldn't want either of us to get into trouble, he was quiet and looked serious. "You're right! We'll keep my radio receiver out of this!" He began coming over to the fonda for English lessons after dinner, with Doña Lutgarda's blessing.

"Juan José is a serious person," she nodded her approval, a good boy. "I've known his family all my life, honest, hard-working people. His ambition is to join the Spanish Navy, to better himself. He has the brains and the perseverance to succeed." She was as happy to see me begin to make friends with people she approved of as Pearl would have been. My feelings of loneliness began to dissipate.

Pepe Mendibles

Pepe-Mendibles the carpenter and joiner. He built the most beautiful furniture out of wood, such as the bed-boards and mirror-frame behind him.

One day, only two or three short blocks from the plaza, in a side-street just off Calle La Alhóndiga, I passed a workshop where a joiner was bent over a circular saw, confidently cutting boards to size. His saw-blade whined and clouds of yellow sawdust spurted into the street, forcing me to hold my breath and speed up to escape. When I returned later that afternoon, he'd cut the various boards to size, clamped several together to make the headboard and the footboard for a double bed, and was expertly running his hand-planer over the bedrails. When I passed a day or two later, he was carving an intricate pattern into the headboard with expert passes of his wood-chisel. I stopped, he looked up, gave a quick grin, and turned his attention back to his work. When he'd finished that part of the pattern he'd been carving, he looked up once more, smiled and extended his hand. "Pepe Mendíbil." I shook it. "Orlando."

"I know! You're el Extranjero who lives with Doña Lutgarda at the Pension Méndez." Pepe was about my height, 5'7', maybe in his early forties and his broad smile took up almost the entire lower half of his

48

face. He was fair but well-tanned, and his high cheekbones and steady confident eyes reminded me of Polish army officers who'd been billeted in my grandmother's house in Coupar Angus during World War II. I used my fledgling Spanish to compliment him on his fine carving. "Beautiful!" He was pleased.

"Look at this one!" Deeper into his crowded workshop he showed me the headboard of an even grander bed that he'd completed just days before and was polishing into a fine finish. It was a work of art.

I stroked the light, polished wood and the stylized rose patterns that he'd drawn out of it with such perfection, using his razor-sharp wood-chisels. "You must have been a carpenter for a very long time." He nodded, the huge smile never left his face.

"This is not carpentry, this is cabinet-making. I'm a cabinet-maker as well as a carpenter." He used a word I didn't know, ebanísta, with the stress on the final syllable. I repeated the words carpintero, then ebanísta; carpintero, ebanísta; carpintero, ebanísta! We both laughed. Within two minutes flat, I'd increased my vocabulary and my ability to speak with greater precision and, best of all, widened my circle of friends.

Everybody in the village seemed to be known by a nickname and when I asked Pepe if he had one he beamed, "Of course! Pepe is the diminutive of José. But because there are so many Josés and therefore many Pepes, they've found ways to distinguish us. They call me Pepe Mendibles. It's a play on my surname. My surname is Mendíbil, but it's difficult because it's unusual. So me? I'm Pepe-Mendibles!" Everything including his eyes was absorbed into his smile.

Daily, I'd stop and talk with Pepe. If he was too busy because he had an order to fill by a particular deadline, he'd tell me and I'd wave and go on. If he'd no urgent deadline, he'd show me the different woods he worked with and the range of tasks he undertook as the only carpenter-cabinet-maker in the village. He made window frames, stools, tables, chairs, beds, and grand double wardrobes. Factory-made furniture, he told me, was unknown in Buenavista so, before a couple married, he had the job of making what they would need to set up their house. As in Scotland, they didn't order everything at once. They started with the essentials – bedroom suite and the kitchen table and chairs. The baby's cradle was next. The rest followed as needed and if money was available. Pepe looked at me to see if I was following. I was.

"Do you like boats?"

"You make boats too?" I was prepared to be astonished by his woodworking skills.

"No, I don't make boats, but a friend in Los Silos owns a small fishing boat, a falúa, a boat with an inboard engine. Occasionally on a Sunday he picks me up and we putt-putt down the coast and round the headland together to visit the Torrero at Teno." He gestured in the direction beyond the road, beyond the village, past the cliffs.

"¿Torero?" I'd seen a bullfight in Spain but hadn't imagined there might be bullfights in a tiny, isolated village like this. Actually, one bullfight had been enough to satisfy my curiosity for life.

Pepe laughed again. "Listen to me, Orlando: torero, torrero; torero, torrero; torero, torrero! You hear the difference?" I did. A single 'r' was pronounced with one flap of the tongue as in Scots; a double 'rr' was pronounced with two rapid flaps of the tongue the way the English would when they tried to mimic us Scots.

"Right, so what's a torrero?"

"It's not a real Spanish word," he laughed, "It's the nickname we invented for the lighthouse keeper at la Punta de Teno just off the tip of the island facing into the Atlantic. If a man who fights a bull – toro with a single 'r' – is a 'torero', then a man who looks after a tower – torre with double 'r' – must be a 'torrero'!" Pepe loved common logic. "We're friends, the torrero and I. He and his wife welcome visitors."

"I'd love to visit the torrero and his family!"

"It's quiet there. There's a little-used, long and dangerous path over the mountains but the simple way is to go in one of the fishing boats. There's little to do there except talk and fish. You can just make out two of the three closest islands from the lighthouse, La Gomera and La Palma."

I was hooked! Getting to know people, having someone welcome you to his carpenter's shop for a chat or having someone drop over to the fonda to practice speaking English now took the edge off my loneliness and made me feel I was beginning to belong.

Though I might be known as the foreigner, el Extranjero, simply because I was the only one around, I promised myself that I'd do all I could to learn how to live in Buenavista del Norte in a way that made them see that I was no more exotic than they were.

7. First day at work

Women would collect bundles of herbs and grasses to feed the rabbits they bred for meat at home.

It was still dark when I woke at 6.30. The noise of the front door being opened and locked back and the usual kitchen sounds below told me I wasn't first up and that breakfast would soon be ready.

"Sit there!" Doña Lutgarda indicated the table closest to the kitchen alcove and then raised her voice, "Obdúlia! Pastora! Are you fine ladies up yet? I won't tell you again!" Every morning, the younger pair of girls were needed to rise early and make innumerable trips back and forth to the communal water tap below the plaza in order to fill the cisterns with water for the day's business, before getting the tables ready for guests.

Doña Lutgarda laid a large empty cup, a jug of milky coffee and a dish of what looked like course brown flour on the table in front of me. "It's too early for bread, but this is better – gofio! It's guaranteed to keep a man going from before dawn until midday." For emphasis she puffed out her cheeks and flexed her biceps. Her lively impersonation reminded me of the World's Strong Man at Billy Smart's Circus when, once a year, it came to that cinder-strewn piece of derelict land in Dundee called Gussie Park. Thankfully, Doña Lutgarda wasn't wearing leopard-skin tights.

"Gofio?" This was the first time I'd heard the word. "What is gofio, Doña Lutgarda?"

"It's roasted corn flour or roasted barley flour. Remember, you're a working man now!" There was pride in her voice. She filled the cup half full of coffee, added several spoonfuls of brown powder and stirred briskly until the contents turned into a mixture the colour and consistency of diarrhoea.

"You'll like it, but some don't!" I regarded the brown sludge in the cup and knew why some might not. "But it's the best thing for a labourer to start the day. Try it!" She pushed the cup towards me. It had a musty scent like the inside of the ancient grist mill on the River Isla at Blairgowrie. Gingerly, I licked some off the spoon. It tasted pleasant. The thought of this sustaining me till lunch time, perhaps putting me in line as a candidate for the title of the World's Strongest Man, encouraged me to continue. It was the Tenerife equivalent of brose or peasemeal. My grandfather sang the benefits of breakfasting on both. Brose was course oatmeal mixed with boiling water, a pinch of salt and a dash of white pepper; peasemeal likewise.

Through slitted eyes, Doña Lutgarda watched me. "I like it!" Her broad face broke into a warm smile. Happy, now, she removed the empty cup, knowing that on this, my first day of work in Buenavista del Norte, I'd be fine till lunch time. Satisfied, she bustled back into her kitchen and the day's preparations. It was she who had found me a job as a labourer with her cousin, who went by the name of Pata Cabra, meaning Goat's Foot. Nick-names in the village ranged from the complimentary to the caustic, yet nobody seemed to mind. Pata Cabra was an agricultural building contractor and agreed to try me out because she asked him.

As the taste grew on me and I refilled my empty cup with the remaining café con leche and stirred in more gofio, Obdúlia and Pastora trudged reluctantly down the stairs and into the open courtyard. They were rubbing their eyes. "What time of day is this to come down! It's almost seven! Look! Even the Extranjero's up before you!" My intentionally virtuous smile was met with hostile glares. "There's lots to be done. First, water!" They ignored their mother's scolding. Each dutifully placed a cloth ring on her head, placed an empty 10-litre can on top and walked with stately grace to the door leading to the still-dark plaza and the communal water tap, to join the line of other young women and begin the first of their daily chores.

After Doña Lutgarda was satisfied that I'd supped enough gofio to guarantee I wouldn't collapse from starvation before noon, she reminded me what I had to do. Pata Cabra had been through the procedure with me just a couple of days before, but she wanted to make sure I got things right.

I was to be out in the square by 7.15, no later, and wait along with the other workers till the lorry with the foreman arrived to pick us up. The lorry would take us to the construction site out on the barren scrubland that lay between the main road and the rocky shore. There, I'd be assigned my duties.

"My lunch?"

"Pastora will bring it to you. That way, it'll be fresh and still warm."

Unclear about how the day would unfold, or how far we would be from the village, I was taking everything on trust. I certainly didn't want to go without lunch and Doña Lutgarda could see my concern and so she repeated, slowly and clearly, "Pastora will bring you your lunch at midday!" She bustled me out the door into the darkness and herself back into her kitchen.

Slightly apprehensive, but also eager to be starting work and earning a daily wage to boost my dwindling funds, I crossed the road and joined a group of a dozen men and women waiting quietly in the plaza. Some, I knew by sight. All knew me: ¡El Extranjero! – the Foreigner! They introduced themselves by their nicknames and shook hands with me. Everybody in the village, it seemed, went by a nickname. Surnames appeared to be superfluous since everybody knew everybody else as well as everything about one another.

At 7.20 an old one-ton Bedford lorry drew up and an athletic man in his mid-twenties with high cheeks that gave him a slightly apprehensive air, jumped out of the passenger seat of the cab. He greeted by name and shook hands with everybody. The called him Juan. When it was my turn he scratched his head. Plain, Extranjero – Foreigner, somehow didn't seem quite right as a direct address, so he asked "What's your Christian name?"

"Ronald," I told him. The workers crowded round curiously, surprised that I even had a Christian name. I'd been el Extranjero since turning up three weeks previously. Juan looked puzzled so I repeated, in two distinct syllables, Ro-nald. The women in the fonda chose to call me Orlando but I wanted to give my workmates at least the opportunity of getting my name right. Juan looked at the older men in the group for help. Some had worked in Cuba or Venezuela and so were considered authorities on all things exotic. One of these sages nodded, "Orlando!" Ah! Now everybody smiled. I could see that I wasn't going to shake the name Orlando, nor el Extranjero when being referred to. The women in the fonda had been right after all!

I decided to accept both as nick-names and they made me oddly proud. Orlando was obviously Spanish and so made me feel more fully part of the village. El Extranjero acknowledged my unique status as the one and only foreigner living in the entire region, at least that I knew of.

In time, anywhere within several hours walk of Buenavista or in any of the many villages in the district, if a workman I happened to pass regarded me with a quizzical look, I would introduce myself, "Soy el Extranjero!" and they would immediately nod in recognition. "Of course, you're the Foreigner! From Buenavista! We've heard all about you! Orlando, isn't it?" And I was immediately accepted.

Juan offered his seat in the cab beside the driver to a very small, dapper, silent older man who was smoking a pipe. When Juan had introduced me to him, I'd caught his name as Maestro. Without a word, Maestro now handed me his canvas tool-bag as if presenting me with a precious gift. I climbed onto the back of the lorry with the rest, lugging Maestro's bag. Already piled onto the bed were picks, shovels, sledgehammers, long steel crowbars, several wheelbarrows and a score of woven rope baskets, suggesting the kind of work we were in for. Once we were all hanging tightly onto the high, wood-slatted side-boards, we lurched northwest out of the village towards the arid plain.

With day breaking, we jerked and swayed along a rock-strewn track past a few isolated, walled banana plantations the size of football fields, past the occasional un-plastered cottage, and acres of cactus and sweet-smelling shrubs that grew here and there out of the barren, yellow ground. A kilometre to our right, towards the main road that led to Santa Cruz, I could see fields of irrigated tomatoes. Pickers with straw hats and coloured scarves already at work. A kilometre to our left, beyond the great waves breaking spume against the rocks, the vast blue-green Atlantic Ocean stretched all the way to Cuba and the Gulf of Mexico. As the long, lingering lines of swell gently rose and fell, I caught an occasional glimpse of a two-man fishing boat here and there, well offshore. These cobles would disappear, reappear only to be plunged once more into the depths of enormous troughs.

"¡Ya llegamos – Here we are! Everybody out!" The lorry stopped. Juan got down with the men who gallantly helped the women off and then, showing equal care, the tools. "Orlando, you're going to work with Maestro right here. The rest of you follow me!" They traipsed after Juan into an area bigger than a football field, marked with a footing of concrete round its entire perimeter, taking all of the tools except one wheelbarrow, a sledgehammer, two bags of cement and Maestro's heavy canvas tool-bag. Maestro gestured at these, so I placed them all in the wheelbarrow and silently followed him until he stopped half-way along one of the footings. He turned to me and announced: "Here, you and I are going to build the principal entrance!"

"The principal entrance?" I was puzzled. "To what?" There was nothing but an acre of barren land with a concrete footing around the perimeter. Fortunately for me, Maestro's approach was to talk quietly but clearly as he went methodically about his task and so I had two sets of clues to help me understand: what he did and what he said.

"First, we're going to measure the entire length of the wall." He paced it out. "Now we find the midpoint." He paced halfway back. I marked the midpoint with chalk. "Now you'll mark points three metres on either side of the midpoint." He handed me a steel tape measure. "That's our gate opening, so we leave it vacant. But here," he took the chalk and drew a line, "and here," he drew another, "we'll build columns to mount the gates on and then a wall two metres long and two-and-a-half metres high on each side." I was beginning to see it.

When we'd reinforced the chalk-marks to make them obvious, he pointed to a pile of grey-black rocks, roughly split, that had been dumped inside the perimeter. "¡Basalto! – volcanic rock! That's what we're going use to build."

And we spent the morning doing just that. It was like building a drystane dyke in Scotland, but here and there he used very small quantities of grout made from cement and a little sand, that I mixed with a shovel on a broad wooden board. My responsibility was to keep Maestro supplied with a continuous flow of both grout and stones of exactly the size that he needed as he surely and steadily built. He progressed without any visible effort as if assembling a well-loved jig-saw puzzle. I was getting the hang of his technique and so was soon able to anticipate accurately the exact size and shape of the stones he needed and exactly where and when he wanted them. From time to time I had to use the sledgehammer to break up the larger ones into just the right size and with the right angles to their faces to suit a particular need.

Every movement he made, every stone he laid, every tap with his stone-hammer, contributed faultlessly to the growth of an elegant, grey-black wall made up of thousands of closely-fitted rocks. By lunchtime he'd laid the entire two meters of wall on one side of the opening to the height of his waist. He lit his pipe. We both stood and complemented the morning's work. The flat faces of all the many stones locked together as assuredly as the pieces of a puzzle, a work of art. Maestro smiled and I smiled back. He was a craftsman whose modesty, skill and quiet confidence made me want to please him.

Once, when cycling in Caithness in northern Scotland, I'd stopped to watch a stonemason split stone in a quarry. He'd examine an enormous rock from different angles and then place his chisel just so, and tap it lightly with his stone-hammer. A sheet of stone an inch thick and the size of my bicycle would separate itself from the mother rock. He'd lay the grey-green sheet gently on its side and repeat the performance. "How do you do that?" I'd asked, amazed. "Once a man understands a rock," he mused, "all he needs to do is tap it and it will open like the pages of the Bible!"

"Where did you learn to lay stone like that?" I asked Maestro.

Maestro explained. "Laying stone has been my lifetime's work. I started in Orotava, not far from here, when I was ten years old. I've built walls in every municipality on this coast. I worked in Cuba for many years. When I'd saved enough money, I returned home. I don't have to work, but I enjoy laying stone. It's in my blood. So now I take on only the very difficult jobs, the jobs that require skill and caring. Jobs where a plantation owner wants a truly symmetrical entrance, a thing of timeless beauty, and doesn't argue with my fee."

Suddenly, the penny dropped. His Christian name wasn't 'Maestro'. Maestro was an honorific, a title he'd earned for the excellence of his work. He was referred to as 'el Maestro' – the Master – out of respect for the skill he possessed to build not just walls, but perfect, beautiful facades that engendered awe and admiration.

He took my hands in his and examined them. After four hours, the skin was split and bleeding. The stone was rough, porous lava. Rock that had, thousands of years ago, poured molten down the sides of Teide, the volcano in the very centre of the island. The lava had cooled into a mass that looked like burnt treacle-toffee. Each of the thousands of tiny perforations created by gases bubbling out of the magma were razor-sharp.

"Go and pish on your hands!" Did I hear him correctly? He had used the word for animals!

"Pish? On my hands?" He nodded.

"Uric acid! That'll harden them up. By the end of the week, when we've finished this, your hands will be hard and calloused like mine." I looked at him to see if he was joking. He wasn't. I felt embarrassed trying to hide behind a scanty shrub to ease my hands, especially as the rest of the work-gang, men and women alike, had broken for lunch and knew exactly what I was up to. Nevertheless, I followed el Maestro's instructions. It helped ease the pain and stem the bleeding.

"Here's your lunch coming, Orlando!" I rejoined the group in time to see Pastora approaching, head high, straight-backed, on the path from the village, carrying what looked like a tall round aluminium can on her head. It turned out to be a set of three cans that clipped one into the other and kept different food items separate. She'd walked all that way, at least a kilometre-and-a-half, just to bring me my lunch fresh. I felt embarrassed. In Scotland, I'd worked on many a farm but had never seen a woman bring a man his lunch. He took it with him in an ex-army haversack when he left home at 6.30. If it happened to be cold or soggy or stale by the time he ate it, no matter. He'd be hungry enough not to notice.

Slightly humbled, I nevertheless wolfed down the whole fried boga fish, the potato-and-onion omelette and the banana. We all drank water from the same botijo – a porous clay jug with a spout that sent a stream of cool water into your mouth without your lips ever having to touch or even come near it. Several of these botijos were brought each day, kept in the shade and used by all as needed. The water inside seeped through the clay and evaporation kept it cool.

While I ate, Pastora chatted with the other workers, men and women alike. When I'd finished, she gathered the three dishes – polished clean with my last piece of bread – clipped them together, and set off back to the village, eyes up, back straight, the empty container perfectly balanced on her head. Almost two hours out of her busy day – at least half-an-hour's walk each way and another 30 minutes' wait. I made a mental note to insist on bringing my own lunch with me in future, as most, but certainly not all, of the other workers did.

By five o'clock, I was exhausted. When Juan called, "¡Bueno, muchachos, vámonos!" – "That's it, folks! Let's go!" I was thankful to glance admiringly at the growing wall, clean the remnants of cement off the board and help load our tools onto the lorry. Right there, in my presence and to my extreme embarrassment, Juan asked el Maestro, "Does el Extranjero work well? Should I tell him not to come back tomorrow?". My workmates stopped what they were doing and listened. El Maestro paused, took pipe and tobacco out of a buttoned pocket, silently thumbed a thick wedge of moist flakes into the bowl, lit a match, and puffed. The sweet fragrance reminded me of Coupar Angus and my grandfather. He removed the pipe before speaking. I held my breath.

"¡Está bien!" – "He's not bad! I'm happy to have him come back tomorrow. Ask him if he wants to continue working with me."

"I do!" I volunteered even before Juan had time to ask. Most of the men and women nodded. Perhaps one or two looked slightly disappointed, having secretly hoped to see el Extranjero either be sent home with his tail between his legs or voluntarily relinquish his post, as being too arduous.

"That's settled then," Juan nodded to me. "Same time tomorrow!"

El Maestro looked at me through curls of blue smoke, stepped towards me and shook my hand. Praise indeed! I swung myself up onto the truck bed to show I still had the energy. But half way home, when my eyes were beginning to close with exhaustion, the lorry shuddered to a halt alongside a pile of soil and a waiting, empty, two-ton lorry, larger than ours.

"Right, all men off, bring a shovel, we have to load this soil before we go back to the village." And we did. I was glad to see that I was not the most tired!

As we finally lurched homewards workers in ones and twos banged on the cab roof to be let off close to their homes. In the plaza, Juan had to help me down. "Well done, Orlando, we'll see you at 7.15 tomorrow." I staggered across the road, through the double doors and into the courtyard. Immediately Doña Lutgarda and all four girls surrounded me. "How was it?" "Did you find the work hard?" Did you have enough to eat for lunch?" "Wasn't it a good idea to have the gofio for breakfast?" "What work were you given to do?" "Are you going back to work tomorrow?"

I hid my bleeding hands and smiled brightly at all of them. "I loved the work. I'm el Maestro's assistant. Together we're building a lava wall. Tomorrow? Of course, I'm going back!" They nodded eagerly. They were as happy as I was that I'd passed an important rite of passage that brought me closer to being embraced as a legitimate member of the village.

After I'd showered, changed out of my working clothes and had dinner, I strolled out into the plaza with deep feelings of renewal and validation, distinctly taller than my 5'7". Men out for an evening stroll, some with their wives and children, stopped and shook my hand. Word of my acceptance had circulated. I felt honoured – and tried not to wince at the pain. By 8.30 I was sound asleep in bed, dreaming of the Spanish names for a dozen different shapes and sizes of volcanic rock and pishing merrily on my tender hands.

The arid plane between Buenavista and the sea had been eroded by wind and rain.

8. Don Juan-Pedro, School Teacher

From Monday to Friday, at precisely 7.15 in the morning, Don Juan-Pedro kicked his well-worn, blue, two-stroke BSA Bantam into a faltering cough, circled the plaza to comfort the engine and braced himself to tackle the steep, zig-zag gravel road up to the hamlet of El Palmar, a thousand feet above Buenavista. As often as not, El Palmar was shrouded in moist, cloudy isolation. And every afternoon at precisely 2.30, after a victory lap around the plaza, Juan-Pedro returned to park in exactly the same spot. He struggled to dismount, limped to a solitary yellow table set out on the pavement in front of the cafe, and lingered comfortably over a dark fragrant cortado.

Don Juan-Pedro was in his early thirties and modestly built. He was the only man who taught at the one-room school up in the clouds. His score or more of pre-adolescent pupils came either from the hamlet itself, of perhaps 100 souls, or from families who worked tiny share-cropped fields even higher up in the mists but within walking distance of El Palmar.

"The legal obligation to attend school isn't strictly enforced," Don Juan-Pedro told me, "but mountain-dwelling Canarios, especially those whose lives are brutally harsh, value education as the means to better prospects. So a six or eight kilometre round trip by foot is no discouragement. Not even when each child's day, out of necessity, begins and ends with the drudgery of farm and household chores." His fellow-teacher, a woman from El Palmar itself, taught the six to nine-year-olds and both she and Don Juan-Pedro had their respective classrooms crammed with eager pupils. Neither he nor she was under any romantic, utopian illusion about the way of life of the share-croppers on the mountain terraces. "Struggle is etched into their faces from the time they begin to walk," Don Juan-Pedro told me.

In Spain as in Scotland, primary school teaching was a career that tended to attract women. Don Juan-Pedro was a man but, regrettably, a man-with-a-disability, and in those days, a man-with-a-disability in Spain was sorely handicapped if he chose to pursue a more traditionally masculine path in life. Sadly, the disadvantage wasn't limited to the workplace alone, but extended into every sphere of life, both personal and private. It made difficulties in finding a partner to help keep life's loneliness at bay, as a comfort in life's sorrows, and with whom to share the pride, joys and occasional heartaches of raising children and watching them grow.

Don Juan-Pedro's left leg was shorter than his right. His jerky sailor's roll, the hesitation followed by decisive effort when stepping off the kerb onto the road, and his determined two-handed grip onto the stair-rail followed by his crab-like, one-step-at-a-time slapping ascent, drew covert glances of pity from women and girls. Men and boys, after they'd overcome the urge to stare or mimic, either cloaked Don Juan-Pedro in a kind of embarrassed invisibility or displayed a forced bonhomie born of there but for the grace of God go I!

Since, in those unenlightened days, a single disability tended to constrain the sufferer's entire range opportunities in life, Don Juan-Pedro considered himself blessed for enjoying the opportunity to earn his living teaching uncouth but willing children in a mountain hamlet. Happily, in return for the grace with which he accepted his role and performed the taxing task with faithful and good-natured dedication, he was quietly and sincerely respected.

He was a favourite in the fonda, where, from Monday to Friday, he ate and slept and from early morning until mid-afternoon, he strove to teach reading, writing, arithmetic and respect for El Caudillo – ¡Viva Franco! – and Spanish patriotism – ¡Arriba Espana! – high up in glistening clouds that swirled around the white-washed houses, tethered goats and scarlet geraniums of El Palmar.

The hamlet of El Palmar where Don Juan-Pedro taught. The villagers cultivated gardens on the terraces and often used donkeys to take their goods down to Buenavista for sale,

During my walking excursions within Buenavista and far beyond, I was beginning to discover many different sorts of roads. There was the single asphalt road that led out of Buenavista and snaked north up the coast and then east over the mountains to Santa Cruz. There was the gravel road that ran zig-zag up the hill to El Palmar. There were tracks of beaten earth or dusty hardpan that allowed lorries to reach plantations and isolated farms though often with great reluctance. And for every road used by vehicles, there was always a grassy footpath or narrow track that would take a sturdy walker to the same destination and invariably in much less time.

There were even trails that took you to places where no vehicle could ever reach: up the precipitous sides of dark cliffs, skirting treacherous yellow scree that threatened to slide you into the spiny clutches of cactus plants, or up impossible stone staircases that appeared to have been cut into the very rock itself. These led to unimaginably isolated groups of houses crouching moistly, high in the clouds.

Residents depended, for the most part, on no one but one another and what their stooped labour produced in the way of food. There in the clouds, the inhabitants patiently raised aromatic herbs and perfect onions, squat orange carrots and purple-topped turnips, brown lentils and yellow chickpeas. They bred rabbits, milked goats and made moist, circular blocks of sour-smelling, pale, deliciously-crumbly cheese. From time to time, a small train of sturdy men and women, in single file, would tightly pack these hard-won treasures in used potato sacks and carry them on broad shoulders and strong backs or in baskets perfectly balanced on erect heads, all the way down the mountainsides to Buenavista to exchange for cash.

Pilgrim's Way, the lane that led to the hamlet of El Palmar in the mountains.

61

When I met such a group on the mountain, I'd stand to one precarious side of the track as a chattering, laughing family came springing goat-like down from rock to rock without ever putting a rope-soled foot wrong. "¡Adios, Extranjero!" --"Greetings, Foreigner!" Though I might never have, to that point, visited their hamlets or farmed terraces, they knew me and laughed at my slow trudging sweat. Admirable as they undoubtedly were, fit and supple in their youth, the undeniable physical demands of their way of life would age them all too soon. An emergency or an accident would likely be fatal. Their lives appeared romantic and free, I thought, as I observed their confidence and strength, but in all likelihood ended brutish and short, leaving the next generation to repeat, with relentless exactitude, their parents' and grandparents' struggle; or to seek liberation via migration or emigration.

After only two or three weeks in the village, I'd hiked most of these paths and tracks and could find my way about, with relative ease, over an area of many square kilometres. One of my favourite trails was the one that led up to El Palmar. Whenever I walked up its steep slopes, invariably alone and feeling solitary in these early weeks after my arrival, I imagined myself to be on foot with Chaucer and his assorted band of Canterbury pilgrims. The track was unevenly laid with smooth stones the size of large cobbles worn by countless devout feet and hooves, over quiet centuries. Rough terraces were carved into the hillside and kept in place by stone dykes, and the same winding dykes bordered and protected the trail itself.

The branches of fruit trees and nut trees spread over the track, most of which I'd never before seen growing. Initially, they were leafless but on my countless walks, they budded, leafed and bloomed. Some bloomed pink and white and prolific even before they leafed and caused me wonder. Back in the fonda over dinner, I'd tell the girls what I'd seen. They'd ask me to describe the leaves or the blossom and then cry with delight in recognition, "Ah! That's an almond tree! Or a walnut, or an apricot, a peach, a míspero or a membrillo."

"What's a míspero?" The were amused by my ignorance.

"It's small, round. It has soft sweet pulp inside and large glossy seeds."

"And a membrillo, what's that?"

"¿Membrillo?" Pastora laughed. "You eat it for dessert, preserved, when there's no fresh fruit. You know what membrillo is!"

The absence of sugar in Scotland during and after WWII guaranteed that we children developed no sweet tooth and so, instead of cooked dessert, the girls at the fonda learned to bring me fruit. When there was no fresh fruit, they'd bring me a slice of a fragrant, amber-coloured, jelly that was neither too sweet nor too tart and felt cool and slightly gritty in my mouth. I had no idea what it was and their confusing attempts to explain never enlightened me.

"When there's no fruit? But it's a fruit!"

"It's a fruit preserve."

While I rack my brains, Pastora hurries to the kitchen and returns with what looks like a dark, malt loaf. "¡Membrillo!" She plonks it down on the table. "You take fruit this size," she cups her hands to the size of a bulky apple, "You boil them with sugar, pass the liquid through a flour bag and squeeze out the last drops into a pot. The pig gets what's left in the bag and you boil the liquid again until it thickens, so!" Pastora prods the dark, slightly sticky loaf. "You let it cool and shape it with your hands, until you have this." Another prod. "In a cool place, it keeps for months."

And then it comes to me! Every year from as early as I can remember, Pearl made jams and jellies using the fruit we all picked from her mother's garden in Coupar Angus. First the strawberry then the rhubarb and then the raspberry, blackcurrant, redcurrant and gooseberry and finally, in autumn, the apple jelly. And every year, Vivian and Euan and I helped her by carefully washing, drying and arranging the empty jars. From a safe distance, we'd watch intently as the copper jam-pan quietly boiled. Pearl would always ask us to make the most important decision of all – to decide when enough liquid had evaporated to the precise point where the jam or jelly would set firm when it cooled. Our task was to watch a scant spoonful of the sweet liquid on a cool saucer. If we told her it jelled within less than half a minute, Pearl would turn off the gas and begin to ladle liquid into the sparking one- and two-pound jars. Well-made jams and jellies must spread evenly on your bread; they should not run off onto your fingers or, heaven forbid, onto the table-cloth. A country-woman's jam in Scotland and even more critically her jelly, because jelly was the greater challenge, was judged by just how well it had set.

"Aye, you're a dab-hand at making apple jelly, Pearl! What's your secret?"

Pearl's secret was a triple one: Vivian, Euan and I served as her quality control. At her prodding, we announced the precise moment when the gas under the jam-pan should be turned off, the scalding pan carefully removed from the hot stove, and the fragrant jelly ladled into the waiting jars. First, a metal soup-spoon had to be placed into the jar to absorb the heat and prevent the glass from cracking. Pearl crowned us lords of the jams and jellies. We were convinced that without our contribution, neither their colour nor consistency would have been nearly as perfect. She taught us to bear responsibility, weigh up the evidence, develop trust in our own judgement. That's how we mastered the art of doing things 'just right', before we even started school.

"Making jam's just like living life," she'd say, "do it right the first time and you don't have to give up and start over again." She was grooming us not to repeat the great mistake she had made.

"Do you understand what membrillo is now?" Pastora's query brought me back.

"I understand how it's made," I told her. "I don't know for sure what the fruit is in English but it might be 'quince'." The word 'quince' had a satisfying, medieval ring to it. Later, to my delight, I discovered that my guess was correct. Membrillo was the quince, boiled with sugar and reduced.

When Don Juan-Pedro invited me to visit his school up in the clouds to address his pupils, or at least for him to present me with a view to showing them what an 'extranjero' looked like, he explained that his motor-cycle wasn't powerful enough to carry both of us up the mountainside. I readily agreed to walk. My favourite Pilgrim's Path never failed to present something new and interesting. So I set off early on the half-hour walk.

As soon as the pupils caught sight of el Extranjero at the open door, they fell silent in embarrassment and confusion. Don Juan-Pedro introduced me. "This is Don Orlando, el Extranjero who is living in Buenavista." They gazed at me in silence. He prompted them into a rehearsed chorus "¡Buenos días, Don Orlando! Goo moneen Meester!" As promised, Don Juan-Pedro had pinned a physical map of Europe to the blackboard. The word England was printed across the entire United Kingdom from the Shetland Islands to the English Channel.

Stretching my limited Spanish resources to breaking point, I showed them approximately where I came from – a little village north of the Firth of Tay just beyond the Sidlaw Hills. As did they, I told them, we in Scotland grew corn, potatoes, various kinds of berries and apples in the area of the map shaded in green. In the higher areas shaded in dark brown, we raised sheep. On the more extensive light-ochre areas in between the lower and the higher land, we raised beef. Without being so ungenerous as to accuse their Ministry of Education of wrongly labelling the map, I told them that the northern part of 'England' was called Scotland. Pointing to the many sea-lochs I showed them that at no point was anywhere in Scotland very far from salt water, and so was a fishing nation. 'England's' great fishing fleets netted the entire coastline and much further afield. I tried to focus on similarities between our countries and steered clear of politics and how government was conducted, as Don Juan-Pedro had quietly requested.

The pupils were less interested in a geography lesson, however, than in the opportunity to question the first extranjero that any of them had the chance to meet. "Was my name really Orlando? What was my father's name, my mother's name? How old was I? Had I been to La Peninsula"? – which was how they referred to Spain as opposed to their beloved Islas Canarias. "Would I marry a girl from Buenavista del Norte? How many years had I gone to school?"

When, in response to their last question, I told them trece, 13, they were unwilling to believe me. That was a life-sentence! So I wrote 1942 on the board and below that wrote Orlando! Alongside 1942, I drew an arrow and wrote 1947 and below that escuela primaria. Then an arrow to 1954 and wrote escuela secundaria, then 1960 and below it the word terminar to show I'd left school just a few months earlier. Then I wrote the arithmetic calculation 1947 minus 1942 = 5 to show them I'd begun school at age five and then wrote 1960 minus 1947 = 13 to show them I'd attended school for 13 years. Uproar ensued; the pupils all talked at once, asking the teacher questions I couldn't follow. He eventually quietened them down with a long explanation that required constant gestures in my direction, pitying looks and sad shakes of the head.

"What's that all about?" I asked Don Juan-Pedro, but my allotted time was up and he promised to explain all to me that evening back at the fonda. He did promise, however, not to divulge my age. In my earnestness, I'd inadvertently shown that I was 18 years old, information I'd successfully kept from Doña Lutgarda and her family – and still wanted kept secret.

I strode back down Pilgrim's Way, greeting and receiving greetings from individual farmers working alone. I stopped to talk to a young well-built man I often saw ploughing narrow terraces with a single ox, sometimes with a pair, and a wooden plough. Small groups of field workers who were planting or harvesting vegetables that grew all year round on the long narrow terraces waved.

Later that evening, Doña Lutgarda called me down for dinner and I found a special table set for Don Juan-Pedro and me together. Pastora, América, Obdúlia and Lula stood around in anticipation. I drew up a chair for Doña Lutgarda. Don Juan-Pedro proudly explained how he had primed his students for the visit. I praised their English, explained to Doña Lutgarda and the girls how they'd greeted me, "Goo moneen Meester!" in perfect Queen's English thanks to Don Juan-Pedro. He accepted their admiring glances.

I'd explained to his pupils, he told them, the economic geography of 'England', how they'd laughed uproariously when they learned that in the part of 'England' that I came from – the part called Scotland – the men wore pleated skirts and played the discordant gaita just like the Gallegos in north-west Spain.

He told them how I'd surprised them by admitting I'd attended school for 13 years but thankfully avoided telling them that I had left school only months earlier. When he'd finished, I asked, "Why did the information about how many years I'd attended school surprise them?"

"Well," he paused, "here, especially in the rural areas, it's not uncommon for pupils to go to school for only three or four years. Most girls and boys will be out working very early. They simply couldn't understand how anybody could still have anything to learn after going to school for five or six years, let alone 13 years!"

"So, what did you tell them?"

He hesitated, uncomfortable. "I told them that you'd gone to school for so many years so that you could learn everything there was to know." I felt pleased. "But," he went on, "they wouldn't believe me – they told me that it was common knowledge in El Palmar that el Extranjero didn't know very much at all." I winced. "Much, that is, about anything that matters, like pruning fruit trees and harvesting onions

My friend the ploughman. I never failed to meet him on my long walks. At my request, he taught me how to plough with his oxen and guide them with the long, pointed prod he's holding in his left hand.

or the best places to graze goats or the milk-cow. They also pointed out that el Extranjero couldn't even speak Spanish properly!" Doña Lutgarda and the girls nodded in agreement. I felt inadequate.

"But you explained some more and they finally seemed to agree with you!"

Don Juan-Pedro looked at me apologetically. "I told them," he refused to meet my eyes, "that in England the people are, unlike we Canarios, very slow learners. They are so slow that they have to go to school for many, many years to learn as much as people like us learn in three or four!"

Doña Lutgarda and the girls laughed uproariously. To my embarrassment, I could see that they secretly believed him.

Worshippers at the Church of Nuestra Señora de Los Remedios created sand-pictures in honour of their patron saint.

9. *How to build a banana plantation from scratch.*

One evening, a couple of weeks after I first began working as el Maestro's assistant, we completed the stone columns and wall that gave elegant entrance to the banana-plantation-to-be. I set about cleaning the tools and putting them in order. Although Juan-the-Foreman had checked regularly on our progress, he now came to inspect for the last time and give his seal of approval. Standing calmly beside Juan, his straw hat shading his face, el Maestro reamed his pipe, tapped out the burnt ash, thumbed the bowl full of fresh tobacco, struck a match on his nail, sucked in the flame, and contentedly blew a cloud of fragrant smoke into the cool evening. The stone entrance was a work of art, each of the thousands of irregular pieces of porous basalt tightly fitted together by hand, one at a time. It possessed a symmetry and balance that satisfied the eye as comfortably as the stone arch that invites you to enter a medieval church.

As we'd progressed, el Maestro had built into the wall the four, huge, gate-hangers made of forged steel, two on either side. On these, the great wooden gates would be hung using two metre-long double-strap hinges. The V-shaped gate-hangers, too, had been almost two metres long and we'd set them deep into a layer of cement over which enormous blocks of basalt had been laid and grouted in so that even the heaviest gates wouldn't sag or scrape. "Make certain the gate hardware is installed firmly into the wall! Then, the gate will always swing freely. It's easier to do it right the first time, Orlando, than to be called back in two or three years to fix it." The principle of 'do it right the first time' was, fortunately, well known to me from having worked on farms back in Scotland during Easter and summer school holidays. Farmers strove to do a job just once. They needed to be sure that the results would bear the test of time.

Juan uncoiled a rope from around his waist, looped it over the first of the steel pins that stood ten centimetres proud of the columns. He put the entire weight of his 70 or so kilos on it. Then he did the same with the other three. He scrutinized the tight, neat stonework and examined the narrow, concrete irrigation channel that linked the plantation-to-be with the irrigation system that networked the entire region.

Since there were no sources of surface water and no wells outside the village, all cultivated areas were given access to water that came from underground sources at the base of the mountains. Water was made available in certain regions on predetermined days of the month. A farmer who wanted water let the 'key-man' know and the key-man would make sure that the appropriate sluice gates were opened, using his keys to direct the water to where it needed to go for the time required.

Juan stepped back in line with el Maestro. "It's good!" Juan-the-Foreman, like most country-folks, wasn't given to elaborate praise.

El Maestro puffed and nodded. "Then don't blow it up!" I was at a loss to understand what he meant. Blow it up? But because my ear was still attuning itself to my new language and so missed quite a lot, I shrugged and thought no more about it. Juan shook hands with el Maestro, who nodded for me to sling his tool bag onto the bed of the lorry. His job here was done.

When the lorry growled into the plaza that evening, both el Maestro and Juan got down from the cab. El Maestro shook my hand and then held it up to take a good look at it. "See! Just like mine! Remember, urinate on them regularly!" And with that last piece of advice he climbed into the cab. Juan shook my hand as well. "El Maestro tells me you did a good job for him. I've spoken to Pata Cabra. He wants you to keep working with us. So do I. We still have a lots to do before this plantation is finished."

My work-mates were listening and gave a cheer. "¡El Extranjero!" All of them, even those few who'd shown reluctance at first, seemed genuinely pleased.

Elated that I'd reached a milestone, had been judged satisfactory and fit to go on, I tipped back my straw hat and waved "¡Hasta manana!" as casually as I could and, smiling, strolled across the road to the fonda I now thought of as home. When washed with my allotted half-gallon of precious water and went down to the courtyard for dinner, all four girls crowded round my table. Within the village news travelled instantaneously. Doña Lutgarda herself, smiling her pride, brought me a plate of garbanzas, "Your favourite, Orlando!" Garbanzas was a stew made from the larger variety of chick-peas. The more common word 'garbanzos' was reserved for the smaller variety. Garbanzas were soaked overnight and then simmered together with potatoes, onions, garlic, red pepper, tomatoes, laurel leaves, paprika, cumin and freshly-ground pepper. This evening, thin strips of salted pork had been added for flavour and festivity. They made me feel like one of them, a member of the community. It warmed me to know I was accepted.

In the weeks that followed, as a willing member of Juan's contented work-crew, I learned how Canarios went about building a banana plantation from scratch, how they carved it out of the arid plain that ran for several kilometres between the main road to Santa Cruz and the rocky coastline. The plain was a great, flat stretch of semi-desert; the ground hardpan, a thick layer of hard-baked clay so compact that any rain just ran off into gullies. Most of the rain-water, however, was absorbed into the permeable basalt long before it reached the sea.

Pata Cabra -- Goat's foot -- is supervising the excavation after Juan and I blasted a ridge of basalt with dynamite to make the rock easier to handle. Beautiful stone walls surround every plantation.

Any local entrepreneur with the capital and the vision, along with the willingness to make the investment and take the risks, could buy land in lots more or less the size of a football field. Once he'd bought the land, the entrepreneur would engage a contractor like Pata Cabra, Doña Lutgarda's cousin, to 'develop' it. That meant Pata Cabra would send out a group of labourers, supervised by a foreman like Juan, to do the work.

First, the team had to clear all of the dangerously prickly cactus plants and vicious, thorny shrubs off the lot. Then, once Juan-the-Foreman had marked out the exact perimeter of the plantation, he would set his crew to excavate the site to a depth of a couple of metres, mainly by hand.

When I began working with the crew, about a third of the excavation had already been completed. The ground was so compact in places that we'd have to bring in an operator with a noisy pneumatic drill to break up the offending patch of rock-hard clay. Then, for several days, the men would use pick and shovel to smash the slabs into smaller pieces and shovel those into woven baskets.

It was the women's job to carry these baskets. One would help another swing a laden basket, by its stout, plaited handles onto the padded ring on her head to cushion the load. The woman would then walk straight-backed to the waiting lorry parked as close as it could to the operation. She'd ascend a gangway of wooden planks, and tip the contents of her basket into the open box. It was important for us to neither under fill nor overfill a basket. Overfilling made them too heavy and invited protests; under filling meant they had to make more trips to the lorry. When the box was full and the tailgate swung closed, the women would have a brief respite while the lorry went to dump its load. We men, however, would continue breaking large slabs into smaller ones with picks or sledge-hammers, until the lorry came back empty and the laborious loading process started all over again. In this laborious way, the dozen of us in the work-crew excavated many tons of hardpan each day.

We kept up an unhurried but regular pace all day from eight o'clock in the morning until six o'clock in the evening, with an hour for lunch and breaks to drink water mid-morning and mid-afternoon. The trick of getting heavy physical labour like this done is to find the precise pace that the entire crew can keep up steadily, hour after hour. If you rush, the delicate links in the chain of work break down and with it the crew's morale. If you set too slow a pace, the crew never manages to swing into a comfortable, satisfactory rhythm and the work falls behind. On Scottish farms, I'd been told: "Pace yourself, son! The secret lies in setting a canny rhythm!"

One day, my pick-head gave a resounding 'ding' as loud as the clang of a ship's bell. Painful, jolts shot up the solid wooden shaft into my hands, arms and shoulders. "We've hit a ridge of basalt!" All work stopped. Juan came over to decide what to do. After a lot of prodding and probing with the crowbar, he shook his head, "There was nothing for it! I'll fetch Pata Cabra!

Pata Cabra duly arrived and after he and Juan both had poked around some more, they straightened up and agreed: "Dynamite is what we need!" This was music to my ears. The only explosives I'd ever seen used were on the screen in the cowboy-and-Indian films at the picture-house in Dundee. Invariably, the dynamite or nitro-glycerine was being transported in a stagecoach. The horses ran wild, took off, and horses, stagecoach and of course the baddies as well, were all sent to kingdom come in a spectacular explosion.

That evening after I'd cleaned up and walked in the plaza to relax before dinner and seek company, I remembered el Maestro's warning to Juan: "Don't blow up my wall!" Maybe he hadn't been joking after all!

The following day, the pneumatic drill with its operator and the bulky compressor that powered it arrived drawn by a lorry. As I was the only one who didn't know the operator, I was introduced. His nickname was Pepe-de-la-Perforadora – Pepe-of-the-Pneumatic-Drill! With a deafening sound that sent my work-mates scuttling away, he began to drill a series of blast-holes into the rock as deep as the planned excavation. Juan pointed out exactly where the holes should be drilled. Fascinated, I stayed to watch.

"Location is critical," Juan told me. "If we drill the holes in exactly the right pattern, we'll pulverise the entire seam with the fewest sticks of dynamite!" After six blast-holes were drilled and cleaned out to Juan's satisfaction, the operator, the compressor and pneumatic drill moved on to another job and the most exciting part of our operation began.

Everybody except Juan took their lunch pans and retired a couple of hundred yards to shade and safety. I stayed to watch and offer any help I could. We went to our lorry that had been driven to a safe distance, to get the blasting paraphernalia. Juan handed me a reel of coiled line and a paper bag.

"That," Juan pointed to the reel, "is the detonating cord. "In there" he pointed to the paper bag, "are the firing caps. For safety's sake, I mustn't carry both the dynamite and the caps together." Juan grasped a modest cardboard box. "Here, I've got six sticks of dynamite." He left it to my imagination why it was safer to keep the firing caps and the explosive separate. He also handed me a broomstick handle. "This stick is important!" But he didn't say why.

Juan carefully cut detonating cord to six different lengths and handed them to me. At the first blast-hole, he made careful slits along opposite sides of the paper tube that held the dynamite gel and then gently pressed a blasting cap into the soft, open top. "We want the explosion to come out the sides of the stick, not out the top," I couldn't see how slitting each stick of dynamite would help focus the blast, but I could feel Juan's increased tension and so I decided to listen and keep silent. Then he attached the wire that protruded from the blast cap to one of the detonating cords I carried, slipped the stick into the blast-hole and asked me to pass him the broom handle. Ever so gently he pushed the primed stick of dynamite down to the required depth. By the time he'd repeated this procedure for each of the remaining five blast-holes, I was getting the hang of it. There was a definite logic to setting charges effectively. We needed to shatter the entire basalt ridge into pieces small enough for easy handling. We had neither digger nor any mechanical device, only a dozen pairs of men's and women's bare hands.

The penultimate task was to visit each blast hole, every one now charged with a stick of dynamite, blast cap and wiring, and cover each with a few shovelfuls of loose soil. "This will make sure the explosion goes sideways and not upwards." I was just as puzzled by this comment as I had been when he slit the sticks of dynamite. He seemed to be telling me that the direction of the blast could be relatively easily directed. Finally, he attached the cords from each covered hole to the reel I carried and wound the cord out some hundred yards from the closest charge hole. "This should be enough to protect us from flying debris."

These preparations hadn't taken us more than an hour. Satisfied that all was ready, he fetched the blasting machine from the cab of the lorry. This machine was exactly as I'd seen them in the cinema. It consisted of a metal box with a double-handed plunger that, when deliberately depressed, would send an electrical current through the wires and cause the blast caps to detonate. Each cap would immediately cause the dynamite attached to it, to explode. Juan signalled me lie down beside him once he'd finished.

"Is everybody ready?"

"Yes! Yes!" The voices came from very far away indeed!

"Count the explosions, Orlando!" And Juan pushed the plunger.

At first, I thought that something had gone wrong because nothing happened. But then the ground shuddered and I felt, more than heard, a great thwomp! Then another and another. Six in all. It was over in seconds. Juan looked pleased with himself. For me, it was an anti-climax. I was expecting an almighty kaboom! and a heaving explosion that sent the stagecoach flying into the air and the baddies' bodies cartwheeling like rag dolls to land impaled on the cactus. The only visible signs that there had been a series of explosions were six coils of blue smoke where the blast holes had been, as if goblins were smoking cigars below ground.

Juan didn't move. "How many explosions?"

"Six!"

"You're sure?"

"I'm sure. I counted each one."

"Good, I counted six too. That means all six sticks exploded. We won't have to gouge any unexploded dynamite out of a single blasthole." I looked at him.

"You're not serious!"

"Absolutely serious. I used different lengths of cord for each blast cap so that each explosion is delayed by two or three seconds. By counting the number of explosions, we can be absolutely sure how many sticks have gone off. If one doesn't explode, then we must find out which one. Once we find it, we have to dig the explosive out of the hole spoonful by spoonful." I looked at him askance, but he went on seriously. "We use a special instrument with a long handle made of a material that doesn't cause any sparks when it scratches on rock. If you were to use steel or iron and raise a single spark, BOOM!" His normally worried look intensified.

"Who'd be crazy enough to do that job?"

He looked at me without blinking, "Today, it would have been you, Orlando. You're the only one I'd trust to do it without blowing us all sky-high!"

I peered at him out of the corner of my eye, wondering how seriously to take him. Secretly, I was pleased that he had chosen me to help him lay the explosive charges. It was a vote of confidence that gave me prestige among the others and this news would soon spread around the village.

"Okay, folks. Back to work!" Juan gestured for me to collect the tools of the blaster's trade. The others left their distant hiding places and approached with caution awed by the rubble.

I was deluged with questions. "You weren't scared, Orlando?" "How could you stay so close to the explosions?" "Did you feel the shudders when the sticks of dynamite went off?" "Did you push the plunger or was it Juan?" "Are you going to do all the explosive work from now on?"

I just smiled, shrugged and walked over to the stone wall and gate-posts that el Maestro had built a few weeks earlier. They stood solid and proud; the explosions had been perfectly directed so that only the offending ridge of basalt had been shattered. Now I understood what el Maestro had meant when he'd warned, "Don't blow up my gate!"

My work-mates were still talking about me. "See! El Extranjero is not afraid of dynamite!" "Of course, he comes from Switzerland, and there they use dynamite all the time to build tunnels through the mountains." "Nonsense! He comes from Sweden, they dynamite snow in the mountains there to cause avalanches and then they ride down the avalanches on their skis." "Sweden? Rubbish! He comes from Scotland and Scotland's a place in England and its capital is Londres. A long time ago, in Londres, a Scotsman once blew up the Houses of Parliament, killing the King, the Queen and all their sons and daughters. That's why England had to hire a new king and queen from Holland!" "Scotsmen do it all the time! They go about in their skirts blowing people up with dynamite!"

From that day on, I acquired an undeserved reputation for fearlessness.

The ridge of basalt had been shattered into irregular pieces that ranged from the size of a 12-bottle cardboard box down to jagged rocks the size of a football. We spent the rest of that day, and the following, extracting them from the surrounding clay and piling them just outside the limits of the plantation-to-be so they could be used later for finishing the footings around the perimeter.

The job of excavation by hand continued until, a couple of weeks later, we had dug out what looked like an enormous rectangular swimming pool. Then a crew of rough-work stone masons came in and quickly built a stone footing round most the perimeter, to join up with the main gate el Maestro and I had built earlier. A driver nick-named el Bachillér, the owner-operator of his own lorry, dumped load after load of topsoil into the 'swimming-pool'. Using shovels, we spread and levelled the soil to a depth of a metre. Then the plantation was complete.

We stood back and admired what had taken us the better part of a month. Now we had what looked like a beautiful garden edged with a wide basalt footing and graced with a handsome stone entrance. This moist, brown garden stood in obvious contrast to the baked clay that stretched around it, scattered with cactus and thorn trees.

On the lorry back to the village that evening, Juan told us, "¡Mañana vamos a plantar papas!" – "Tomorrow, we're going to plant potatoes!" I assumed that must be a colloquialism for some kind of celebration. Perhaps we were going to close out the job with a fire and roast potatoes over the embers.

However, at 7.20 the following morning, when we climbed aboard the lorry, there were five or six hundredweight sacks of seed-potatoes, several 45-gallon drums filled with water, and a dozen buckets. "We're going to plant potatoes today!" As we made the bumpy ride out to the new plantation, my work-mates explained that, because banana trees took a year to produce their first piña, potatoes were planted between the rows of young banana plants. Not only could the potatoes be harvested within a few months to bring in revenue, they also served to break up the soil and give the tilth that would promote the growth of the banana tree.

"Where do we get the banana plants?"

"Oh, don't worry, Juan will bring them during the course of the morning."

At the plantation, we jumped down off the tailgate, each with a bucket. Two or three of us unloaded the sacks of potatoes. Each sack had a carton label sown into the top seam. The English words 'Up-to-Date' caught my attention. I looked closely at the label. These were Certified Seed Potatoes from Ireland! It made me quite excited to think that I, the Foreigner in Buenavista and member of a team that had just built a banana plantation, was now going to plant Irish potatoes as the first crop. "Hey! Listen to this!" I read the entire label in English and then translated it into Spanish for them.

"We always plant English seed-potatoes," they told me, "but we've never been able to understand the label on the sacks before."

"Well," I corrected, "these potatoes are not English, they're Irish."

"If the label's in English, it stands to reason that the potatoes must come from Inglaterra!"

I decided against delivering a lecture on political geography and began unloading the remaining sacks and the tools we'd need for the day.

A man with a donkey pulling a type of plough was just finishing work he must have started well before daylight. The entire plantation had been ploughed into furrows. My workmates explained that these furrows were not for planting, they were to allow the irrigation water to soak the soil round the potatoes and the banana trees as soon as we'd completed the job.

We cut each potato into three pieces, making sure that there were at least two eyes in each portion. My hometown of Coupar Angus sat right in the heart of Scotland's seed-potato farmland and I'd spent many days bent double lifting tatties, exposed by a rotating, horse-drawn digger. As I stood on that arid plain outside Buenavista del Norte, I was overcome by the memory of the sweet, rich smell of a newly-exposed furrow near Coupar Angus and the sight of the exposed pink potatoes. I could even feel a chill nip in the air and watch as the autumn mist was burned rapidly off the fields by the rising sun, smell the sweating Clydesdale as it tramped by and I set to work alongside Euan. He and I shared a 'bit' and my mother and Vivian also shared a separate 'bit' between them. It was late September 1950 and Pearl had decided that we really needed to know what it meant to 'pick tatties'. Pearl carried powerful memories of her own childhood and a firm conviction of what had for her been important character-building experiences. She constantly sought to expose us to similar experiences because she considered them invaluable for our physical, moral and intellectual development. She firmly believed that there were priceless benefits to be found in life. The best of them couldn't simply be purchased; they had to be lived. Some of these included the music of longing like Mendelssohn's:

"On wings of song, I'll bear thee,
My heart's love far away.
Speeding fast over the palm trees
Where Ganges' blue water play.

Where, hidden in glorious garden,
Beneath the gleaming moon
The lotus flowers are longing
to see their sister soon."

Some experiences bestowed a visual blessing, like the view of the rail-way bridge curving over the rippling, tidal Tay seen from Airlie gardens in front of Queen's College in Dundee. Some were adventures as when, in the middle of August, we children would walk with her down to the Taybridge railway station, buy day-return tickets to St Andrews and spend the late morning and early afternoon walking round the stalls of the Lammas Fair. We'd hurry to take a quick swim in the outdoor swimming-pool that changed its water with every rise and fall of the tidal Forth.

Some were trials of character and others ordeals to be endured. Harvesting potatoes served both these purposes. When the time for the tattie-harvest came around, we rose early, supped porridge made the night before and trotted after her at breakneck speed – the only pace Pearl seemed to know – for a mile to catch the bus to Tealing. There, we'd spend the entire day, from eight till five, filling heavy creels with freshly dug Kerr's Pinks or Golden Wonders – potato varieties all had names. We'd struggle to keep up with the digger, almost fall asleep from exhaustion during the lunch-break when we ate rolls and cheese and drank sweet tea from a thermos. We'd continue the ordeal all afternoon, and finally fall asleep during the 30-minute bus-ride to Dundee before trotting the mile back home for tea. Then we'd all tumble into bed early, only to be wakened by the urgent alarm clock the next morning at six. We'd repeat the entire, back-breaking ordeal for days. We learned never to complain because we knew Pearl's only response would be, "It's good for you! In 20 years' time, you'll thank me for this!"

"Orlando!" One of the crew dragged me back into the present. "Here's Juan with the banana plants now." We finished planting the potatoes left in our buckets and went to help Juan unload the banana plants. When we dropped the tailgate, all I could see was a high pile of several hundred clods that looked for all the world like the muddy severed feet of a herd of elephants. I wondered if they were kidding me. "These are not banana plants!" But Juan came to my rescue.

"Banana trees are not trees at all," he explained, "they grow from a root-ball." He let me examine one of the corms. "Out of this, a palm-shoot will grow to a height a little over that of a man, in about six or eight months. Then a stem with a flower will form. The flower will grow and you'll see the tiny bananas forming all around the flower stem, after the petals have been shed. These bananas continue to grow and in a couple of months they'll be ready to harvest. The average piña of fruit is so heavy, around 20 kilos, that the stem, thick and strong as it is, bends over with the larger bananas at the top of the inverted bunch and the smaller, newer ones around the bottom."

Often, when we were heading home in the evenings, we'd see another lorry lumbering along, laden with these huge, green conical piñas. They'd be carefully cushioned with blankets to stop them bruising. I'd no idea where they were going or what happened to them after that, but in my next job, I would learn.

After a spur of rock was blasted using dynamite, the construction workers, including the author in the picture, had to break up the boulders so they could be more easily handled.

For the rest of that day and the next, we planted potatoes. Then we undertook the harder job of planting the banana corms so that their tops were flush with the surface of the soil. When we'd finished planting the corms, the key-man was called in. The key-man had an intimate knowledge of all the channels that brought the water from the galleries at the foot of the mountains down to the plain. While we tidied up the site, made sure there were no tools left behind and that the track was clear of rocks or debris, the key-man directed fresh water into our newly planted plantation. A couple of the more experienced men from our crew used large hoes to slow down the flow thereby avoiding erosion and to soak the entire surface of the plantation, portion by portion.

Successful irrigation was a skilled job that required understanding and speed. Water was sold by the hour and so every drop had to be made to count. All the potato rows and the soil round the banana corms had to be soaked to a depth of half a metre. I began to understand the process of manual irrigation. Water flows to the lowest level. While I had assumed we'd been building the plantation perfectly level, its entire surface was in fact tilted slightly to the south and sloped very slightly downhill towards the coast. The sweet, cool irrigation water flowed within its concrete irrigation channel at the top end of the slope and entered the plantation. Those responsible for irrigation used their wide-bladed hoes make soil dams and direct the water from left to right along the entire length of each furrow, one furrow after the other. In this way, the water was allowed to move along each furrow and then down into the next and the next until the entire plantation had received a good soaking. The volume and speed of flow had to be controlled so that it didn't carry any soil with it. The purpose was to soak the soil and give the plants life, not to move earth.

At the end of that day, as we were about to climb on the back of the lorry, Juan told us: "That's it, lads and lasses. No more work for the moment. I'll call you again as soon as I need you." The men and the women on the crew took this news with calm nods. Most of the men, I'd learned, had small plots of land of their own where they grew a few rows of bananas, some fruit and vegetables for the house, and fattened a pig or kept a hutch of rabbits. The women had families to

look after, clothes to repair, meals to prepare, neglected household chores to catch up on, fruit to bottle, and when the pig was killed, they'd salt, smoke or cure its every part to make it last as long as possible. I, on the other hand, had little in the way of finances to fall back on.

But the Fortunate Isle was kind to me; I was soon to be offered a new job.

We had to irrigate banana corms immediately after planting.

10. La Empacadora: The banana-packing warehouse.

The employees of the banana-packing station used pine needles, straw or hay to protect the banana stalks for transport. We favoured pine needles because they had no other practical use, whereas hay and straw was also cattle-fodder.

That evening, no sooner had I sat down to dinner, at my usual table in the courtyard, than Don Salvador stood up and invited me to join him.

Don Salvador stayed overnight in the fonda every few weeks. At six feet tall and dressed in spotless khaki shirt and creased slacks, he'd no sooner unfolded himself from his car, which he always parked on the edge of the plaza close to the church, than people flocked to greet him. The dark-framed spectacles couldn't hide the laughter lines round his eyes; his neat black moustache added distinction to the warmth of his smile and a sense of well-being was conveyed by the unhurried way he had of looking around him as if all was gloriously well with the world. I knew little about him other than that he lived only 50 kilometres or so away in Puerto la Cruz with his wife and daughter, that he exported bananas bought from the plantations around Buenavista and that he seemed to be known and liked by everyone.

If he happened to meet me in the plaza, he'd open his eyes wide as if in delighted surprise and shake my hand. "Still here, Orlando? It's clear that Scotland's not a patch on Tenerife! How are you enjoying the work with Pata Cabra?" I would express my general satisfaction with life in the village. He'd listen attentively and then: "Your Spanish is getting better and better! Now it's almost native-like!" We often encountered each other in the dining room but we ate at separate tables. Initially, my limited mastery of the language was responsible for my isolation at meal times, but as I watched and listened, I began to appreciate that there were other more fundamental reasons why guests tended to keep to their own tables.

Most of the guests who stayed overnight in the fonda and even the clients who occasionally came in for lunch or dinner were engaged in business of some sort. Don Salvador, I gleaned from the girls, came to discuss with plantation owners how the banana crop was progressing so that he could plan his purchases and his exports. Well in advance, he needed to negotiate with European buyers and reserve the space he would require on a cargo ship from Santa Cruz to Oslo, Stockholm or Helsinki. From time to time, he and a plantation owner would lunch or dine together to go over the details of their agreements.

Even if he wasn't talking business, exchanging local news with one of the girls or pencilling in numbers on the clipboard he carried permanently with him, Don Salvador, like all the guests, had much in common with each other. They were all Canarios, born and bred. They knew one another or had at least heard of one another's families. They shared a culture and a history and a set of social conventions that were foreign to me. Any attempt, by Don Salvador or any of the other guests, to engage me in conversation, required them to make an enormous effort for relatively little reward.

Their simplest, most well-meaning questions elicited from me answers that drew on a geography, a history and a way of looking at the world that was different and puzzling. The world my words conjured up was so remote from theirs as to be alien, inaccessible and, judging from their reactions, far less attractive than their own. Even after a month or two, Doña Lutgarda and her daughters still shook their heads in disbelief at a culture that permitted me, a mere boy in their eyes and penniless to boot, to quit the family home and explore a distant, little-known country where a foreign language was spoken, strange food eaten, and bizarre customs observed. Spain was a country almost entirely cut off from the rest of Europe and had been shunned since the end of the Spanish Civil War more than 20 years earlier. Europe knew little of Peninsular Spain and Peninsular Spaniards knew virtually nothing at all about the rest of Europe or of Europeans. The Canary Islands, though a Spanish possession, was more than 2,000 kilometres from Madrid and almost 3,000 from Dundee.

Shortly after my arrival in the village, Doña Lutgarda had brought to my attention some of the social rules that governed behaviour in the village. She let me know that it was my duty to watch, learn and adapt if I wanted to be accepted into the life of the fonda and of the community as a whole. That the onus to adjust fell on me, the incomer, made perfect sense and so I strove to observe, find out and comply. As a result, I was beginning to fit in rather well, I thought, even though it was clear I'd always be el Extranjero.

Initially, I wasn't entirely comfortable with my nick-name because I thought it sounded faintly pejorative. I decided that if I needed a nick-name at all, it should be El Escocés – the Scotsman. Besides being the name of a leading Scottish newspaper it sounded more positive. Most of the villagers, however, had only the vaguest of notions about geography and for a while randomly referred to me as El Escocés – the Scotsman, El Sueco – the Swede or El Suizo – the Swissman.

As a consequence, I gave up insisting and decided, rather than try to manufacture a nick-name for myself, to leave it to them. Nick-names after all, reflect not what you think of yourself but what others think of you. So I went back to being, simply, el Extranjero and came to appreciate that it wasn't derogatory, merely a description of my unique status.

As the one and only foreigner in the village, I saw my first duty as doing all I could to fit in at the fonda because Doña Lutgarda had offered me a home there. It's where I slept, was greeted pleasantly when I went downstairs for breakfast, lunch and dinner, where my laundry was washed, hung out to dry, ironed and put back into my room neatly folded and smelling of fresh sea air and detergent. Knowing I had little money, Doña Lutgarda even went so far as to reduce my weekly tariff if I agreed to forego the luxury of selecting dishes from the menu and accept whatever plate she decided to serve me. That was no hardship whatsoever. Everything that came from her one-woman kitchen was delicious. I loved the basics like chickpeas, beans, lentils, rice and potatoes.

Had I made even a small social blunder, I had no doubt that Doña Lutgarda would tell me bluntly that my room was needed and I would have to leave. Fortunately, both at home and at school in Dundee, we'd been reared to detect others' sensibilities and to respect them, even if that meant curbing our own personal desires. And because the fonda with its attached venta – the store – were, together, the hub of the village where local gossip was exchanged, the reputation I built for myself there was a matter of factual testimony to my character. It was immediately shared, broadcast and exposed to public discussion, and moral judgment.

The truth was that I found it no great challenge to live according to the norms of the fonda and the customs of the village. Life in Coupar Angus, where I'd spent the first few years of my childhood and then visited frequently until my grandmother died in the mid-1950s, was, in terms of person-to-person relations, essentially similar to life in Buenavista. All villagers knew and treated one another with respect. Differences in role and status were not questioned, simply accepted. Some villagers required labour and so employed. Others needed a secure weekly income and accordingly contracted their services for a weekly wage. There were those who worked the land and those who owned it. For those willing to bear the risks, there was the option of share-cropping – a process whereby the owner offered the land, a worker his labour, and the income from the produce, be it great or small, was shared in an agreed ratio. There were those who worked within the village, those who went down to the sea and fished, and those who commuted daily to plantations on bicycle or on foot. Some dressed for business, some for manual labour.

Houses I'd known in rural Scotland, were simple and without luxuries, some lacked basic conveniences. Here in the fonda, there was no central plumbing, light bulbs were of low wattage and switched off unless absolutely required. There was no running hot water, even cold water was used sparingly since the girls brought it from the communal tap near the plaza. Residents greeted one another affably and went about their daily business in a way that suggested a community comfortable within its own limitations and the range of its own diversity. The village appeared to be free from the discord that arises from jealousy or resentment. Individuals were free to pursue their own ambitions. Individually they could choose to make greater or lesser efforts in school or at work. The ambitious cultivated entrepreneurial initiative while others were satisfied with an easier pace of life that would take them along a more predictable, more modest path. There was no dishonour in choosing a more casual route through life and yet those who showed the initiative, passion and zeal to exceed the accomplishments of their parents were accorded admiration and respect.

As in Scotland, emigration was one of the escape valves for serious discontent or determined ambition. For well over 100 years, Canarios had been tempted by the prizes offered by leaving all behind; they also knew the personal sacrifices involved. In the village, there were many who had gone off to Cuba or Puerto Rico and come back to buy fertile acres that would be worked by willing sharecroppers, allowing the new owners to live in relative ease. Every villager knew of family members, friends, neighbours or acquaintances who, in the not-so-distant past, had taken a cheap passage to find work in the thriving oil industry around the Gulf of Maracaibo. From time to time, one or two of them would return, fashionably dressed, to spend leisurely weeks broadcasting the opportunities that offered themselves to the daring. Such tales of success, embellished or factual, inspired some to follow these adventurers in search of similar triumphs. In others, the stories of sacrifice, isolation and hardship stirred even deeper satisfaction with the familiar daily cycle of family and friends and companionable village life in Buenavista, where custom offered more comfort than money could buy in alien lands.

There was however, one difference that I found myself incapable of adapting to. In our family, we'd been brought up to attend the Presbyterian church. Just as I bore the unquestioned certainty that to have been born Scottish was a matter of supreme good fortune, I enjoyed the confidence that Presbyterianism trumped all other sects. If asked why, I would have found it impossible to give a reasoned explanation. It had occurred to me, as I'd visited, simply as a tourist, cathedrals in France and Spain, that Roman Catholics might regard Protestants as the lesser. They might deride our aversion to pomp, hierarchy and public display and our refusal of the sacrament of confession that leads to absolution.

My fledgling doubts about the significance of divisions within Christianity, however, had no base in substance or theology. They gave me no insights that might allow me to overcome my prejudices so that I could take part in the daily worship within the substantial church on the plaza, Nuestra Señora de Los Remedios, even though I appreciated that the rites and rituals gave the village a good portion of its dignity and cohesion. Fortunately for me, the number of respected villagers who didn't attend mass was sufficient that my failure to do so was not quite beyond the bounds of acceptable behaviour.

By allowing me to live as a guest in the fonda and even actively encouraging me to prolong my stay, by finding me my first job with her cousin Pata Cabra, Doña Lutgarda and her family were sending a message to the entire village. It said that, despite my youth, my foreignness, my spoken errors and odd accent, I was acceptable, decent, and presented no threat to the integrity of the Pension Méndez, the community, or to any of its members.

My colleagues in the banana packing station preparing 'cushions' to protect banana stalks for transportation.

Don Salvador's invitation to join him for dinner was further evidence that my Spanish had improved to the point where my conversation was now tolerable and my public acceptance as an honorary villager was at least being considered. We shook hands. Pastora served us fried fish and salty, wrinkled potatoes, a delicacy loved by every Canario.

"How good is your arithmetic, Orlando?"

"Very good!" Had he said 'mathematics', I might have hesitated. I'd passed my school maths only at the second attempt, a weakness that explained, in part, my refusal into Agriculture at Aberdeen University. However, in all Scottish schools, by the end of primary, we could add, subtract, divide and multiply easily, often without the need to resort to paper and pencil. Skill in 'mental arithmetic' was considered a basic.

"How would you like to do some counting for me tonight? I have a lorry to be loaded at the empacadora – the banana-packing station – after dinner. I'd be obliged if you would confirm that the kilos loaded correspond to the kilos written on the sales order."

He detached from his clipboard examples of the different kinds of paper receipts his export business used. There were separate sheets for sales quotes, purchase orders, packing slips and acknowledgement of receipt and delivery. "What I want you to do is to make sure that the employees load the lorry with the exact weight on this sales order. The weight of bananas on the lorry must correspond within a kilo or two to that on the packing slip that our driver takes with him to the docks."

"I'd be happy to do that!" I vaguely wondered why the counting couldn't be done by one of the employees at the packing station or even by Don Salvador himself but I was learning to be patient. Explanations were not always readily self-evident, at least to me, in Canario culture.

"You've never seen our empacadora. Come with me. I guarantee you'll find it interesting, Orlando." Half an hour later, we were on our way together across the plaza and up a cobbled side-street I was unfamiliar with, on our way to the packing station.

"That's the lorry we use to collect bananas from the plantations and to take the piñas, once they're packed, to the port in Santa Cruz!" Don Salvador pointed to a smart green Ford Thames with high wooden-slatted sideboards parked outside the open doors of a warehouse. It was very similar to the one that el Bachillér had used to deliver soil to the plantation I'd helped construct. At the tailgate, a tough, middle-aged man with an authoritative manner was giving instructions to a very tall young fellow who appeared to be the driver.

Before we entered the warehouse, Don Salvador first introduced me to the smaller of the two men. Don Pancho was Don Salvador's business partner. He was in his fifties, fit and hard-bitten, the kind who sum you up accurately in seconds. He crushed my hand without smiling. His combed hair was wet as if he'd just showered and he smelled of fresh soap. He struck me as a man who had worked hard all his life and would give no quarter to others. Don Salvador then introduced me to Ángel, the lorry driver. Ángel was a pleasant, rangy lad in his early thirties, smelling of petrol and sweat, whose hair stood up as if he'd recently got out of bed.

Just inside the warehouse stood the smiling packers lined up to greet Don Salvador. There were several pleasant women in their 30's and 40's wearing faded brown warehouse coats and coloured headscarves tied tightly over their hair. Most of them I recognized from the store attached to the fonda. There were only two men. Epifanio, middle-aged and quietly self-assured, shook my hand. His look was friendly and approving, as if he'd been waiting to meet me for a long time. Miguel was a pale, lanky lad about my own age. I detected a slight suspicion as if my presence made him uncomfortable without his being aware of it. Both were dressed in well-worn khaki twill pants and shirts, the ubiquitous uniform of manual workers. Black, indelible stains on their clothes told that they worked with bananas. They all greeted Don Salvador warmly and me with curiosity. It was obvious that this was a happy work crew.

"This is where we pack the piñas. A piña is the entire banana stalk." Epifanio gestured to row upon row of large, round tubular packages wrapped in thick brown paper and tied firmly with sisal, stacked against the wall. From the wider end of each package protruded the end of the thick stalk that had had to be cut with a machete from the plant it grew on in the plantation. There was also a lower stack of green piñas against the interior wall as if waiting to be packaged. The air was dry and smelled pleasantly of straw, of the huge rolls of sisal treated with tarred oakum and fresh, brown packing paper. Three bare 60-watt bulbs high in the ceiling cast a pale-yellow light in the darkness.

"Show el Extranjero how you pack a piña!" At Don Salvador's request, the crew sprang into action. Willing pairs of women took up positions on opposite sides of the long, wide, wooden trestle and placed a sheet of brown packing paper about one metre wide and two metres long onto the table's surface. Epifanio grabbed an armful of clean, aromatic straw from a crib and shook it out to cover the sheet evenly and form a thick cushion. A pair of women immediately placed another identical sheet of paper on top to create a thick, protective pad. Then Miguel and another woman, also working from opposite sides of the table, gently laid a whole banana stem – the piña – complete with its 5 or 6 tiers of curved bananas, onto the pad.

Working swiftly and in unison, one pair rolled the padding round the entire stem, tightly tucking in the paper at top and bottom. Another pair, using pre-cut lengths of strong-smelling sisal string, firmly circled the pad to ensure that the protective roll would be kept in place and so cushion the fruit from the weight of other piñas that would be piled on top of it during transport. The outer skin of the banana is delicate and easily bruised. Although the fruit inside would suffer little, buyers judge the desirability of a hand of bananas by how uniformly yellow and free of blemishes the individual fruit are. The final pair expertly knotted the twine, cutting off the excess, and Epifanio pasted a large colourful label, bearing the words 'Alhambra Bananas, Buenavista del Norte, Tenerife' squarely onto the brown paper exterior. He raised his hand to show the task was complete. The women and Miguel beamed.

The entire crew looked up at Don Salvador expectantly, proud to have taken just a minute or so to complete the series of routinized, shared tasks that made up the entire operation. "Well done!" It was clear to me, from watching how they expertly synchronised their every movement, that they had worked together for a long time to reach such a level of skill and that they took pride in doing a good job and in pleasing Don Salvador.

"You see, Orlando? That's how our team packs each and every

piña for export. Despite being simple, local and cheap, the packaging guarantees that every piña can be loaded onto the truck, unloaded into the hold of the boat and so on, until it reaches its destination in perfect condition. The importer in Helsinki will sell it when the fruit is still green. Once it reaches a fruit shop, each piña will be cut up and sold hand-by-hand and just beginning to turn yellow, to happy customers. One of the most important secrets of exporting bananas successfully lies in the packing. Another lies in timing."

Ángel said something to Don Pancho and Don Pancho nodded. "Let's go! Time to load the lorry! Ángel has to be at the docks soon after midnight to wait in line. Our fruit must be loaded onto the ship before the sun rises and things get hot."

Don Salvador explained. "The ship will begin loading at 5 a.m. but there will be a long line of trucks waiting. Ángel likes to arrive there a few hours early so as to be among the first in line. That means our fruit will be loaded before the sun is up and while the air is still cool. A low temperature lengthens the life of the piña. It must still be green when it gets to Helsinki and it's up to the fruit merchants there to allow it to reach the stage of ripeness their customers prefer."

"What weight do we need tonight?" Don Pancho was getting impatient.

Don Salvador consulted a paper on his clipboard. "Two thousand four hundred kilos."

"Right, let's get at it!"

Ángel and the boy, Miguel, climbed up onto the bed of the lorry. Epifanio and one of the women lifted a piña, read out its weight written in purple crayon on the round face of the cut stem, 24.5 kilos, and placed it on the head of the first woman, who walked swiftly to the open tailgate of the lorry. Don Salvador handed me a pencil and a clipboard containing sheets of lined paper, each line numbered sequentially, some 20 to a page.

"As Epifanio calls the numbers out, Orlando, please write the weight of the first piña on line one and so on. If you don't hear a number clearly, ask Epifanio to repeat it. Your record must be 100% accurate."

Even while they were working, the eyes of the entire crew were on me as Epifanio called out the weights and I entered them onto the sheet. Don Pancho bade us "¡Buenas noches!" and retired to his house, the side door of which was inside the warehouse.

Ángel and Miguel lifted each piña off the woman's head and began to lay them gently on the boards against the cab, always with stem facing out. On the operation went, at a smart pace, until all but 25 or so of the tubular packages were neatly stacked up to the height of the wooden, slatted side-racks that held the load secure and about a single row from the tailgate.

"Orlando, what weight of fruit have we loaded?"

Everybody rested, eyes on me as I counted up the tally, page by page and then made the final sum.

"A total of 73 piñas, giving a weight of 1,978 kilos."

"Are you sure?"

"I'm sure."

"Absolutely sure?"

"Absolutely!" I felt as if I were being tested.

Don Salvador consulted his own clipboard. He'd been recording as well. There was a pause. Everybody was silent and their eyes moved from Don Salvador to me and back. I held my breath. He looked up; smiled. "I get the same. A total of 73 piñas, giving a weight of 1,978 kilos."

The audience, wide-eyed, nodded to one another.

"El Extranjero can count!" Miguel seemed impressed.

"Of course he can count! He's not a thick-head like you!" There was general laughter.

I winked at Miguel. "I'll show you how." He seemed mollified.

The entire crew looked at me with respect. They were all clearly impressed.

"What weight are we short?" Don Salvador looked at me.

I calculated quickly. "We're short 522 kilos."

"How many piñas?"

Again, I made a quick calculation. "Between 22 and 25 approximately."

There were more murmurs of admiration. "He's guessing!" Miguel announced. There was more good-humoured laughter.

As the human chain began loading the final score of banana stems, I kept a running total in my head. When we were just 39 kilos short of 2,400 kilos, I called out to Epifanio. "Bring these two, please!" I pointed to two of the dozen or so packages that had the purple numbers 22.5 written on the round, cut-end of the stalk. The last two were laden, patted gently into place, and Ángel cast a driver's critical eye over his load to guarantee its balance and safety.

"We've got 2,406 kilos on the lorry," I announced.

"Why did you overload?" Don Salvador asked.

"It's impossible to get the exact weight given the remaining piñas we have to choose from. I thought it makes better sense to overload by five or six kilos than to be a kilo or two short."

Don Salvador nodded. "A good decision! When Ángel drives onto the weigh-scale at the dock, he won't run into any difficulties." He seemed pleased and showed me how to make out the delivery slip in quadruplicate.

"Right Ángel, off you go!" Ángel held out his hand for the copies he needed to give to the port authorities and to the ship's officer in charge of loading. Carefully folding and tucking these into the breast pocket of his shirt, he waved "¡Adios!" climbed up into the cab of his lorry, started the engine and slowly began to make his way up the lane towards the main road to the port of Santa Cruz and the docks, where the Finnish ship lay berthed and waiting.

Smiling warmly, Don Salvador thanked everybody and exchanged a few short, personal words with each. "¡Bueno muchachos! That's it for now! We've no export shipment going out until the week after next. Don Pancho will let you all know when we'll be collecting, in about seven or eight days' time." There were murmurs of agreement, thank-yous and handshakes. The women took off their protective warehouse-coats and removed the scarves tied around their hair, shook the dust off them in the street and hung them up on pegs on the wall. Together, Don Salvador and I made our way across the silent, empty plaza to the fonda.

Don Salvador (right) is supervising us unloading freshly-cut banana stalks we'd just collected from El Rincón.

"What do you think of the empacadora?"

"I find it very interesting. I've helped build a plantation and planted the corms that will turn into trees, but I'd no idea how bananas were packaged for export."

"There's a lot to know about this business. If you want to learn more, come and work for me."

"What will that involve?"

"You'll be part of the crew you were with tonight. Together with Ángel and the truck, you'll have to collect the piñas from the various plantations I buy from in this region, and take them back to the packing station. Then you'll pack them to the weight that coincides with the timing of an export order. It's not a 9-to-5 job though. It's entirely dependent on the fruit available and the orders I'm able to win from my customers in Northern Europe. Sometimes the crew works days on end from morning till night. Then there will be days with little or no work at all. There will be nothing for the next week or so."

"That kind of work would suit me fine."

"I really need someone who's entirely reliable and good at record-keeping and numbers. Keeping accurate track of the produce is essential. You've shown you can do that."

We stood on the pavement outside the fonda while Don Salvador gave me details of hourly pay and how he would let me know when I was needed. Just as we were finishing, Doña Lutgarda came out to swing the main doors shut and bolt them.

"Isn't it time you two gentlemen came in? It's late. The day's work is over." She didn't appear at all surprised to see us talking together.

Don Salvador gave her his winning smile. "Doña Lutgarda, I want you to meet my right-hand man, Don Orlando, el Escocés!" It didn't surprise me that a banana exporter mastered European geography.

"So," she looked at me approvingly. "You finished with Pata Cabra today, Orlando, and you've already found another employer!" She exchanged a knowing look with Don Salvador. Once again, Doña Lutgarda had put in a good word for me. As I climbed the wide stone staircase to my room. I couldn't help feeling that my arrival at La Pension Méndez had been fortunate indeed and my decision to remain as a guest was one of the best I'd made in my entire life.

I knew that one day, I would scale El Teide, Tenerife's majestic volcano that last erupted in 1909.

11. Between jobs

Expedition to El Barranco Negro

After my experience as a member of Juan-the-Foreman's crew, I'd grown in confidence. My Spanish had improved; I'd shown I was as reliable a worker as any and keen to learn. The men knew I always pulled my weight; the women appreciated me because I respected them and never overloaded the baskets they had to carry on their heads. Now, when I walked in the plaza I was constantly greeted. "¡Buenos días Orlando! ¿Qué tal? How's it going?" No longer did I feel like the outsider I undoubtedly was when I'd arrived. The villagers were beginning to treat me more like a neighbour. I had a stake in the village. My growing acceptance pleased Doña Lutgarda. She had taken a risk when she made me her protégé, first by approving my continued residence in the fonda and then by recommending me to Pata Cabra as a suitable employee. I was pleased to be repaying the confidence she'd shown in me.

Now, with a whole week free, I ventured further afield on my exploratory walks with greater confidence, using the dozens of footpaths that criss-crossed the district. Mostly I explored alone, occasionally with one or other of my new friends.

I'd long heard the girls in the fonda mention el Barranco Negro – the Black Ravine. "On your walks, Orlando!" they would warn, "avoid el Barranco Negro."

"Where exactly is it?"

Lula took me upstairs to the terrace and pointed. "Look southeast towards the mountains. Can you make out that black cleft below the dark cloud? That's the Barranco Negro. Don't go near it!"

And so, one morning shortly after dawn, without being explicit about my plans, I set out for el Barranco Negro. There was a light, salty breeze from the ocean, and the sky was dotted with puffy, white cumulus. Cocks were crowing; donkeys braying for hay. I felt exhilarated by what I was about to do. Superstitious fears were not for the likes of me!

Although on the north-western side of the island we enjoyed light from around seven or so in the morning, the sun didn't crest the mountain ridge until an hour later. The first sign was a golden glow around the dark crenelated tops. Then, like fresh water rushing down a mill-race, the warming light would flush first the ocean and then the countryside into colour. Dark breakers turned green; the arid plain turned yellow and tall cacti stretched their morning arms like green soldiers; shredded banana fronds waved above the cinder-grey walls that tried to protect the fruit from the constant Atlantic breeze. As the sun rose higher, the village shed its modesty to boast the petal-soft mustard, lemon, ochre, and honey walls that lined its narrow streets and offered privacy and protection to waking villagers. Bougainvillea and geraniums glowed like stones in a treasure chest.

I reached the edge of the village just as the sun sprang free of the craggy ridge and flushed its warmth onto the green and brown terraced fields I was crossing. The welcome warmth encouraged a lone farmer hoeing weeds to straighten his back and raise his straw hat to savour the day's promising kiss on his face. Pale yellow canaries chirped, "Life is blessed."

To better get my bearings, I climbed atop a high stone wall. Several kilometres ahead, the hillsides were still in shade. Half way up, a bank of mist was rising to expose the tiny hamlets that clung there, surrounded by their narrow terraces of vegetables and grazing goats.

Two of the principal footpaths that led in the general direction of the mountains were familiar to me from previous excursions. The one I'd christened Pilgrim's Way; was an ancient, cobbled path that snaked up the hillside to El Palmar. The other veered abruptly to the right, past la Casa Blanca, one of the larger, more prestigious estates in the area. Its spotlessly-white-washed, rambling hacienda gave the impression of aspiring to a self-contained, walled village – what in Scotland we'd call a ferm-toun. The word conjures up an intimately-connected group of weathered, stone buildings with crow-stepped gables, a two-story farmhouse, a set of workers' cottages and a clutch of stables, steadings and warm barns.

La Casa Blanca stood staunch and respectable behind its rough, whitewashed wall. Its patron and farm-hands, I knew from experience, tended daily to well-managed fields of vegetables and rustling plantations that might have been there from time immemorial. Just two or three rocky kilometres further and I'd reach the base of a great wall of dark cliffs, that seemed to soar into the clouds. The farm there was called el Rincón, the Retreat, a natural alcove in the surrounding cliffs. I'd heard it said, however, that the villagers from Teno Alto, a loose cluster of cottages on the high plateau over 1000 feet above, knew, but kept secret, an almost vertical path, a veritable staircase that they used to get up and down the cliff whenever they wanted. To an untrained eye like mine, that rumour seemed more myth than truth.

My destination today however was neither El Palmar nor el Rincón. By my reckoning, el Barranco Negro lay approximately half-way between these two paths and so I was forced to start cutting across country, making use of the stone dykes that divided the small properties and the concrete irrigation channels that provided water to the terraces. These terraced fields had long ago been carved out of the sloping land. The incline progressively increased the closer I got to the base of the mountains, and the terraces became more and more narrow.

I wasn't certain if I was allowed to use these dykes and verges as a freeway and so, when I spotted an isolated farmer here and there, bent over his narrow field of onions or strawberry plants or drills of potatoes, I'd purposely make my way to where he was working and call out a greeting. Farmers and field-workers, I'd found, were always happy to pause in their task, lean on their hoe and exchange a few words about the weather or the state of the crop and glean a scrap of news. They knew who I was by reputation and were pleased to get to meet me in person. They'd have something novel to talk about when the day ended and they returned home.

None of the smiling farmers I greeted that morning, some of them women, gave even the slightest hint I might be trespassing. That reassured me. All were naturally curious about where I was going. If I was heading for El Palmar I was too far to the right. If El Rincón was my destination, I was too far to the left. They tried to be helpful without appearing to be blatantly curious. They were too polite to ask me the direct question: "Where are you going and why?" When I finally relieved their curiosity by volunteering, "I'm heading for el Barranco Negro," they would raise their eyebrows and cross themselves. "El Barranco Negro? Why there? That's not a good place to go!" Of course, their alarm made me all the more determined.

As I progressed up the slope and approached the foot of the abrupt cliffs, the terraces narrowed to little more than a metre wide and then stopped altogether. The slope was now too steep for cultivation but was densely overgrown with small trees and shrubs that suggested fertile soil. The going was tough, so I stopped often to rest. At one steep spot, I turned and looked back down the long, arduous way I'd come. I could see my journey in reverse. The descending terraces grew in width till they became almost the size of respectable fields before eventually reaching the edge of the compact village, crouched like a sand-crab on the plain. The clock-tower and spire of Nuestra Señora de los Remedios rose proudly above palm trees, walled streets and coupled houses. I could imagine the villagers greeting one another in the flowered plaza as they began their daily tasks. My feeling of belonging came, in part, from being so familiar with the morning sounds of renewal and the predictable routines of the villagers.

Rest and reflection at this vantage point also allowed me to make a good guess at how the entire area might have been formed. Dr Brown, who'd taught us physical geography at the Morgan Academy, had an inspiring technique designed to make us think about landscape and the factors that shape it. He would pin a coloured, but untitled poster to the blackboard. Then he'd encourage us to ask searching questions, drawing exhaustively on all visual clues that could help us determine what kind of landscape the picture illustrated. "By what forces of nature or man might it have been formed?" "Any hints in land or sky to signal the latitude and longitude?" "Clues to suggest the driving economy of the region?" "How might people earn their living?" As we refined our questions and conclusions, the intimate life of the location revealed itself. Eventually we'd be able to determine its most likely location in the world, its climate, and how the population survived. I applied Dr Brown's techniques to the view in front of me.

Over millennia, periodic showers of rain, carried in on Atlantic westerlies, eroded the volcanic mountains, allowing vegetation to cling, then thrive. Steadily, ash-laden minerals accumulated to a great depth at the foot of the mountains inviting further vegetation. Soil was gradually transported down the steep slopes until the incline gave way to the more gently sloping plain that stretched all the way to the coast. On these slopes, early farmers built horizontal stone dykes to make level terraces wide enough to cultivate vegetables in the moist alluvium.

The founders of Buenavista del Norte in the early 1600s began building on that part of the plain precisely where the rich soil cover ended and the hard, bare clay began. The moderate incline was ideally suited for larger fields and plantations. Below the village however, towards the coast, the plain lacked any soil that would sustain more than cactus and shrub thorn. This explained why, when we built the plantation, we needed lorry-loads of black earth before planting the seed-potatoes and the banana corms. Man's ingenuity was modifying the natural landscape to allow a village of hard-working people to thrive.

Here, where I now stood close to the mountains, the soil was rich and deep, with a thick covering of woody shrubs. The soil became even richer and deeper, the closer I got to the foot of the cliffs where it had accumulated over millennia.

In the stillness, I caught the call of voices raised over a thrumming diesel engine. Making my way through the shrubby undergrowth that grew higher than me, I found a mechanical shovel loading a lorry with fresh soil. The drivers were startled to see me emerge from the shrubbery. "¡Hombre! It's el Extranjero! What are you doing up here in this godforsaken place?"

"¡El Bachillér! ¡Buenos días!" I was pleased to be able to greet the lorry-driver by his nick-name. "You two started work early this morning!"

El Bachillér – literally, the Graduate – owned the lorry that had brought the soil to establish the banana plantation I'd recently helped build. Barely in his 30's, he exuded confidence. He owed his nickname to the fact that unlike most, he had completed school. All the others had left at the first opportunity to supplement their family income. Entrepreneurial and tireless, el Bachillér had invested in a lorry. As a proud owner-operator, he a offered reliable bulk carrier service to building contractors within a radius of a score of kilometres around his home, a hamlet close to Buenavista. He'd taken a liking to me when he'd learned that I too had completed school. In celebration of our educational bond, he would greet me with noisy blasts on the horn whenever he spotted me. He was respected in the region, and some of the deference paid to him rubbed off on me merely for winning his friendship.

In response to my comment about their early start, El Bachillér rubbed forefingers and thumb together to indicate that if there was a job that paid well for his services, he would be there to oblige. He had confided to me that if his business was to maintain itself, he needed to earn 4000 pesetas a day – over £200. By comparison, I earned less than 50 pesetas. He hadn't stayed on at school for nothing!

After introducing me to the loader-operator, the three of us talked about the geological formation of this part of the island and el Bachillér confirmed the conclusions I'd come to about how the landscape had been created. He added that the periodic addition of volcanic ash resulting from Teide's occasional eruptions, the last only 50 years earlier, enriched the mix because the minerals it contained were ideal for plant growth.

His lorry loaded, el Bachillér was about to drive down a near-invisible track back in the direction of Buenavista and offered to give me a lift. "Thanks, but I'm heading for el Barranco Negro." The loader operator immediately launched into a series of reasons why I should steer clear of that unholy place, but El Bachillér silenced him.

"Nonsense! Like I am, El Extranjero is a man of deep education. Didn't you see he knows all about how this island was formed thousands of years ago by a volcano? People like us don't believe in old wives' tales. Evil spirits! Haunted places! Rubbish!"

"Have you ever dared to visit el Barranco Negro?" The loader driver asked him pointedly.

"No, but only because I work so hard and don't have time!" His excuse earned him a sceptical look. El Bachillér climbed up into his cab, waved and began to creep down the incline in low gear, engine growling in protest under the load and the steepness of the incline. "¡Adios!"

Now I was in deep shade, the cliffs towering above me and the dark defile of the Barranco straight ahead. The place, I had to admit, had an uncanny feel to it. Through the hanging ferns and verdant shrubs growing out of the steep cliff-face, I could see moist, white clouds and blue sky far, far above. The clouds slowly rose and fell and sent glistening, probing wisps drifting into the upper darkness of the canyon with eerie effect.

Should I continue? Go back? I was in two minds. My timid side said: Nobody will ever know if I don't actually enter the gorge! My curious side said: Since I've come this far, I may as well see everything there is to see!

Doña Lutgarda had a way of prising information out of a stone. Under her questioning, I would be embarrassed to admit I'd walked all the way to the Barranco but had been too scared to penetrate its mysteries. I examined the dark canyon in detail, giving myself time to muster courage. The rock on either side of the defile was slightly lighter in colour from the black, porous basalt of the interior. This darker interior rock intensified by the permanent shade within the gorge was what gave the Barranco its distinctive black – negro – appearance, even from a great distance.

As I made my cautious way inside, the gorge narrowed abruptly. Loose rocks moved under my feet and made the going laborious, even dangerous. What if I sprain my ankle? Or break my leg? Just as I was about to give up and turn around to retrace my steps, I noticed, quite motionless and only yards ahead, a forlorn donkey, head bent almost to the ground, and behind it, the dark mouth of a cave. I'm not alone! My presence, I realised, must inevitably have been noticed. Now I felt the need to account for myself to demonstrate, to whomever, that I meant no harm.

"¡Hola! ¡Buenos días! I'm el Extranjero. Orlando, el Extranjero from Buenavista del Norte. I'm just doing a little exploring!" I paused. Only my echo, eerily complete, replied!

I moved into an open space where anyone watching would be able to see me easily and repeated my announcement. Clear as a bell, my words echoed uncannily back. The donkey didn't even raise its head. The cave was obviously being used as a home. There was a ring of blackened stones containing ash but no flames. Behind the fireplace, I could see a pile of jute sacks and a battered aluminium pot. Age-old soot clung to the ceiling and crept round the roof of the opening to spread velvet fingers up the cliff-face. After forcing myself to wait a few more minutes, I carefully withdrew from the Barranco and began to walk slowly along the base of the cliff.

Now I could smell something unsettling – a pungent scent I couldn't identify. Gingerly, I moved towards its source. In the centre of a small clearing, I came upon a tumulus of what was undoubtedly freshly-dug, moist soil. The very earth, however, appeared to be smouldering. Curls of white vapour rose off the entire length of the grave-like mound. The smell was not unpleasant, but gave me no hint of what seethed within. I stood rooted, far from comfortable.

My eyes searched for clues; my mind searched for understanding. Stifling alarm, I began to put one and one, then two and two together. A silent hermit, nicknamed El Carbonero, visited Buenavista from time to time with sacks of charcoal tightly roped to the back of his donkey. Doña Lutgarda was one of his regular customers. When I'd asked, she'd told me: "El Carbonero lives up that way, quite alone!" She'd gestured vaguely, uncertainly towards the mountains.

The tumulus wasn't a suppurating source of malevolence or corruption, nor a gruesome burial ground. It was charcoal in the making! Although I'd never seen an 'earth burn' before, I'd read about the process in books that dealt with traditional country skills, like building dry-stane dykes, and making shepherds' crooks from a single branch.

This must be where el Carbonero lives and where he makes his charcoal! Where better? He has a free home and no neighbours to disturb his privacy. He has a ready, inexhaustible source of branches from woody shrubs easily cut to size. There's soil enough around to pack over his neat pile of dried sticks in order to keep the air out and so produce a slow, prolonged, flame-free burn. Denying oxygen to the fire by covering the sticks with sod and soil, I'd read, guarantees that the wood will be carbonized, not consumed. The result, when the burn is complete and the soil removed after three or four days, is a neat pile of short, charcoal rods, ideal for use in kitchens like Doña Lutgarda's.

To my enormous relief, I'd resolved the puzzle of the donkey, the cave and the smouldering, seething tumulus! My mission, to explore el Barranco Negro, had been accomplished.

Something still bothered me however. El Carbonero must have seen and heard me, but hadn't chosen to appear. That could mean only one thing – my presence was unwelcome! My being there was an invasion of his privacy, of the place that he had, perhaps over his entire adult lifetime, taken elaborate precautions to discourage even the most inquisitive from visiting. Maybe he himself, had initiated and promoted the malevolent reputation associated with el Barranco Negro. With such thoughts in mind, I called out in as friendly a tone as my uneasiness would allow, "Adios! I'm off now. I won't come back!" and made my way noisily down the slope, hoping to reassure him. I didn't look back.

When I reached the lower level where the cultivated terraces began, I came across a mulberry tree heavy with fruit. Using my straw hat as a basket, I filled it with the dark, bramble-like berries that lay in profusion on the ground. The berries still on the branches were well above my reach. As soon as I arrived home, I presented them to Pastora and Obdúlia to distract them from asking where I'd been "We'll have our mother do something with them!" Delighted, they went off to the kitchen, purple juice oozing through the crown of my hat.

That night, at dinner, Doña Lutgarda came to my table with a slice from a fragrant, moist tart she'd made in her oven. "I'm always asking my girls to go and collect mulberries but they complain, saying the trees are too far away. Gracias, Orlando!"

She turned on her daughters. "See! You scoundrels are from here, my own flesh and blood. Yet it takes a foreigner, who seems to know the countryside better than you, to bring me mulberries." The girls laughed. Seldom did they take seriously their mother's scolding. I smiled too, happy that my gift had given her so much pleasure. The slice of pie was delicious and all too small.

"Of course you didn't go to el Barranco Negro?" She regarded me from slitted eyes.

"I did!"

"Right inside?"

"All the way inside!" I was relieved to be able to tell the truth.

"And what did you find there?" Doña Lutgarda and the girls crowded closer to hear about the forbidden place.

Searching for just the right words to heighten and prolong the mystery, I told them how I'd found the Barranco, entered its darkness and discovered signs that it was inhabited. I mentioned sacks for a bed, a fireplace, a cooking-pot, and fingers of probing soot. I invented sharp, non-human eyes glinting malevolently at me from the dark depths. They shrieked and hugged one another. "Didn't we tell you! Brujas! – Evil spirits! So it is haunted!" Heads nodded in unison to confirm what they had always believed.

But haunted by whom, I decided, was information best kept to myself. I said nothing about the Carbonero's donkey. That would have been one clue too many.

Of boats and fishermen

The cove where the Buenavista fishermen keep their rowing boats. Note the narrow gap they have to exit in order to put to sea.

If I chose to walk the two kilometres or so from the village across the dry plain to the coast, I'd be sure to run into fishermen also on their way to the shore. On days when the wind provoked the waves into churning whitecaps I'd see them tightly wedged for safety between tumbled black rocks. Below, waves crashed and the backwash seethed and sucked and dragged long banners of golden seaweed to and fro.

Each fisherman would rig his cane with hook and stout line and use bait to prize protesting fish from foaming water. In place of a cane, one fisherman might have a shallow wire net that dangled from a steel hoop attached to a long pole. He would lower his net into a shallow pool or a wide crevasse between two rocks and wait for a surging wave. Then, just as the ferocious backwash sucked the water back out to sea, he'd raise his net sharply and toss a good-sized fish onto the rock behind him.

They were always willing to tell me exactly what variety they were after. "Fish are creatures of habit," I'd be told time and again. "Each kind has its preferred territory and sticks to it. Some choose the protection of rocks, some prefer clear water; some like to be closer to the surface, others seek security in depth."

On fine days, I could get a glimpse of the occasional two-man coble, borne to the crest of a wave before the following wave plunged it down out of sight. I'd assumed that the fishermen in these boats were from the neighbouring village of Los Silos and the Buenavista fishermen fished exclusively from the shore with cane and wire net. Los Silos had a small harbour that any traveller could see clearly from the road, whereas Buenavista, to my knowledge, had none. However, while talking one day to a pair of Buenavista cane-fishermen, they explained that they normally fished offshore but on wild days like this, it was unwise to put to sea.

On days when the waves were too high for the fishermen to launch their boats, they would fish from the rocks using long, home-made canes.

"So where do you keep your coble? In Los Silos?"

They walked me along the rocky shore it rose and we were standing on top of a hundred-foot cliff. "Look down there!" I followed his finger. I saw a tiny cove and a pebble beach. Both were overhung with rock that formed an almost hidden cavern. They led me down a precipitous path right to the water's edge. Under the overhang, a dozen two-man cobles were drawn up, invisible from the clifftop. They were brightly-painted, between four and six metres long and elegantly slim. A surprising feature was that they were symmetrical, pointed at both prow and stern.

"That's so we can row in either direction. With two prows, we never need to turn the coble. In the huge rollers offshore, turning would be dangerous." His tone was matter-of-fact. Hazards were ever-present for fishermen, risk an unavoidable part of their daily work.

The cove was created by a pair of rocky arms that extended into the sea to create a pool of water that rose and fell as the force of the tide swept in and out. To launch their boat, they explained, they dragged it through the gravel to the pool, then the first man jumped in and took the oars while the second man held the boat steady. When they spotted an ideal wave, the second man shoved off and leaped in while the oarsman pulled up onto the face of the wave, over the crest and down its back. Once safely past the rocky arms, they were on the breast of the open ocean. I listened in awe as they explained the dangers in as matter-of-fact a way as a city-dweller might talk about crossing a busy intersection.

A fisherman and his son repairing tears in a large wire net they used to catch 'viejas' offshore.

"We're fishermen. ¡Es nuestra vida! – It's what we do!"

A day later, well before dawn, after asking for their permission, I rose and walked the couple of kilometres down to the cove to watch these fishermen launch their boats, exactly as they had explained. All my life I'd enjoyed rising early. Dawn offered so much promise and renewal. Though almost three hours before sunrise, the sky was clear. The moon and the stars and the ocean's phosphorescence gave enough light to see all that was necessary. In near silence, lifelong partners dragged their cobles down the rattling pebble slope to the pool. One would board and stand with oars at the ready, the other would hold the vessel steady. At the urgent, "¡Ya! – Now!" the second man would give a powerful shove and leap aboard. The oarsman, standing erect, promptly dragged expertly on the long oars, and the coble would cut into the wave, rise to its crest and be sucked down into its trough, missing the rocks on either side with little room to spare. Then the oarsman dragged it up the face of the following wave, and coble and fishing partners were gone, swallowed by the darkness. Boat after boat launched in this way until I was left standing on the noisy pebbles, alone.

From the top of the cliff, I could just barely see Buenavista's entire fleet bunched together on the ocean. Each coble had its two fishermen, the standing one stoutly rowing, the sitting one preparing the equipment they'd need when they got to the fishing grounds they'd chosen for that day. Slowly, singly, the boats dispersed, each to probe the secret places where they knew, from hard-fought experience, the fish they sought would be feeding.

Back at the fonda for breakfast, I told Doña Lutgarda and the girls where I'd been and what I'd seen. Though they knew of it, none had ever been right down to the cove where the cobles were kept. Fisherman, they explained, were a group apart. They lived as a close-knit clan at their own edge of the village, observed their early hours and never failed to sell everything they caught. Doña Lutgarda had her own contacts. They supplied the fonda daily with the fish she needed.

Enthused by the romance of what I'd seen, I wondered aloud if a pair of fishermen might take me with them one day. The girls raised noisy objections. "It's far too dangerous!" But Doña Lutgarda understood my curiosity. Like Pearl, she was a wise woman who knew the futility of trying to scare or forbid those of us who are driven to probe and discover. I'd already visited el Barranco Negro against all advice!

"Your Spanish is good now, Orlando, why don't you ask? They'll take you."

I did ask and the answer was as she'd predicted.

So, a few days later, I found myself seated on the centre-thwart in one of the cobles a mile offshore with two experienced fishermen and the sharp tang of salt in my nostrils. They might not have agreed to take me had I been anybody other than el Extranjero. As the sole foreigner, I enjoyed the freedom to be just a little bit eccentric, and pursue unorthodox interests. That freedom, I understood, was extended just as long as I respected the norms that respected the peace and harmony that guaranteed the continued integrity of the community.

The launch from the cove, in starlight, was breath-taking. Oscar and Vale, the two fishermen who'd agreed to take me, adapted to accommodate the weight of one additional live but quite inexpert body. Oscar launched the coble on just the right wave; Vale expertly guided it through the narrow opening then pulled strenuously up and over the approaching wave and into the open ocean.

I was conscious of my uselessness to their purpose. The realisation humbled me. The few items aboard were carefully selected for the value they added to success of the expedition. I was an unnecessary liability. Oscar and Vale could read the slightest threat from each wave. A visceral intuition effortlessly adjusted their bodies to balance and ease the boat's progress. The pair worked in perfect harmony. Despite being as

Fishermen's wives would clean the fish their husbands had caught as soon as the boats returned to the cove.

superfluous as a sack of potatoes on the pillion of a motorcycle, neither fisherman uttered an impatient word.

Initially, I was overwhelmed by the sheer, unfathomable power of the ocean. The rounded waves were enormous, evenly spaced, smooth-sided as glass. They advanced on us with unforgiving regularity. Each bore us up to its transparent crest, held us captive for a few heart-stopping moments and then tipped the boat over the peak and drove us down into the dark green depths of its trough. Terror and euphoria gripped me in equal measure.

Our coble, narrow and maybe five metres long, was an insignificant piece of flotsam on the heaving ocean. From trough to crest, the waves were twice as high as our boat was long. The distance between crest and crest, however, was three or four times that length, and so I had the feeling of having been shrunk to a fraction of my size, like Alice in Wonderland! Even the three stormy days aboard the *Ciudad de Cádiz* hadn't prepared me for an ocean with such alien majesty.

While our oarsman hauled seawards, his partner began to prepare the fishing equipment. It included several lines with large hooks that he baited with chunks of strongly-smelling, rotted fish, nets of metal mesh suspended from a steel hoop like the ones I'd seen used from the rocks, and a metal biscuit-tin with a thick glass bottom. Holding it tightly, the second mate suspended the biscuit tin over the side of the boat, let it sit in the water and peered into it. I'd been told not to move and so just sat on the thwart and tried to get used to the mechanical, rise-pause-and-fall. I was facing the shore, and could see from the crest of each successive wave, how the cove and the compact village were drawing further and further away.

Just as I was getting used to the routine of our passage, the waves began to get less steep and the troughs less abyss-like. Oscar, sweeping at the long oars, was able to reduce his effort. Vale indicated we were coming into our fishing grounds and peered into the biscuit-tin with increased concentration.

"¡Ya! – Here is good!"

At the command, Oscar held the boat steady, Vale handed me the biscuit-tin and gestured for me to have a look while he slowly lowered one of the hoop-nets into the water.

"When you see fish in the net, give me the signal!"

Through the glass-bottom, the ocean suddenly became perfectly transparent. An entirely new world came into focus. I could see into the green depths as if examining an aquarium in a dentist's waiting room. At first, I could see only solitary fish, this one grey, this one pink. They swam unhurriedly into view and just as leisurely, out again. As if through a prism, I spotted the conical weighted ring-net slipping beneath the boat and then a shoal of dark fish blocked the wire ring-net from view by their number.

"¡Ya!-- Now!"

Hand-over-hand, Vale hauled on the rope bringing the ring-net swiftly to the surface. In its shallow maw were half a dozen of the dark fish I'd seen flipping over one another, silver-sleek in the new sunlight. They were larger than they had appeared through the biscuit tin. I held a canvas bag open while Vale deftly transferred the fish, each the size of a plump herring, and pulled the drawstring tight at the top. Then he scooped sea water onto the bag to lengthen their lives.

"The fresher they are, the better the price."

Over the next couple of hours, we repeated the exercise, moving every thirty minutes to find a new shoal, or perhaps following the same one, lifting the dripping net to trap a few fish each time, until the canvas bag was bulging. I marvelled at Oscar as he swept the boat expertly even further from the shore, which was now so distant that our village was just a white smudge on the dry, yellow plain.

"We have all the bogas we need. Now we'll see about hooking some viejas." Bogas were the most common fish we ate in the fonda and were usually fried. Viejas were more of a luxury and were served poached in broth. Both were delicious and served whole. The ease with which I forked the flesh off whole fish surprised Doña Lutgarda and the girls.

"It's how we eat fish at home in Scotland." When we were still little children, I explained, Pearl had taught us the simplest way to eat a whole fish. She patiently showed us exactly where the rows of different bones were located and how to methodically strip them of every piece of flesh, including the two button-like cheeks between eye and mouth, the two soft matching flakes at the back of the head and the nutritious skin.

We learned that if you eat a whole fish the way it should be eaten, there should be nothing left except the stripped head and the tail still joined by the perfect spine, a cluster of small bones from the dorsal fin and the ribs. At the end of a meal, Pearl would inspect each of our plates. "Perfect! Now you'll do yourselves proud even if you're invited to Buckingham Palace!" She took a delight in preparing us every eventuality, even the most unlikely. Her coaching and the confidence she showed in each of us encouraged us to strive. The discipline of those early years served us well.

When we reached a patch of ocean that was almost still, Oscar shipped his oars. Vale had prepared three lines each with baited hook and sinker. After we'd taken a quick glance through the biscuit tin, each of us lowered a line to exactly the same depth and let it hang there. As soon as we felt a tug on the line, we'd haul it smartly up into the boat, take it off the hook and place it in a space over the ribs of the coble made by removing a length of one of the bottom boards. We poured seawater over them and they lay on their sides giving the occasional flip. The vieja was larger and more fleshy than the boga and commanded a higher price.

Fishermen had to contend with powerful waves and jagged rocks. These rocks would be submerged one minute and the next, would rise like hungry sharks from the deep.

At about 10 o'clock, my friends decided we had enough fish for the day. The equipment was cleaned and stowed tidily. Since our coble had two prows, there was no need to attempt the dangerous manoeuvre of bringing her about. Each fisherman took one oar, and standing, one fore and one aft, began the long, ponderous haul back towards the cove. As we rowed with the slow high rollers, we caught glimpses of other boats also heading steadily back. One or two had been fishing even further from shore than we had, where bonito, small tuna, fed. These boats were using one long oar as a mast with a piece of canvas rigged to it. The advantage they gained from the wind allowed them to overtake us even though they'd come further.

Once close to shore, each coble waited its turn and chose the wave that would lift it high between the rocky arms of the cove and carry it safely into the quiet pool beyond. Hands were ready to pull each boat up the shingle under the overhang of the cliff. Wives and daughters waited to unload and clean the catch. At the top of the cliff, I was surprised to see a couple of merchants with small vans, from far beyond Buenavista, exchange cash for fish and then hurry off to their more distant markets. I watched the calm, methodical work of gutting, bargaining and loading, with the warm conviction that I had somehow grown in stature as a result of the timeless experience of the morning. Somehow the ignominy caused by my having been refused a place in agriculture at Aberdeen University seemed less significant beside the comfort of being an integral part of this scene.

In single-file and silence, we fishermen walked back across the stretch of arid plain, past the isolated campo santo – the local burial ground – and finally into the narrow, walled village streets. Oscar and Vale each shook my hand warmly and smiled wordlessly into my face. Both they and I knew that no words needed to be said, given the glorious and close companionship as well as the danger we'd shared since before dawn. Oscar presented me with a whole, gutted vieja. I raised my hand as they trudged off and then I crossed the plaza to my home in the Pension Méndez feeling quietly exalted.

Doña Lutgarda had a broth boiling on the charcoal stove. For lunch, I enjoyed the best cut from the vieja I'd hauled fresh from the sea only a few hours earlier.

Fishermen in their small cobles always worked in pairs.

12. To the Lighthouse: la Punta de Teno

"I need your help, Orlando!" Pepe Mendibles, the carpenter, found me alone at dinner, in the courtyard of the fonda. "I've finished the window frames for the lighthouse at la Punta de Teno. Can I count on you to help me install them?"

Pepe and I had become good friends since first meeting at his workshop on Calle Cruz. His business took him all over town and I'd see him in the most unexpected places, measuring up doors or windows or delivering a wardrobe or a dining-room set he'd made for a customer. Pepe Mendibles worked at his own pace, enjoyed life and always carried the smile that engaged his whole face.

"Of course!" I was flattered to be asked and curious to visit the lighthouse.

"Saturday morning, then, 5.30 a.m. at my workshop! I've hired a car to take us and the windows to Los Silos. We'll go to la Punta del Teno in the falúa from Los Silos." He smiled ¡Buenas noches! to Dona Lutgarda in her kitchen and was gone.

"So you're leaving early for the lighthouse with Pepe Mendibles? I'll be down here to give you breakfast before you go." Although that meant her getting up a good hour earlier, I didn't try to talk Doña Lutgarda out of her plan. I knew that no matter how much I protested, she would rise to give me breakfast. Looking after people was her sacred duty. "It'll take you a couple of hours in the falúa. Be prepared for a rough passage!"

The Buenavista fishing boats were powered by men plying oars. A fishing boat with an inboard motor was called a falúa, and the closest was owned by a fisherman in Los Silos just a few kilometres north of us. The same word, falúa, was also used to refer to the Civil Guard fishery patrol boat. Now that vessel inspired fear, because nobody could ever be quite certain where the Guardia's powers began or where they ended. I knew that when Pepe said we'd go to the lighthouse in the falúa, he didn't mean we'd be hobnobbing with the sinister Civil Guard.

In the dark pre-dawn of Saturday morning, Pepe and I loaded half-a-dozen fresh-smelling, newly-made wooden window frames into the trunk of José-María's glossy, black, 1955 Humber Super Snipe along with wrapped panes of glass, putty and putty-knives and an unopened can of white paint, and drove to Los Silos.

José-María, a native of Buenavista, had gone off to work in Venezuela for a few years. When he had saved the money he needed, he had returned to the village and bought a brand new Super Snipe sedan that could seat up to eight people, if the two fold-down seats were used. With this elegant limousine, he had set himself up as a Pirata – a Pirate! That is, he operated an illegal taxi service from Buenavista to Santa Cruz, at prices and hours that competed very favourably with the official bus service.

Still in darkness, the owner of the falúa, Sebastian, and his experienced first-hand silently helped us to load the windows and stow them safely so they'd be out of reach of our feet. The clinker-built falúa was between eight and ten metres long ample space for four people and a few window frames. As I boarded in the pale-yellow light from the lantern, I noticed traces of silver scales glistening on the woodwork. Sebastian's tidy boat smelled of recently-caught fish, dried fish-bait and diesel.

The single-cylinder marine engine coughed twice and then settled into a comforting sputt-sputt-sputt, reminding me of the lobster boats at Arbroath and Auchmithie. We headed directly into the waves for ten minutes or so to get beyond the breakers and into the more comfortable swelling rollers. Then we swung south-west, parallel to the dark coast. Now, instead of taking the rollers head-on, we were running between the waves. To avoid being swept towards the shore, however, the helmsman had to take each roller at an oblique angle. This meant long, anxious minutes of a disconcerting tilt to port as we took a wave on, agony as the falúa reached the crest and seemed to hesitate, and then, mind made up, tipped decisively to starboard and began the slow, oblique slide down into the depths of the following, glassy trough.

In order to have some indication of how worried I should be during these disconcerting manoeuvres, I kept my eye on the first-hand who stood at the helm. He was a weather-beaten man in his forties with an impassive face. He'd no doubt had kept a true course in seas far worse than this. I took his placid concentration as a sign that all was well and allowed myself to relax. Soon, I was enjoying the trip. Pepe began naming the seething rocks and surging headlands we passed as we slowly crawled towards the south-west. Since it was before dawn, all I could see was dark land and contrasting white spume as waves broke on distant rocks.

Pepe stretched his arm out into the darkness, finger pointing. "La Punta del Casado – Husband's Point!"

"Why's it called that?" Pepe shrugged.

"Los Guinchos – the Winches."

"Why?" Again, Pepe shrugged.

"El Risco Pajero." "La Punta del Roque Negro." "El Fraile. See how that rock stands up looking like a friar in his cloak? That's why they call it el Fraile." He was happy to offer an explanation for at least one name.

Time passed. The falúa rose, paused, and plunged; rose, paused, and plunged. The silent helmsman steered his oblique course. Now the profile of the island of Tenerife, with the perfect cone of Teide in its centre, was silhouetted against the velvet-blue sky that was slowly turning bright orange.

"¡El Callao de Márquez!" Pepe pointed. All I could see was surf. "Callao is the word we use for a rocky beach. There's a great flat rock there just off el Callao. When the tide's just right, a good seaman can get close enough to the rock to allow a nimble passenger to either leap ashore or to leap onto the boat."

"That sounds dangerous!"

"Oh it's dangerous! I've only heard of it being done, never done it myself! Miscalculate by a fraction of a second and…" He left the image of chaos and drowning to my imagination. Beyond the breaking surf, I could now make out a broad, dark, desert plain scattered with tall cactus and almost entirely surrounded by thousand-foot high cliffs.

"Why would anybody be there in the first place or why would anybody want to go there?" I asked.

"Long ago there used to be a tiny village there called Teno Bajo – Lower Teno. Entirely cut off from the rest of the island. The only access by boat is by that rock. There's only one other way in and out, but it means following a very dangerous path up over the cliffs to a hamlet on the plain above. The hamlet's called Teno Alto – Upper Teno. From there, a fit person can walk all the way down to Buenavista."

"Long ago? And now?"

"Now?" Pepe looked away. "Now only Daniel lives there, with his wife."

"What does he do in such an isolated place?"

"Do?" He shrugged. "Daniel's a kind of custodian, a self-sufficient man." Now Pepe was pointing to new sights. "La Punta Morro de Diablo – the Devil's Promontory, la Punta Delgada – the Slim Point."

That Pepe hadn't wanted to expand on the abandoned village, nor on Daniel and his wife, made all the more intriguing to me the fact that a couple could live, apparently from choice, in such utter isolation.

Triumphantly, the sun sprang free of the mountains and we were blessed with a light that gave a deep-green tint to the sea that a few moments before had been as dark and smooth as a wine bottle.

"Look! There's la Punta del Muerto – Dead Man's Point." I followed his finger and saw a rocky promontory entirely devoid of plant life.

Why aren't more of these identical, barren, wave-crushed promontories called Dead this or Dead that? I wondered. Were there, perhaps, gradations of death? Were some locations even more dead than others? Or might there be a more sinister origin for a place called Dead Man's Point? But when asked, Pepe only shrugged.

Sebastian-de-la-Falúa, who'd been almost silent up until now, having exchanged no more than a few short words with his first-hand, called out something that I didn't catch. From the urgent tone, I guessed it was a warning. Pepe sank down onto the thwart and gestured me to do the same. "Two tides meet here, Orlando. Hold on tight, for all you're worth!" He braced himself with his hands. I glanced ahead as I braced myself just as Pepe was doing. The sun was warm to port now and I could see massive, near-black cliffs rise vertically out of the sea and on a promontory beneath them, I could just make out the stubby stone tower of a lighthouse and its attached white-washed buildings. We were two thirds of the way there! What was there to be concerned about?

No sooner was the question framed in my mind than, without the slightest warning, the sea grabbed us and savagely hurled the falúa this way and that in the most terrifying dodgem-car ride of my life. With no experience of the sea, I couldn't begin to guess what was happening. Because I had my arms tightly wrapped around the thwart, I didn't feel in danger of being tossed out, but I did feel that the falúa was out of control and in imminent danger of overturning. My eyes were just above the gunwale and so I looked around desperately for anything that might offer help if I found myself in the water, which appeared very likely.

We'd entered a maelstrom of enraged, choppy waves competing violently against one another, battering our boat from all directions. In my mind's eye, I saw Corryvreckan, the whirlpool in the tidal straights between the Inner Hebridean Islands of Jura and Scarba. Our Boy Scout Troop had made a special trip to see it when camped near Oban in the summer of 1956. At a certain moment each day, the tides and their backwashes rebound from the two neighbouring islands. They start to compete and flow in different directions. Powerful currents build, unite and form a gigantic whirlpool that can draw in a full-size boat and suck it wind-milling down into its gaping vortex that leads directly to the centre of the earth. Or so the story goes.

Pepe looked as scared as I felt but was doing my best to disguise.

I glanced at the helmsman. His impassive face hadn't altered but the intensity of his concentration seemed to have doubled. I glanced back at Sebastian-de-la-falúa. He understood my concern and shouted: "Hold tight! It won't last long." I relaxed, breathed freely again. All was well if he said so. As I concentrated on watching the beauty of orange sunlight chasing the darkness from the rusty desert and turning the cliffs to fire, the boat steadied itself and emerged into the more familiar, more comfortable green rollers once again. The helmsman's hands relaxed and Pepe gave me one of his huge smiles.

"Almost there!" I followed his finger and saw more clearly now, the tip of a stubby, black peninsula and on its highest point, a low, white building attached to a short tower built from local stone with glazed lantern atop that caught the sun. Finally, la Punta de Teno!

Sebastian-de-la-Falúa took over the helm as we approached the concrete landing where the lighthouse keeper, his wife, three small children and an older man waited for us. A formal welcoming party! The landing was a concrete appendage on the leeward side of the black lava promontory on which the lighthouse had been built. The landing was modest, no more than a long, steep set of sea-washed, concrete steps. The top step had been extended to form a narrow platform about five metres long. The growth of brown seaweed up the score or more of concrete steps stopped at about the fifth from the top. Neither the higher steps nor the concrete platform bore any traces of seaweed and so were obviously above the high-water mark.

The reason for the extreme caution with which Sebastian-de-la-Falúa was approaching the dock became immediately obvious. As a wave approached, the number of steps visible was swiftly reduced from more than 20 to about two or three. There was a brief pause and then the row of stairs became visible again one after another as the wave spent itself and retreated in backwash that sucked the gleaming belts of leathery, brown weed after it. Somehow, the helmsman had to inch the falúa parallel to the quay. Then he had to hold it there so as to allow each of us, one at a time, to step from the boat onto the flat concrete at exactly that brief moment when the boat paused level with the quay and before the backwash tugged it back down three or four metres.

This is where the first-hand came in. He picked one or two of Pepe's packages up, balanced himself of the gunwale, and precisely when the wave raised the gunwale to the level of the concrete, he stepped smartly off and stowed his packages safely on the dock. Pepe and I watched, fascinated, as we plunged four metres with the backwash. Then he waited till the next wave raised the boat up again and stepped smartly onto the gunwale once more. In this laborious way – indeed there was no alternative – he transferred everything that was to remain at the lighthouse – the window frames, the glass, and finally the materials and tools for their installation. There were a dozen packages in all, because this was a regular supply trip as well as Pepe's opportunity to install windows.

I watched the intricate ballet between Sebastian, the first-hand, the boat and the dock, very carefully and began to get a feel for the repeated, predictable rhythm and split-second timing that made it possible. And so, when my turn came, with a little assistance in maintaining my balance from the first-hand, additional support from the lighthouse keeper at the critical moment when the boat paused atop the wave, and a "¡Ya! – Now!" from Sebastian, the operation seemed positively simple although it left my heart pounding. From the safety of the dock, I watched the falúa plunge four metres down into the trough of the backwash.

Now Pepe, smiling even more broadly than ever, was standing safely alongside me. The first-hand waved solemnly to our little group of seven, and Sebastian expertly backed the falúa away, touched the throttle and steered his craft out of sight round the rocky headland to the north. Only then, safe from the fascination of imminent, mortal danger, did we turn to excited introductions, welcomes, hugs and cheek-kissing.

The Lighthouse-keeper's Family

The locals had given the lighthouse-keeper, José Sánchez Acosta, the nick-name, el Torrero. El Torrero, with the double 'rr', means the Keeper of the Tower. However, for any Spanish speaker, this unusual sobriquet Torrero, pronounced with a trill like somebody exaggerating a Scottish accent, would immediately conjure up the similar and by-far more common word, el Torero, the Bullfighter! The result of this inevitable association would be, for someone meeting José for the first time, to expect a slim, agile, arrogant and colourful individual. What he would find, however, would be a man dressed in the plain, undecorated, white uniform of the state-employed coastguard service, in his early thirties, who appeared amiable and slightly pudgy. At the very first sight of him, it would be clear that José would never battle a fighting bull, bleeding from the neck, merely to entertain a thrill-seeking crowd.

José's nick-name, el Torrero, embodies the subtle and ambiguous play on words so greatly valued by Canarios. José's single concession to ostentation was his flat, officer's cap with discreet, gold embroidery on the brim. He wore it more to shield his distance-seeking eyes than to impress.

As soon as we had regained our balance on the pier, Pepe proudly presented me to José. José, in turn, introduced me to his wife Mary Carmen and their three children. There was Pilar, a pretty girl of about six and twin boys a year younger, Pepito and Toñito. The twins introduced me to their grandfather, Abuelito. The family were Peninsulares from Murcia, a town close to the Mediterranean coast in the south-east of Spain.

"Come on! Breakfast's ready for all of you up at the house." I thought that 'all of you' was an exaggerated way of referring to Pepe and me, but we picked up the window-frames, the tools, the paint and putty and followed the family up a steep, winding path to their home at the highest point on the narrow peninsula. As we walked, José, Mary Carmen, Abuelito and the children smiled and chattered to us all at the same time. Visitors were few and far between, a luxury to indulge in.

We stopped in front of the modest stone that rose to a height of 7 metres or so. Its lantern room with its complex chunky lenses behind thick glass windows in metal frames, sparkled atop the tower. Round the tower's outer circumference ran a circular, steel balcony that served as access to allow exterior cleaning. Judging by the gleaming windows, José was diligent in his duties.

"The light is 60 meters above sea-level!" José was getting ready to brag about his charge.

"José, please! Our guests have been fighting the waves since before dawn this morning, they must be desperate for cof-

The lighthouse keeper, Don José, at La Punta de Teno. Seldom was he without his official cap. We were waiting for the launch to take us to Los Silos.

fee!" José relented and Mary Carmen led the way into the white-
washed, stone house attached to
the tower. She seated us at a long
wooden table by the open window that gave us an awesome
view of 2,000-foot black cliffs
away to the south-east and a tur-
quoise sea bordered by white lace
that lapped their feet.

The eight of us had no sooner sat down and had our cups
filled with milky coffee, than Sebastian-de-la-Falúa and his first-
hand joined us. I'd assumed that
they'd gone fishing and would return for us the following day, but
no, they had moored the falúa
in a safe place and returned by a
narrow path that linked the peninsula to the mainland. Maybe
their plans had been mentioned.
My Spanish, however, was still at

The lighthouse keeper and his family. They were always happy to have visitors.

the stage where I could miss even important information, especially
when it as embedded in general conversation and everybody was speaking at once.

I experienced little misunderstandings like this, and occasionally
more significant ones, quite frequently. They always took me by surprise and served to draw my attention to the difficulty of mastering a
foreign language to a point where all the cues, including the non-ver-
bal ones, are automatically captured and processed as the speaker has
intended. Doña Lutgarda and the girls in the fonda insisted that I now
spoke Spanish like a Canario, but they spoke directly to me and I to
them and invariably about simple, concrete matters. Seldom was I ever
engaged in an informal conversation among multiple friends who had
all grown up together and where shared cultural presuppositions were
taken for granted.

One day, I had used the word rana, Spanish for frog, as a pejorative
to refer to a shopkeeper in Santa Cruz who had unscrupulously over-
charged me for an item I'd bought. Since I had so little money, I was
extremely careful about my spending and I'd arrived back at the fonda
annoyed at having allowed myself to be short-changed. Doña Lutgarda

and the girls had looked at me blankly. "Rana? The shopkeeper was a frog?

"Doesn't that mean a scoundrel?" I was sure I'd heard it used in that way.

"No, it means frog!" Doña Lutgarda appeared about to squat to represent a frog. Fortunately, Lula shoved a chair under her and her dignity was preserved.

"Well," I was feeling defensive, "on my walks about the country-side I hear mothers calling their children rana when they do something wrong!"

They shook their heads. When have you heard a mother call her child a frog?"

"Just the other day! I was passing a cottage where an older child was splashing mud on her younger brother. Their mother came out and shouted, "¡Basta! Usted es sinvergüenza, más, rana!" – "Stop that! You're shameless! And what's more, you're a frog!"

This sent them off into further gales of laughter. Doña Lutgarda had to hold on to the edge of the table to stop herself falling off the chair.

"What's so funny?" Now, I felt mocked. In the context, I had understood the mother's use of 'and what's more, you're a frog' to be the ultimate affront and was proud to have been able to make use of it myself at what I considered to be an appropriate moment.

When the laughing ceased, Lula kindly explained. "What the mother actually said was, '¡Usted es sinvergüenza! ¡Marrana!' 'Marrana' means a pig, an object of filth." And off they went again into further gales of laughter at my having misheard 'marrana' as 'más rana'. It was an understandable mistake on my part, since Canarios generally failed to pronounce a final 's' at the end of a word.

It didn't surprise me, therefore, that I'd missed some of the casual conversation between Pepe and the fishermen. Nevertheless, I wondered to myself, "Will I ever be able to say that I have really mastered Spanish?"

Mary Carmen laughed to see Pepe and me and the two fishermen all spoon gofio into our coffee and then enjoy supping the thick, cereal mixture. "If we stay here in Las Canarias long enough," she admitted, "we're going to become aficionados of gofio as well. The children love it! Since we don't have any bread here unless I make it myself, gofio's a great substitute at breakfast time."

After I finished, I left them all talking about local and national politics, went outside and stood at the low stone wall taking in the magnificent vista. From my vantage point 60 metres above the water, the shimmering, green-blue sea far below was in silent perpetual motion. Looking south, I saw lines of near uniformly-spaced rollers moving steadily in from the west and crash in white spume against los Acantillados de los Gigantes, the 2,000-foot black, basalt Cliffs of the Giants. I turned north and looked over the desert plain where Daniel lived with his wife. Its western boundary was the rocky coast beaten by waves coming all the way from the Americas; its eastern boundary a wall of craggy cliffs rising abruptly into grey mist. The clouds were forever climbing, falling back and rising once more. When they rose for just a few seconds, they exposed bald, barren tops. The plain itself was bright red and strewn with many varieties of cactus. From where I stood, I could see nothing of the ghost-village of Teno Bajo. The idea of an abandoned village intrigued me. It brought to mind verses from Goldsmith's haunting poem The Deserted Village that we'd learned by heart at school:

"Sunk are thy bowers in shapeless ruin all,
And the long grass o'ertops the mouldering wall;
And trembling, shrinking from the spoiler's hand,
Far, far away thy children leave the land
Ill fares the land, to hastening ills a prey,
Where wealth accumulates, and men decay."

José came out and stood by my side, interrupting my thoughts. Pepe stood a little further back, smiling. I had given him my camera and with it, he had taken the picture used on the cover of this book.

"Look over towards the south-west! The island of Gomera! It's more than 30 kilometres away." I followed José's finger and could see a long, dark disk and just make out a tiny smudge of white. "That's the village of Santa Catalina." He turned further to the west. "And over there," on the horizon I could just make out the hazy-blue outline of another island, "that's La Palma. It's more than 80 kilometres from where we're standing!"

I turned back north, content for the moment with the Island of Tenerife. "Have you ever visited the abandoned village of Teno Bajo, José?"

"Not yet. We haven't been here that long. During my four months on duty, I can't really leave the lighthouse at all. As soon as our two-month leave is due and my replacement arrives, we take the falúa straight to Los Silos and then go on to Santa Cruz to stay with my mother- and father-in-law. We remain there until our leave is over and I

117

have to resume my duties here. But Daniel comes to visit occasionally. He loves conversation and he brings us fresh goat milk and meat."

"I'd like to visit him one day."

"Then come back and stay with us when you have a few days free." José was encouraging. "Get a fisherman to drop you off here at the pier. Then, after a day or two with us, you could walk back over the plain to Teno Bajo and meet Daniel and his family. He'd welcome the company."

"I'd have to be picked up again from here. Pepe Mendibles makes being taken off at El Callao de Márquez by boat sound like a nightmare!"

"He's right! But you wouldn't need to leave that way!" He pointed to the craggy cliffs with their shrouded tops. "I've heard that there's a path from Teno Bajo over the mountains to Teno Alto. From Teno Alto, I'm told, there's a path down the other side of the mountains to El Rincón, just a few kilometres from Buenavista."

"I'd like to do that!" I should have pursued the matter a little deeper given his 'so I've heard' and 'I'm told' but I was too busy recalling a poem by Douglas Young:

"That old lonely lovely way of living
in Highland places, - twenty years a-growing,
twenty years flowering, twenty years declining-
father to son, mother to daughter giving
ripe tradition; peaceful bounty flowing;
one harmony all tones of life combining-
old, wise way, passed like the dust blowing.
That harmony of folk and land is shattered,-
the yearly rhythm of things, the social graces,
peat-fire and music, candle-light and kindness.
Now they are gone it seems they never mattered,
much, to the world, those proud and violent races,
clansmen and chiefs whose passioned greed and blindness
made desolate these lovely lonely places."

The sentiment, intended for the Scottish Highlands, seemed equally appropriate here.

"Fine! Plan on it! José made it sound simple.

Pepe appeared. "Orlando! Did you come here to help me or just to chatter to el Torrero?"

"How many times do I have to tell you, Pepe Mendibles," warned

José in a mock-angry voice, "I'm el Farolero, not el Torrero. I look after the 'faro', the light, I don't fight bulls! José was as sensitive about his nick-name as I had at first been about mine. However, given the propensity Canarios possessed to capture precisely the characteristic they intended to highlight when they chose a person's nick-name, he wouldn't have much luck persuading them to change.

I went off with Pepe to give him a hand to fix each pane in place with glazier's points, putty the joints and then prime the window-frames. José kept us company while we worked. The lighthouse, he told us, had been built in the 1890s and had been manned ever since. However, Madrid was considering replacing it with a more a more technologically sophisticated light. "Madrid?" Pepe showed typical Canario contempt for the distant government in the Peninsula. "All they do there is talk!"

We looked with satisfaction at the row of frames propped against the wall, newspapers protecting the stonework from the fresh paint. "We can start installation after dinner."

Sebastian-of-the-Falúa and his first-hand had spent the afternoon fishing with the children and so dinner was fresh fish fried in garlic and 'papas arrugadas', small potatoes that we'd brought with us, boiled in sea-water until it had evaporated and only the potatoes left with white, powdery salt crusted around their skins.

After we'd eaten, Pepe and I installed the first couple of frames and left the rest for the following morning. José showed us guests into a whitewashed, stone room devoid of any furniture except for four narrow, single beds. I was lulled to sleep by the sound of waves breaking regularly on the rocks far below.

The following morning Pepe and I installed the remaining windows before breakfast. As we worked, I explained to Pepe that José had invited me to visit him and his family again so that I could walk back across the plain to visit Teno Bajo and then take the path across the mountains down to El Rincón. Pepe looked doubtful when I talked of walking over the tops. Thinking it was because he himself had never made the trip, I failed to ask him what dangers there might be. However, he offered to show me the safest way off the rocky peninsula where the lighthouse stood, onto the mainland.

And so, after breakfast, the two fishermen, Pepe and I and the oldest child all made our way down from the lighthouse and across the narrow, natural causeway that linked the lighthouse to the mainland. Judging from the seaweed growing on the rocks, the causeway was above the high-tide mark most of the time but at certain phases of the moon, the sea could come swirling round to the narrowest point of the peninsula and meet at the causeway, causing a powerful current to flow in and out in an unpredictable way. Sebastian-de-la-Falúa had moored his boat in a sheltered cove on the north side of the causeway and it there it sat, gleaming blue and white in the sunshine.

The ground on the mainland side was made up of red and black cinders that gave way to red hardpan strewn with cactus and stretching away into the distance where the steep, rocky cliffs blocked the plain in and separated it so mysteriously from the rest of the island.

"I've been told that if you make your way north across the plain on a line a third of the way from the shore and two thirds of the way from the cliffs, you'll eventually come to Teno Bajo."

"Is there a path?"

"There's no path. Nobody ever comes this way." These scant instructions would serve as well as any for my next visit, I reckoned.

Our excursion was cut short by José calling to us urgently from the wall that surrounded the lighthouse above us. "There's rough weather on the way. You must leave before it's too late!"

Sebastian-de-la-Falúa sent his first-hand to bring the boat around to the dock and we all headed back across the causeway and up the rocky path to gather our belongings. We had few. Mine fitted into a small duffle-bag slung over my shoulder. Pepe's bag was similarly modest; his toolkit was heavier. We made our way down the steps cut into the rock to the pier. The first-hand brought the boat in close and Sebastian stepped expertly aboard before it plunged ten feet and then rose again on the next surge.

It was only then that I discovered that we were charged with taking all three children and Abuelito, their grandfather, with us on the return journey. The little girl went to school in Santa Cruz where she stayed with her grandparents, and the twins were accompanying her.

Abuelito held the little girl in his arms, Pepe and I each carried one of the twins. Sebastian helped us each aboard, with the children clinging to our necks and we distributed ourselves as instructed so as to keep the boat in balance. To fond, goodbye waves from José and Mary Carmen, the first-hand expertly backed the falúa away from the pier and steered her towards the sea, giving a wide berth to the tip of the promontory where waves were already breaking with momentous force as the wind rose. He then headed north, holding course about a kilometre off-shore at an oblique angle to the waves, which meant we were constantly rising and falling, rising and falling.

Scudding clouds hid the sun, curtains of rain obscured the horizon and a rising onshore wind battered each wave noisily into our bow as we maintained a safe course well clear of the rocky headlands. Sebastian-de-la-Falúa had Pepe and I, each with a clutching child, re-position ourselves along the port gunwale, the easier to cut, with increased weight, into the waves driven by the on-shore tide. He'd positioned me closest to the bow which rose and plunged in a way that alarmed me. I held Pepito all the more tightly in my arms. I'd unbuttoned my shirt and he was clutching me with both tiny arms around my neck like a monkey in the zoo. I had positioned him so that my shirt would protect his face from the worst of the stinging spray.

The strain of trying to both keep myself from being tossed over the side and protect the gripping child, was beginning to cramp my back and arms. I kept my eyes on Sebastian and the first-hand. Their sober expressions suggested intense concentration but no alarm and so I managed to control my fear. If these seamen were fine, then so was I and my charge likewise.

Suddenly, Sebastian called out a warning. I recalled the same sharp alert he'd uttered the previous morning. This time, I understood its urgency and braced myself for the impact. The falúa was brutally snatched by the battle of the tides, and tossed into the maelstrom. The pitch of the engine rose as the first-hand sought to increase the boat's grip on the capricious water. For several breath-taking moments, the boat seemed to lose confidence in itself and we were hurtled this way and that by the competing wash and backwash of surging swells thrashing from all directions.

To keep my mind off my rising fear, I mentally rehearsed each step in the rescue training I'd received to gain the embroidered emblem from the Royal Lifesaving Society that I'd proudly worn on the sleeve of my Boy Scout shirt. Taking the practical Lifesaver examination had been Pearl's idea. "Learning to swim is not enough," she'd insisted with Scottish common sense. "You need to learn how to save a life in addition to your own!"

After rehearsing all the steps in my head, I felt more confident and looked at the others. Bodies rigid and faces betraying alarm told me that Pepe and Abuelito too were hanging on by little more than a need not to distress the children. Our strategies was obviously working. Each child wore a trusting look that showed complete confidence in us, their guardians. My principal concern was how, after the falúa capsized, I was going to manage to drag myself and Pepito safely from the water without being dashed to death on jagged rocks. Our lifesaving training, taken in the Dundee Corporation Swimming Baths, had not foreseen that eventuality.

I felt something comfortably warm running down my chest. Pepito was gently vomiting up all the gofio he'd eaten for breakfast. I almost laughed aloud as I registered the fact that it smelled of nothing other than coffee and toasted maize. Here we were, apparently fighting the cruel sea for our lives, and I had my very own source of central heating to help me through the ordeal! Then I noticed similar vomit stains down the shirts of the other two adult passengers.

Just as suddenly as we'd entered the maelstrom, we were out of it and back into the slow, rhythmic pattern of climbing, cresting, and falling, climbing, cresting, and falling. We drew level with the rocky beach of El Callao de Márquez and headed further out to sea in order to safely pass the headland that would bring Buenavista into sight. It was a great relief to know that we were going to make it back to Los Silos without my having to put my Royal Lifesaving training into practice.

For the final 30 minutes of the voyage, the temperature dropped abruptly and we were pelted with hailstones, but the discomfort seemed tiny by comparison with all we'd been through. To my surprise, my mind was completely distracted from the increasing chill by the odd appeal of the loud hissing sound that the hail made as it struck the surface of the sea.

Sebastian-de-la-Falúa and his first-hand smiled for the first time during the entire voyage as they handed us passengers easily onto the quay at Los Silos. José-María was waiting with his limousine to take grandad and the three children, now completely recovered, on to Santa Cruz. But first he drove back to Buenavista and dropped Pepe and me in the plaza. We shook hands with that new-found bond of friendship, deepened by shared danger and fear overcome.

When I walked into the fonda, Doña Lutgarda and the girls were waiting for me. They looked at my dishevelled state and the gofio-stained vomit on my chest and shirt.

"Upstairs and shower! You can't come into the dining-room looking like a ship-wreck victim! Remember, it's Sunday!"

13. Apprentice to the banana business

*At the docks in Santa Cruz. Stevedores are transfer-
ring wrapped banana stalks from our lorry onto a
cargo ship bound for Scandinavia. Angel, the lorry
driver, supervises from atop the sideboards*

One evening, more than a week after my introduction to the packing
station, as I was dining alone in the courtyard, Doña Lutgarda
emerged from her kitchen wiping her hands on her apron. "Don Salvador will arrive right after breakfast tomorrow. He asks you to meet him
here. It's going to be your first day of work for the empacadora!"

The next morning, through the open doors of the fonda, I watched
Don Salvador park his car at the edge of the plaza close to the church
and emerge, immaculate in his khakis, holding his ivory Panama hat in
one hand and his overnight attaché case in the other. His dark-framed
glasses and black, pencil-thin moustache looked all of apiece. He'd no
sooner straightened and pushed the car door closed with his knee, than
he was greeted by an acquaintance. He had to clamp the Panama on his
head and switch the attaché to offer an appropriate handshake. He had
to repeat the greetings and the handshake several more times before he

reached the shade of the fonda. I was proud to be going to work for such
a popular personality. It was less than two weeks since he'd introduced
me to those at the the banana packing station and had me demonstrate
my skill in basic arithmetic. But since then, acquaintances in the village
would greet me: "Orlando, I hear you're going to work for Don Salvador!" Words certainly got around and their tone told me that this was a
prestigious job and I was fortunate to have been offered it.

"Ready to start, Orlando?" Don Salvador stooped and shook my
hand.

"I'm always ready for work, Don Salvador."

"Good! You sound just like I was at your age!" He opened his attaché, removed his ubiquitous clipboard and sheaf of papers, closed the
case and passed to Pastora who'd come to the front door to greet him.
"Please put this in my room, Pastora. Orlando and I will be back for
lunch, but quite late." We turned and walked across the plaza together
and up the side-street to the empacadora. He explained briefly what the
work-plan was for the next couple of days.

"While it's still relatively cool, we'll go out to one of the largest
plantations in the area, la Casa Blanca. There, we'll collect piñas, weigh
them, and bring them back to the warehouse. We'll pack them this afternoon. Tomorrow morning we'll collect more, but from a different
plantation. After we've packed these, we'll load up Ángel's lorry and
he'll drive overnight to the docks in Santa Cruz. Bananas are always
the last item to be loaded so nothing heavy is packed on top of them.
They'll begin loading fruit just after dawn."

"It sounds like a tight schedule." The challenge appealed to me.

"To export delicate fruit successfully, everybody has to respect a
very tight schedule. The owners have to harvest on time; we have to
collect the fruit, pack it, and deliver it to the dockside on time; the stevedores must load quickly before the sun heats it and the ship mustn't
delay in getting to its destination. The banana demands precision timing. You'll see!"

Ángel's green Ford Thames, with its high-sided, slatted racks and
open tail-gate, was parked outside the open doors of the warehouse in
the morning sunshine. Ángel, tousle-haired, was up in the empty box.
The smiling, women, coated and headscarved to protect them from dust
and dirt, were handing up piles of folded red blankets that he stacked
into neat piles behind the cab.

"¡Buenos días, todos! Ángel! I see you're all ready to start." Ángel
grinned beneath his unruly thatch.

"Only the scales to load!" Epifanio disappeared back inside the
now very tidy warehouse. He carefully removed a slim steelyard hang-

ing high up on the wall out of harm's way. The counterweights, neatly ordered light to heavy, sat on a shelf below it.

When I was in charge of Captain Bentley's berry-fields at Balmuir Estate just north of Dundee, one of the many farm jobs I'd had during holidays and at weekends since reaching my teens, I'd used an identical steelyard for weighing raspberries and was familiar with its simple operation. The one Epifanio was now holding was the most beautiful I'd seen. Instead of tarnished steel, this one was made of polished brass; the counterweights too. It was a simple bar a metre long with three hooks, one above the bar and two below. The top hook, the fulcrum, was used to suspend the bar; the lower hook closest to the fulcrum was used to suspend the fruit, the counterweight was hung on the hook furthest from the fulcrum. The person in charge would select the counterweight that was most likely to closely match the weight of the fruit at the other end. That portion of the bar further from the fulcrum was graduated in individual kilos and grams. A smaller counterweight could be moved carefully along its upper surface to bring the heavy counterweights and the fruit into perfect balance. That point would be visible to all because then the steelyard would lie perfectly horizontal, since the fruit and the counterweights would be equal. The exact weight of the fruit, in kilos and grams, could then be read off to the nearest gram. Whereas on the berry-field we weighed bulk berries to the nearest half-pound, we only had to weight banana stems to the closest half-kilo.

"All aboard! We're off to la Casa Blanca!" Don Salvador folded himself into the cab, the rest of us climbed onto the bed of the lorry. With a smiling "Hold on tight!" Ángel locked the tailgate in place before pulling himself up behind the steering wheel and easing the lorry slowly up the cobbled street to join the road that would take us to Casa Blanca. The four women sat on piles of blankets; the balance and its counterweights lay safely on another. Epifanio, Miguel and I hooked our arms into the wooden slats of the rack and accepted the lurches delivered by the uneven road.

On my walks, I'd passed la Casa Blanca with its venerable old farm-house and attached outbuildings protected behind a whitewashed wall. I now looked forward to getting a closer look, but Ángel didn't stop until we had left it well behind. He parked at the open wooden side-door of a large walled plantation. A row of recently-harvested piñas lay alongside the wall. They carried a thatch of banana leaves to keep them cool. The entire team sprang into practised action. I had to figure out how best to be useful.

Ángel swung a hinged bar out from the side of the lorry-rack closest to the banana stalks. Epifanio hung the steelyard balance on it and placed the counterweights to hand. Don Salvador, clipboard in one hand and pencil in the other, took up his position alongside the steel-yard while casting a practised, critical eye over the piñas that the plantation workers were now uncovering. Miguel and the women dragged the piles of blankets to the tailgate.

"We'll need the 20-kilo counterweight." Epifanio hung the lead-filled counterweight on the hook hanging below the longer arm of the scale. Then Miguel and one of the women carefully lifted the first of the piñas and laid it onto Miguel's shoulder, padded with a folded blanket. Miguel carried the piña the 10 or 12 paces to the scale. Epifanio slipped a short loop of rope round the cut end and Miguel slowly crouched until the piña hung from the hook that dangled from the shorter arm of the scale. As Miguel crouched, the weight of the piña brought the short arm down. The longer arm holding the 20-kilo counterweight rose to compensate for the opposing excess weight of the banana stalk. Ángel ran the smaller counterbalance along the top edge of the long arm until the steelyard levelled and lay perfectly horizontal. All eyes were on the steelyard until it stilled.

"Twenty-three-and-a-half," called Epifanio. He took a purple crayon from his hatband and wrote 23.5 clearly on the still damp, recently-cut end of the stock. Don Salvador made an entry on the first line of the page on his clipboard. Miguel and one of the women carried the piña to the tailgate and placed it on an open blanket. Two women up on the tailgate expertly rolled the blanket around the piña and carried it to the corner of the truck behind the cab, where it lay in its blanket waiting for the rest to be placed alongside.

"Orlando!" I'd been so interested in the process that I hadn't realised that Miguel and I had to take turns lugging the heavy piñas from the shade of the wall to the scale and making our obeisance. Quickly, I folded a blanket over my shoulder and prepared myself to take the load, but almost crumpled under the unexpected weight.

"See, I told you! These Extranjeros don't have the strength of a Canario!" Miguel quipped.

"Tell the girls in the fonda to serve you more gofio for breakfast, Orlando!"

"Would you like to have a rest now, Orlando? Take a siesta in the shade!"

I staggered to the steelyard.

"Thirty-two and a half!" A roar of good-humoured laughter went up. Relieved of the weight, I wrote 32.5 on the freshly cut stalk with my purple crayon.

"You did that on purpose! You had the heaviest piña reserved for el Extranjero!" Don Salvador was still laughing.

"Who, me?" Miguel adopted an innocent look but was pleased by his prank. The plantation workers grinned, betraying their collusion with Miguel who'd chosen the most out-sized banana stalk to surprise me. Fortunately, all the other piñas were in the low twenties.

And so we continued, hour after hour, until there were no piñas left to load, Don Salvador had filled three or four pages with numbers, and the lorry had only space enough left for us all to sit on the tailboard, legs dangling, as we lurched back to the village.

Loading freshly-weighed and cut banana stalks at a plantation near El Rincón. Behind, the terraces that reach the foot of the almost impenetrable mountains. El Barranco Negro -- the Black Canyon -- isn't far from there.

I commented that we hadn't piled the piñas as high as we had done the night when Ángel had driven to the docks in Santa Cruz. Epifanio explained why. "That's because the blankets alone don't offer enough cushioning. If we were to go more than three or four rows high without the paper and straw packing, we would damage the fruit. It usually takes at least two trips to the Fincas to bring back enough for a full lorry-load of packed piñas to go to the docks." That made sense to me. I was beginning to learn that many, careful, well-thought-out steps had to be followed in order to fill an export order successfully.

"Maintaining quality at each step of the process is the key to success," Don Epifanio continued. He sounded as if he were repeating word-for-word what Don Salvador might have said. "Repeat orders from fruit wholesalers in Europe depend on how well we Canarios manage the fruit." I sat, half-listening, with my legs dangling, and realised that until that very moment, I'd never given any thought to how a banana reached our greengrocer in Scotland.

Although it was noon by the time we reached the warehouse, we had to unload all the piñas into the cool interior and stack them with great care before we could go for lunch. Don Salvador was welcomed through the side door into Don Pancho's house. They had business to discuss.

As all the members of the crew dispersed for home, Don Salvador reappeared. He and I walked back to the fonda together. "Look!" He held his clipboard out to me. "These are the records we must keep. The nick-name of the plantation, the weight of each piña, and the total number."

Plantations as well as people here have nick-names?

"They do and they're very important. For example, la Casa Blanca is an estate made up of many vegetable and tomato fields and several banana plantations. Each of these areas has a nick-name. So that has to be written in brackets to keep the record clear. If there's a problem with any of the fruit, we need to know precisely where it came from. We have to write down the exact weight of each stalk because that's the weight we pay the owner and it's also the weight we use for invoicing our importers and receiving payment from them. Everything has to tally exactly."

"I understand." The process was logical.

"You, Orlando, must calculate the weight you bring in to the warehouse with every load. It's essential that we know how much fruit we have stored in the warehouse at any given time. We make our profit exporting bananas but we can only export the weight our buyers in Northern Europe ask for. If one wants 2,500 kilos and we send him 3,000 kilos, he'll pay us for only 2,500. The importer calls the shots. We must conform in weight and quality."

"What happens if you're left with excess weight in the warehouse after Ángel has left for the docks in Santa Cruz?"

"Bananas are harvested while they're still green but even then, they ripen relatively quickly – within a couple of weeks. We can't have piñas waiting about in the warehouse until our next order. All the piñas in a single order have to have been cut within one or two days of each other."

"So what does happen to any excess of piñas left in the warehouse?"

"Well, it's my job is to see that I buy as close to the exact weight that I need for any given export order as I can. I buy maybe 60 or 80 kilos more than the order asks for to replace any that get damaged either on the lorry or in the warehouse. Anything left over in the warehouse has to be sold for local consumption. The price is much lower, even if the fruit is export quality."

"So, there's a difference between export quality and that for the local market?"

"You noticed when Epifanio was weighing the piñas that any bunch that weighed less than 20 kilos was put aside? Weight is one of our quality criteria; we don't export anything below 20 kilos. So I don't buy any."

"You also laid aside any piña that had even the slightest tinge of yellow on the fruit."

"Exactly! That's equally important. All of the fruit must be uniform and at least two weeks shy of ripening. If even one hand begins to ripen in the hold of the ship, it encourages the others to ripen prematurely. Neither we nor the importer want that."

"So the plantation workers have to be careful about what they harvest."

"We don't leave that decision to the plantation workers."

"Then who decides when a piña is ready to be cut?"

"Epifanio does. Regularly, Epifanio visits every plantation we buy from around Buenavista. He inspects every plant and puts a mark on the stalk of each piña that he estimates will grow to meet our export standards."

"I'd no idea. I thought he worked part-time in the packing station like the rest."

"Oh no! The packing station is just one step in the long chain of processes that we have to control. Making an accurate judgement about the fruit when it's still on the plant is critical. That takes experience. Managing my business means I have a lot to think about and I and those I employ must manage every single step very carefully. I want you to start learning."

An entirely new dimension of what, initially, I had thought was a simple business was opening up before my eyes. Working for the empacadora was promising to be more interesting than I'd imagined.

We'd reached the open doors of the fonda. "Orlando, show me your hands!" I held them up to Don Salvador. They were coal black and very slightly sticky. "Look at your shirt and pants!" I looked and saw that they too, were stained.

"That's juice from the banana stalk. Immediately it's exposed to air, the juice oxidises. The stain is very difficult to remove from your hands but from clothing, impossible! That's why you have to fold the blanket over your shoulder to catch the drips."

I washed my hands without making the slightest impression on their colour and sat down for lunch. Doña Lutgarda and the girls begged me to show them my fingers and when I held them up to expose black river deltas on each palm, they were delighted. "Now you're a true Canario! Every Canario has had his hands black with banana-stalk juice at some time in his life. And these clothes! All they're good for now is for work!" I felt that I'd passed another test of belonging without my having had all that much to do with it.

Before Doña Lutgarda left us alone to eat, Don Salvador gave her the outline of my schedule. "Orlando and my crew will be working all afternoon packing the piñas we brought in this morning. They won't be finished much before midnight!" There was a hum of sympathy from the girls. "Then, first thing tomorrow morning, we'll be collecting another 1000 kilos from El Rincón. Finally, the crew will pack and load these so that Ángel can be at the docks before dawn on Thursday morning."

Doña Lutgarda widened her eyes in mock horror. "Will he have time to eat?"

Temperature and timing were everything in harvesting bananas. Cutting stalks in the plantations; selecting and weighing the piñas; bringing them back to the warehouse still in the cool of the day; packing them in straw-filled paper tied firmly with sisal; loading them onto the lorry in the exact quantity required; and finally getting them to the ship in the best condition possible. This was what the labour-intensive part of exporting was all about. Now I could see why Don Salvador was proud of his team and why he treated them with so much respect and paid them well. They were essential, thinking, human resources in a well-oiled business process. Each job had to be completed well and at exactly the appropriate time. There was no room for tardiness, negligence or cutting corners, if the business was to succeed.

Don Salvador's prediction on timing to Doña Lutgarda was accurate. We were packing piñas at midnight and still hadn't finished.

"Can't we leave the last few until tomorrow?" Miguel looked paler than usual and exhausted.

"No, we can't, Miguel! But I'll tell you what we can do." All tired and dusty faces turned to Epifanio. "If we each pitch in a couple of pesetas. I'll go and get a half-bottle of caña." Everybody agreed and even Miguel cheered up.

"What's caña?"

"You'll soon find out, Orlando!"

We each dug coins from pockets, prickly with shards of straw, and gave them to Epifanio. He stepped out into the darkness and reappeared few minutes later with a bottle half-full of a viscous liquid. A couple of dusty shot glasses were unearthed from a drawer. One woman polished them on the hem of her coat. Epifanio filled each to its rim. The women downed theirs first, instantly rejuvenated, smiling more widely.

I was last in line. "It's not alcoholic, is it?" Everybody laughed. I'd been brought up in a tee-total family. My grandfather had once served as the Chief Rechabite of Scotland. The Independent Order of Rechabites was a friendly society dedicated to promoting abstinence from alcohol as a personal virtue and a social good. My big sister, my wee brother and I had attended the weekly Rechabite meetings in Dundee throughout our youth. We'd entered their annual competitions for recitation, singing and piano-playing. We'd each won prizes. We'd taken the Pledge:

"I promise to abstain from all intoxicating liquors, wine, and spirit as a beverage."

And recited ardently along with all the other members of the lodge:

"Look not upon the wine when it is red, when it giveth its colour in the cup, when it moveth itself aright.
For at the last, it biteth like a serpent, and stingeth like an adder."

And we ended with the crescendo:

"Wine is a mocker, strong drink is raging: and whosoever is deceived thereby, is not wise."

We had loved the rituals, the regalia, the singing. Our grandmother served each of us a thimble-full glass of Crabbie's Green Ginger Wine on Hogmanay. I doubt if she knew it was alcoholic.

"It's a kind of medicine! A pick-me-up for people who have to work late." I was brought back from my reminiscence by the reassuring voice of the oldest woman. She and the others were looking at me expectantly, not unkindly. I made up my mind and took a sip, liked what I tasted despite its having less flavour than green ginger wine, and downed the rest of the glass in one swallow as the others had done. The volatile fumes caught my breath. Then a warm glow spread deliciously throughout my entire body. Fatigue melted away. We returned to work with renewed energy and finished packing the remaining piñas in record time.

131

For what was left of that night, I slept soundly and rose the following morning, bright and early.

"What time did you finish last night?" Pastora asked.

"Half an hour after midnight."

"You must be exhausted!"

"Me? Exhausted? No! We each had a glass of caña. That livened us up!"

"Mamá! Mamá!" Doña Lutgarda came rushing out of the kitchen, alarmed.

"What's happened, Pastora?"

"Tell my mamá!" Pastora looked at me horrified.

"Tell her what?"

"Tell my mamá what you just told me. About the caña!"

"You were drinking caña?" Doña Lutgarda seemed concerned. When I had arrived and sat down to my first meal in the fonda, Doña Lutgarda had asked me if I wanted a glass of wine. "I don't drink alcohol!" She had seemed pleased and the matter never arose again. Very occasionally I'd join a friend in the bar at the upper end of the plaza. He would have an expresso and a Licor 43. Much to the amusement of the other patrons. I would have a glass of gaseosa, soda-water that you squirted yourself from the syphon on the counter and weren't charged for. They would smile and hold their right elbow in their left hand. "¡Codo! – The Extranjero's a tight one!" I would then repeat the joke about the Scottish taxi that was involved in an accident and all 14 passengers had to be taken to hospital. They would laugh. "The Scots know how to look after their pennies!"

"Do you know what caña is?" Doña Lutgarda was looking at me.

"I've no idea, I admitted. It's probably alcoholic though."

"Probably? I'll say it is! It's 60% alcohol! Caña is white rum made from local sugar-cane. One or two of the villagers distil it illegally and sell it on the sly. Who bought it?"

I hesitated. "Epifanio."

That seemed to mollify her. "Well, Epifanio is a good man and he knows the safest caña to buy. If I were you, I wouldn't make a habit of drinking caña when you're supposed to be working." She paused and relented. "However, one glass as a pick-me-up when you're working late will do you more good than harm," but added, "so long as it's from a safe still."

Ten minutes later, Don Salvador and I greeted each other as we were both leaving for the warehouse. "This morning, I'm going to have you record the location of the plantation and the weight of each piña, Orlando."

"Can I make a suggestion, Don Salvador? Why not ask Miguel to do it before you ask me?"

"Oh, we've tried Miguel already and he makes mistakes. He's too easily distracted."

"Well, I think it would be a good idea to have him do at least the first sheet and only then ask me to do it. It might not be a good idea for you to give me an easier job so soon. Carting piñas on your shoulder all morning is hard work." Don Salvador nodded.

Epifanio unloads a particularly large banana stalk onto the head of one of the women workers in the banana packing station.

And so, when we arrived at the plantation known as el Rincón half-an-hour later, parked alongside the cut piñas by the plantation gate, and set everything up ready to weigh the stalks, Don Salvador made his invitation. "Miguel, I want you to record the weights this morning." He handed Miguel the clipboard and a sharpened pencil. A few questioning eyebrows were raised. Miguel, however, looked around at us all, triumph in his eyes.

"Write El Rincón on the top line." Miguel hesitated. "What if I write the name of the plantation and you just write the weights?" Miguel nodded and Don Salvador entered the name and location of the plantation.

One of the plantation workers offered his shoulder to stand in for Miguel and he and I began the arduous task of carting the piñas to the steelyard for weighing.

"24.5!" Pause. "23!" Pause. "28!"

Miguel laboriously wrote the numbers in order. Don Salvador peered discreetly over his shoulder. After we'd loaded a dozen or so piñas, Don Salvador thanked Miguel elaborately and called on me. I handed Miguel the blanket I'd been using to protect my shirt. It was evident that he was proud to have had his moment in the sun but it was equally so that he was now pleased to have been relieved from such an exacting task.

"Yes, Don Salvador, I think it's best if I take over from El Extranjero. These heavy piñas are a bit much for a little fellow like him." I accepted the pencil and clipboard Miguel handed me. He cast me a look of pity for my physical inferiority. But I was happy. He'd had his moment of glory and could now present his decision to withdraw as an act of consideration for me. Nothing was said by the rest of the crew but I could see that they too approved how Don Salvador had handled the situation. My being given apparently easier assignments occasionally was not going to cause resentment within the team.

Don Salvador and I ate a late lunch together. "Can you can handle the numbers required to pack the rest of the piñas and load the lorry tonight, so that Ángel can get to Santa Cruz before dawn?"

"I'm sure I can."

"Good! Then I can go back home to Puerto La Cruz. Here's the pro-forma invoice that shows you the exact weight needed for this export – 2,250 kilos. I'll leave the commercial invoice with Don Pancho. As soon as you and the crew have loaded, no matter how late it is, knock at the house door and Don Pancho will sign the forms and give Ángel the copies he needs for presentation at the docks."

Epifanio, Miguel, the women and I all worked steadily, well into that night, to pack the fruit we'd collected from el Rincón and then load that and the fruit packed the previous day onto the lorry. Each row of packaged piñas was loaded to the exact height that Angel indicated. They couldn't be higher than the side-boards in case they rolled off. I tallied up the weight and we began a new row. It was slightly intimidating to add the columns of figures in silence as the rest of the crew watched me. Most of them could add and subtract, I was sure, and so I could only surmise that I'd been given the task because none of them wanted to take the final responsibility of confirming the exact weight of each consignment.

Just after midnight, when we'd loaded 2,260 kilos of banana-stalks onto the truck, I knocked at the door to Don Pancho's house. After I'd waited a few minutes and knocked again, his son, Haníbal, a young man perhaps a year or two older than I, opened the door.

"It's one o'clock in the morning," he protested. "What do you want?"

"We need Don Pancho to sign the commercial invoice and give the copies to Ángel so that he can leave for the docks at Santa Cruz."

Haníbal closed the door and five minutes later, Don Pancho appeared, fully clothed, blinking sleep from his eyes.

"What weight have you loaded?" His eyes, sharp now, bore into me.

"Two thousand, two hundred and sixty kilos, Don Pancho."

"What weight is on the pro-forma?"

"Two thousand, two hundred and fifty kilos."

He walked round the loaded truck to see that the piñas were firmly packed.

"Why 10 kilos over?"

"It's the closest I could get to the exact number."

He nodded. "You're sure you have 2,260 kilos?"

"Si, Señor!" I was sure.

He turned to me, wide awake now. Don Pancho was my height but far sturdier and in his early fifties; his loose arms and large hands provided evidence that he was well acquainted with hard physical labour. He looked directly into my eyes from his weather-beaten face. "You're absolutely certain?"

"Absolutely certain, Don Pancho."

The author sitting on the wall of a banana plantation. Behind me you can see two good-quality banana stalks as well as how the west-winds tend to shred the leaves of the plants.

He held my gaze for a moment longer, nodded and wrote the numbers on the invoice, signed it, checked that all four copies were legible and handed them to Ángel. "Bring me the chit from the weighbridge at the dock!" I was comfortable in the knowledge that the chit would corroborate my calculation and that Don Pancho would know he could trust me. But he already knew that, I was sure. Don Pancho was like many a Scottish farmer that I'd worked for in Angus. They seldom asked you a question they didn't already know the answer to. They asked simply to confirm the judgement they had already formed of you.

"You've all done a good job here over these past two days. Ángel, you get off to the port now! The rest of you, go home. Be back here next Monday morning. I'll close the warehouse!"

This kind of interesting, intensive work, compacted into a couple of days with the following three or four days free, suited me just fine. I made more than enough money to pay for my room and board in the fonda and had several days to myself to continue my explorations alone and with friends, and to improve my Spanish.

The packing team puts the finishing touches to a shipment of protected banana stalks.

14. How (not) to renew a Spanish visa

My Spanish visa, valid for six months from the date I'd entered Spain's Basque country at Irun, was about to run out and I was alarmed. I hadn't planned to stay this long, but now – urgently – I had either to renew my visa or to leave the Canary Islands for some non-Spanish territory. The choice wasn't difficult. I was happy in the village, I had a job that was interesting and covered my very modest requirements. So, I made the decision to visit the British Consulate in Santa Cruz. Because it was urgent, I decided to buy a seat to the capital in José-María's Super Snipe. I'd be able to accomplish the task in one day – or so I imagined.

Almost nobody in the village owned a car and so the 'pirate' service José-María offered, although unlicensed and technically illegal, allowed people a convenient alternative to the guagua for tasks that needed immediate attention in Santa Cruz. He attracted an older clientele who valued convenience, comfort and promptness.

So, that very Thursday evening after dinner, I went to reserve a seat for the following morning In the evenings José-María was always to be found in pressed slacks, an ironed white shirt with the cuffs folded back and highly polished shoes, at the lower end of the plaza close to the church fastidiously flicking invisible dust from the polished surface of his limousine with a soft yellow duster.

"You've left it rather late, Orlando, but," he appraised my meagre frame, "you can squeeze into the front bench seat with two other passengers. You'll have more room on the way back." I readily agreed. "It's not that the car is full," he went on, "it's that two elderly sisters have paid to have the rear of the car entirely to themselves." I paid him cash just to be sure.

"Six o'clock on the dot!"

"I'll be there." He knew I would. I'd travelled with him a couple of times before when I had to stay clean and tidy. When appearances didn't matter, I'd drive in overnight with Ángel and sleep in straw on the tailgate of the lorry when we reached the docks.

When I woke the following morning just after five, I heard rattling in the kitchen. When I went downstairs to the courtyard, Doña Lutgarda had a bowl-full of warm milk and another of gofio ready for my breakfast.

Her movements were more sprightly than normal. "We're happy to hear you've decided to extend your visa and stay on with us a bit longer." She smiled.

Some days before, I'd told her that my visa was about to expire and that I might try to find a berth on a boat that would take me to Latin America or even to some distant part of the British Commonwealth. Doña Lutgarda was a true Canaria through and through, a woman of the village who put great value in family relationships, community, and the age-old way of life. During her life-time, of source, she'd seen many leave the village, some of them close family members, and been privy to their successes and disappointments. Some returned with money and self-assurance, some with neither. There were those who had called for family members to join them in the Americas and some who'd simply vanished into the tropical interior of Venezuela or Colombia. She didn't attempt to influence my decision, but any time we talked of what I was going to do with my life, she would always make the same remark: "You'll end up going back to Scotland. ¿Quién no quiere a su tierra? Who doesn't love their homeland more than anywhere else?"

At home in Scotland, Pearl eagerly awaited my weekly letters and shared them with Vivian and Euan. They told not only of incidents from my life in the village, at work, and intriguing experiences, but also the longer-term plans I was struggling with. During the weeks I'd spent at the Casa Campello near Alicante in peninsular Spain, I'd talked to many young people from Canada, Australia, South Africa and New Zealand. They all seemed to have saved money for their extended European trips by mining cobalt and uranium in Ontario, hunting kangaroos in the Australian outback or deer in mountainous New Zealand. They'd trapped crocodiles for their skins in the Northern Territories, driven herds of cattle from extensive grazing grounds in the interior to coastal abattoirs at Darwin where the meat was processed for export. Their adventures all had common characteristics that fired my teenage imagination. They were all of them thrilling, out-door, short-term jobs that paid inordinately well and so allowed them to save and then move on to something new. These countries were, according to those young ex-colonials, all desperate for manpower. My mother must have smiled when she read my outpourings and realised that they were the daydreams of a naive young man whose imagination was more ample than his understanding and his experience of life combined. But Pearl possessed a mother's good sense not to tell me so.

These regular letters home, scratched in ink on both sides of flimsy air-mail writing paper and pages long, must have reassured Pearl that I was coping, happy and earning enough to support myself and so allow

138

me to hang onto my tiny emergency savings safely banked in Dundee. She too, had expressed her satisfaction that I planned to remain for the time being in Tenerife. No doubt she thought it preferable to learning that her 18-year-old son, who had never in his life shot a rifle, had sailed off to hunt crocodiles in the swampy shores around Australia's Northern Territories.

What I would do in the longer term, I wasn't at all sure, but to remain for the present in the fonda, work and learn all I could about the banana business while using my spare time to explore on foot, cement friendships and improve my Spanish, seemed an adequate challenge.

So, on that Friday morning hours before dawn, I was supping my warm gofio while Doña Lutgarda, sleeves already rolled to her elbows, busied herself getting the charcoal lit and setting out everything she needed for the day's meals.

I paused at the main door of the fonda and smelled the promise of rain on the breeze that rustled the tall palms around the plaza. Dark clouds scudded towards the darker mountains. Down past the white-walled church, José-María was assisting two older women into the ample back seat of the limousine that, without the arm-rests, usually accommodated four with ease. When he had them settled comfortably, he packed their many packages into the sedan's capacious boot.

"¡Buenos días, José-María!" I handed over my modest bag to stow in the boot since we'd be four on the front seat. I squeezed in beside the two passengers already seated. José-María closed his door and started the engine. Just as we were leaving the silent plaza, drops of rain plopped onto the windshield.

For the first part of the journey, the road ran parallel to the coast and followed its contours through countryside now open, now wooded. It was still too dark to make out anything other than the white tops of the breakers crashing on the rocks far, far below.

The car settled into the leisurely rhythm that José-María favoured and the passengers began to talk. I knew nobody except our driver, but all seemed somewhat familiar with one another and to know all about me. As if I were not present, they exchanged information about the jobs that I had held, incidents they'd heard about my excursions in and around the village, even my life in the fonda and how my favourite dish was goat meat stewed with garbanzas – large chick-peas cooked with herbs.

During those months in Buenavista, I'd come to appreciate that the concept of privacy barely existed. I'd also come to accept, that as el

139

Extranjero, the sole foreigner in this traditionally conservative village, I was a welcome novelty and therefore a focus for their guileless curiosity. They didn't regard their public examination of my life as in the least intrusive and so neither could I. They were as genuinely curious about me as they were interested in one another. When the elderly sisters politely asked the two gentlemen sitting beside me on the front seat, "Why are you going to Santa Cruz today?" they were given fulsome explanations by each, separately, that included all the unembarrassed and perfectly frank why's and wherefore's of what, to my judgemental ears, were confidential family affiliations and intimate medical conditions. I was, I realised, learning to be comfortable with the customs that governed life in a tiny Canario village in Tenerife and wove its inhabitants together, in a web of cherished familiarity.

José-María's voice broke the drowsy silence we had all lapsed into after the initial curiosities had been satisfied. The patter of rain on the limousine's windscreen and the rhythmic swish-swash of the wipers had lulled me to sleep.

"Señoras y Señores," He addressed us formally, "We're going to make a stop in La Orotava. I must make a delivery. Anybody who wants a coffee will be dropped in the plaza. Those who prefer to remain in the car can come with me." We all opted to alight at the café, a pool of weak yellow light on the edge of the still-dark plaza surrounded by the ghosts of colonial buildings. It had stopped raining and we gallantly escorted the two elderly sisters from the car to an inside table where we all sat together. Cafes in Tenerife were always spotless and smelled deliciously of freshly-roasted coffee beans. At this early hour, all was quiet except for the staccato rat-tatt as the puck of damp coffee grounds from the filter cup flew into the waste-bin and the agreeable hiss of steam spluttering into the stainless-steel milk jug. The background harmony of early conversation was just beginning.

The sisters asked for 'leche-leche'. The barman placed two short, clear glasses on the counter and added a spoonful of condensed milk to each. He filled the glass with hot, foamy, steamed milk almost to the top and finally added a shot of expresso. The dark coffee furled into the milk like curling smoke from a pipe. When placed in front of them on white saucers, the sisters proceeded to add sugar and stir. The two men each ordered a 'cortado doble' – two shots of expresso in a tiny white cup to which the barman added a tiny stream of steamed milk, holding back the foam from the jug with a small wooden spatula. They too, added heaped spoonfuls of sugar. Canarios certainly have a sweet tooth, I noted, probably a relic of their sugar-cane history. With my history of war-rationed sugar, I began to sip on my simple, fragrant cortado – a single expresso served in a tiny white cup topped up with scalding, frothless milk. Both sisters uttered expressions of horror as I lifted the cup to my lips.

"No sugar?"

"I don't take sugar."

"But this can't be! You must! Otherwise it'll be too bitter!" One sister urgently pushed the sugar-dish towards me.

"Coffee without sugar is bad for your digestion!" declared the other. When I still didn't touch the sugar, she continued. "You'll suffer for it! Just you wait and see!" They began relating stories of all those people they'd known to suffer from indigestion and much, much worse as, apparently, the direct consequence of not adding sugar to their coffee.

Just as we were crunching the tiny sweet biscuits served in the saucer with our coffee, our limousine returned and cruised to a halt. José-María emerged to escort, with solicitous formality, his elderly passengers back into the comfort of thick, plush seats with wide velvet arm rests. Each sister almost disappeared into the luxurious upholstery and proceeded to fall into untroubled sleep that persisted until we arrived in Santa Cruz. Well, I reflected, neither suffers from insomnia, nor can they have digestive problems given the amount of sugar they take. It required much gentle persuasion from José-María to rouse them, so that they could prepare themselves for their reception at their brother's house, as we approached Santa Cruz an hour later. "Maybe there's something to be said, after all," I thought, "for coffee sweetened with condensed milk plus additional sugar!

I was next to leave the car and bade a cheerful "¡Hasta luego!" to the remaining occupants before making my way to the British Consulate. The consulate was located in a beautiful, lemon-coloured house surrounded by its own gardens near the main boulevard that separated the docks from the town. As soon as I rang the polished brass bell, the door was opened by a smiling, good-looking, well-groomed, Spanish woman I took to be the secretary.

"Good morning. I'm a British citizen. I'd like to speak to the Consul about renewing my visa."

She seemed to hesitate as if puzzled and then: "Please, come in!" She led me across the terra-cotta tiles of the spacious hall to her empty, polished desk. Beyond it, I had a view of an internal garden, bright with scarlet geraniums and smelling of freshly-clipped grass. "Have you previously registered with Her Majesty's Consulate?" I told her I had not. The truth was I didn't really grasp the implication of the phrase, 'register with the Consulate'.

"Can I see your passport?" I withdrew my navy-blue passport

from the bag I was carrying. She accepted it and disappeared through a heavy door of panelled wood, closing it firmly behind her. A moment later, she reappeared and held the door open for me. "The Consul, Mr Foxe, will see you, Mr Mackay."

A relaxed, middle-aged gentleman in a light-weight two-piece suit with a discreet hounds-tooth pattern in it, rose from behind a beautifully-polished desk and came forward, offering a genuine smile and an extended hand.

"Mr Mackay. Thank you for your visit!" I wondered if my fame had spread to Santa Cruz but then realised that he was holding my passport open in his left hand. "Jeremy Foxe, Her Majesty's Consul. How can I be of help you?" We shook hands. I noticed his eyes strayed to the tell-tale, black river-delta on my right palm. His eyes sought out its dark twin on my left.

"I need to renew my visa."

"Your tourist visa expired a few days ago." He made it sound the visa's fault.

"I'm sorry. I've been quite busy."

"I'm sure things can be worked out, Mr Mackay. But first tell me a little about yourself. I see you were born in Coupar Angus, Perthshire and lived in Dundee." He mentioned these places as if he were familiar with them. Within minutes Mr Foxe had me talking about having attended the Morgan Academy and sat my Higher Leaving Certificate the previous summer.

"We played the Morgan at rugby," he told me without mentioning what school 'we' might have been. Judging from his accent, it must have been one the boarding schools, perhaps Dollar or Loretto. Scots who attended such schools spoke 'without an accent', meaning that their English, unlike all other accents in the UK, represented a social class rather than a region. He was interested in my work at Lockwoods canning factory in Monifieth, hitch-hiking through France and Spain and my third-class stormy voyage on *La Ciudad de Cádiz* from the Peninsula to Las Palmas in search of a ship to take me to South America.

"Of course, your parents know where you are!" It wasn't a question and his tone was casual but there was concern in his eyes.

"I write to my mother every week."

"That must be expensive." He was probing, seeking confirmation.

"It is. Even though I write on both sides of the airmail paper, four or five sheets cost me more than 20 pesetas." His eyes registered the confirmation he sought.

"So, you couldn't find a ship out of Las Palmas nor out of Santa Cruz and so you decided to go and stay in Buenavista del Norte? Do I

142

understand correctly?"

"That's right." I wasn't certain where he was going. He let the silence lengthen. "Why Buenavista? Most visitors to Tenerife have never even heard of it, let alone been there."

"Santa Cruz was too expensive. Puerto la Cruz too." I extemporised, beginning to catch his drift.

His eyes strayed back to the indelible stains on my palms. "Of course, you have your own resources." Again, I hesitated. "You're not working." He made it sound like an assertion.

I shook my head. I was beginning to understand the code of this shrewd gentleman's discourse. "I have my own resources," I managed, gratefully borrowing from him.

"Of course! The money you earned by working overtime at the canning factory." He nodded, although he must have known that currency regulations forbade my leaving with more than £40 in cash. "You live economically."

I was back on firmer ground. During and after the War, 'economical' was precisely what we were raised to be. Thrift and parsimony were extolled. To be economical was to practice a virtue akin to godliness, much more important than cleanliness. Nobody I knew could do economical better than I could. 'The best way to save is not to spend,' had been drummed into us from birth.

"With 350 pesetas a week I cover all my expenses."

Impressed, he raised his eyebrows, encouraging me to continue. Cautiously, I told him about the fonda where I lived, that Doña Lutgarda charged me just under 350 pesetas a week for room, board and laundry. I told him I spoke passable Spanish and the villagers treated me just like any other member of the community.

"So you have no need to work." Another assertion. I said nothing. "That's good!" I was grateful for his leading. He went on. "The Civil Guard would never renew your visa if they discovered that you were working illegally."

"The Civil Guard?" Any mention of the Beneméritos made me feel uncomfortable.

"It's the Civil Guard who must provide you with a new visa, Mr Mackay. As the British Consul, I deal only in British visas and, of course, with other matters that pertain to the welfare of British citizens within my jurisdiction."

I could have kicked myself for not having had the common sense to realise this. "Of course!" Now I understood the initial flicker of puzzlement on his secretary's face.

"However, if you happened to fall into the category of a British citizen in need of assistance..." He was leaving the door open for me.

"I don't."

"For example, if, for whatever reason, you found yourself temporarily without resources and needed to be repatriated, we could arrange that. If your mother were taken seriously ill and you had to return home...."

"She's in good health."

"That's just an example." He was quick to reassure me. "In such an eventuality, all costs involved and monies advanced would have to be repaid, of course, but that is the kind of arrangement my position permits me to make on a British citizen's behalf." He made it sound intimate, friendly.

"All I need is to renew my visa so I can remain here. Everything else is fine."

"Of course, it is. I'll have my secretary give you the address of the Civil Guard here in the capital. When you visit their office in the barracks, do remember to apologize for having allowed your visa to run out. Show the officer my card." He scribbled his signature on it. "Tell him I sent you."

"Thank you."

"Before you leave, I'll have my secretary add you to our residents list. I like to keep a current list of the British citizens on the islands I represent." He saw the reservation in my eyes. "It's merely a precaution in case there's another civil war or Teide decides to erupt again, obliging us to repatriate all British subjects." He laughed. "I guarantee you won't be left behind." His voice was sincere and reassuring.

"Thank you. I'll leave my address in Buenavista and the telephone number of the fonda."

"Thank you for your visit, Mr Mackay. Now that we've met each other and you know what we're here for, don't hesitate to call me." He looked at me kindly and I think I saw a twinkle in his eye. He rang a bell and his secretary entered immediately.

"Miss Arozarena, please register Mr Mackay as one of our valued British residents. Oh, and before he goes, show him the sink in the garden where he can wash his hands with pumice-stone."

He looked at me and added, as if sharing a secret, "From experience, Mr Mackay, I know that the Civil Guard view clean hands as a virtue. Enjoy the rest of your stay on Tenerife."

"Thank you, Mr Foxe." I meant it.

The building belonging to the Civil Guard was mostly grim barracks.

Tight pairs of uniformed officers bearing rifle and machine-gun streamed through the arch in both directions. In the covered courtyard was a long counter above which a patterned glass screen obscured a clear view of the officers behind. At regular intervals in the opaque screen were small, arch-like openings behind which brass buttons and polished leather belts over olive-green uniforms glinted. The heads and bodies appeared as a mass of distorted colour. In front of each aperture snaked a waiting line of supplicants. The petitioner at the head of each line, whose business was being attended to, was forced to support himself with one hand on the counter edge and lean down awkwardly to the opening in the glass in order to converse with the officer sitting poker-faced behind. The air was alive with imploring voices and single-armed gesticulations.

I scanned the cryptic words on shingles above each officer's retreat to discover one that referred to visa-renewals. The closest I could find was one that bore the words 'Asuntos Extranjerías' in gold lettering. There was nobody waiting. When I bent down and peered through the arched glass opening, I saw nothing but an empty chair and an extensive set of rubber stamps on inkpads of different colours. In a wooden frame that announced Horario – Hours of Service, individual cards had been inserted: 9-11 and 15.30-17.30. The clock on the wall showed 9.35, suggesting that an officer should be in attendance. I glanced around. In typical public-service manner, nobody would meet my eyes. A hatless officer with gold epaulettes was passing. I addressed him politely.

"Excuse me Señor. Would you know who attends to the business of the British Consul? I showed him Mr Foxe's embossed card bearing his signature." He examined it suspiciously.

"Wait here!" At least I'd found the right place. I waited. Within a couple of minutes, another officer wearing a less-decorated uniform sat down behind the opening, wiping crumbs off his lips with the back of his hand. With one elbow on the counter to support me, I bent down and craned my neck so I could see his eyes and placed the Consul's card in front of him.

"I've just come from His Britannic Majesty's Consul." He cautiously touched the embossed letters on the card. I retrieved the card and placed my open passport in front of him. Pointing accusingly at my expired visa, I stated, "This visa has expired!"

Spanish is a great language for deflecting blame. Instead of being forced to admit, "I have been negligent and allowed my visa to expire and so am now here illegally," Spanish allowed me to use the reflexive to declare, "¡Esta visa se ha caducado!" That form of the verb, uttered in an affronted tone, automatically transfers blame for the transgression from the human culprit to the visa itself. "Just look! This careless visa has allowed itself to expire!"

He nodded wearily, familiar with wayward visas that had allowed themselves to expire.

"El Señor Foxe, the British Consul assured me that you would be able to amend this vexation."

He blinked. "Me? Of course I can!" I'd intentionally aroused his self-conceit. He took my passport and thumbed painstakingly through the pages from back to front, scanning each until he came to the name and photograph. "To whom does this passport belong?"

"The passport bearing the visa that has allowed itself to expire," I declared, "belongs to me!"

He blinked again, squinted, and finally nodded. "It belongs to you." I'd darkened and matured since I'd left Scotland these six months ago. Again, he flicked through the pages with care, blinking at each stamp. I kept silent. "The British Consul sent you?"

"Her Majesty's Consul for the Canary Islands, El Señor Foxe!"

A thin smile finally appeared. "I can arrange for a new visa!"

"Thank you!"

"There is no need!" He assured me haughtily and drew himself up so high behind his opaque glass screen that his face disappeared beyond the capability of my craned-neck.

"Photos!" He stretched his hand out, palm up.

"Photos?" I wondered if this was code for cash.

"Three. Give them to me and I will immediately arrange to renew the visa that has so carelessly allowed itself to expire." The house of cards I'd so carefully built, tumbled.

"There are no photographs!"

"Then photographs must be taken. You will return with them." He was visibly relieved to be released from taxing work.

I thanked him and headed to the photographer's shop where I bought the occasional film or had one processed. The photographer knew me by sight, knew exactly what was required, and said she could have the photos ready within 30 minutes. Within less than 40 minutes I was back at the same counter clutching a tiny cellophane envelope containing my three newly-minted head-and-shoulders. The officer was gone. The cards in the slot had been replaced with one that read ¡Cerrado! – Closed!

I accosted another haughty officer and asked him for information. He pointed to the card and shrugged, "¡Cerrado! means ¡Cerrado!"

"But I was here half-an-hour ago! The card indicated that service is offered until 11 o'clock and again in the afternoon from 15.30 until

17.30. It's still only 10.15."

"Things change!" He showed me his palms and walked away. While individuals in both the Peninsula and in the Canaries tended to offer assistance, members of any public service seemed to consider that they belonged to a privileged elite. A uniform, even a chrome badge, seemed to give them the right to be discourteous to the public. They adopted an attitude that declared, "I possess the power in this relationship. If I fail to perform my duty, there are no consequences for me and so I have nothing to lose by showing you contempt."

José-María expected all new and returning passengers to be by his limousine by 4 p.m. so that he could then attend to his pick-ups and have everybody back home in Buenavista by just after six. If I decided to stay and take the chance that the officer might return at 3.30, I'd have to let José-María know and ask if he'd be willing to wait for me. I decided to have lunch and think the matter over.

Any time Ángel and I stayed in Santa Cruz over lunch time, we ate at a tiny restaurant off the Calle de la Marina. It catered to dock-workers and suited our budget. The menu, in white chalk on a square blackboard, never changed. It began, 'Rancho: 3.50' and ended 'Flan: 3'. Rancho was a thick soup made from a meat-bone, vegetables and chickpeas. It was delicious and filling. Flan was a cup-sized, yellow custard-pudding topped with caramelized sugar. So, for six pesetas and fifty centavos, Ángel and I could stave off hunger.

The restaurant was busy, but a welcoming waiter wearing, as did all the others, a clean apron over black trousers and white shirt, found me a seat at a table for six by a window. I could see a ship being loaded and the line of palm trees and gardens that separated the city from the docks. White cargo ships were moored by hawsers as thick as my arm. Noisy derricks swivelled and stevedores skilfully loaded pallets of tomatoes, bananas, and all matter of mysterious packages into the ship's hold.

Conversation began as soon as I sat down with the inevitable, "You're not from here, are you?" All eyes turned on me. The question was phrased so that the speaker didn't appear overly curious, but was a disguised way of asking, "Where are you from?"

"No, I'm not from here." The questioner's eyes met those of the rest of his table companions to receive their admiration for having made such an astute observation. However, my simple agreement now returned the onus to the speaker to pursue what he wanted to know.

"You're off one of the boats?"

"I'm not off a boat." I knew I could play this game all day, my answers failing to give the information being sought and so drawing more and more indirect questions that required more and more imagination from my inquisitive companions. Occasionally I would draw out the exchanges to discover when the questioners might become so frustrated that they would finally demand, "So where are you from?". But no matter how much I stalled, that direct question was never asked. There seemed to be some cultural taboo against it.

Today, I wasn't in the mood for games. "I'm from Scotland. I work for Alhambra, the banana exporter in Buenavista del Norte."

They looked at one another in amazement. "Buenavista del Norte!" More than likely, none of them had ever visited such a distant and, in the eyes of those from the capital, such an insignificant little village.

"I arrived this morning to renew my visa but the Civil Guard's office is closed. I can't find out if it's going to open again this afternoon. I don't know whether to take a chance or just go home."

If there's one thing that locals love, it's to give advice to an innocent visitor. If the visitor is from a different culture and speaks their language imperfectly, they revel all the more in the opportunity to pontificate. It elevates them to that rare but elusive status of expert. It allows them to indulge their spirit of boundless generosity. They need part with nothing more than words, and bears no responsibility for the outcome enjoyed or suffered by the recipient of their suggestions.

I was bracing myself for an explosion of recommendations and counter-recommendations that would last until I finished my flan. Instead there was silence. The conversation switched abruptly to Los Chicharreros, the nick-name for the Tenerife football team which was gaining a national reputation. I knew that because Don Pancho's son, Haníbal's elder brother, played for them. At the request of the Ayuntamiento – the Municipal Council of Buenavista – he had, one memorable afternoon, appeared in the square, dressed in his home colours. In his white shirt and socks and blue shorts, he delighted the villagers. But before I could boast to my lunch-companions that I had met one of the Chicharreros, they slipped away, as a group.

I should have known! Any reference to the Civil Guard made Canarios and Peninsulares alike profoundly uncomfortable, especially in unfamiliar company. Nobody knew who might be an informer and they knew better than to find out the hard way. As I paid for my bill and left a 50-centavo tip in the waiter's hand, I made up my mind what to do. I would go back to Buenavista with José-María and return the following week when my work-schedule permitted.

That night at dinner, Doña Lutgarda and the girls gathered round my table to share my disappointment. On the way back in the limousine, I'd rehearsed some of the stories I would tell to entertain them. The stop at dawn in La Laguna for early morning coffee with or without sugar; my friendly reception by the Consul's secretary and my long conversation with the Consul; how he had seen my hands and tactfully made it possible for me to clean them with pumice; how I'd won over the Civil Guard with the Consul's fancy card and my successful use of the reflexive pronoun to blame my visa for allowing itself to expire.

I'd even searched my dictionary for several unfamiliar words before coming down for dinner: the luxurious upholstery of Jose-Maria's Super Snipe was 'tapicería de lujo'; pumice was 'piedra pómez'; and idle civil servants were 'agentes públicos ociosos'. They enjoyed my tirades against state bureaucracy. 'Ocioso' sounded like the perfect, sibilant, Spanish for the delicious English word 'slothful'.

"What are you going to do now?" They were concerned. "You can't stay without a visa. After all, Don Eduardo, lives just upstairs. He'll figure out eventually that you've overstayed your permitted time."

"I'll go back to Santa Cruz and try again, once I know my work schedule."

"You said that the British Consul gave you his card? Why don't you call him, tell him of your difficulties and ask for his help?" Doña Lutgarda was a practical woman.

"I couldn't possibly do that!"

"Why not?"

"It's not the kind of thing we English do." I'd adopted the Canary practice of using 'English' instead of British.

"Well, it's the kind of thing we Canarios do all the time."

"But we don't."

"Right now, Orlando, you're not in England. You're here, in Tenerife. The problem is in Santa Cruz. The Consul is in Santa Cruz. Why did he give you his card? He knows what these sloths are like!"

"Maybe you're right."

"Of course I'm right! Tomorrow after breakfast come down here." She pointed to a door off the courtyard. "We'll have the switchboard connect you with your English Consul." There was no point in telling her that he was the British Consul, that he might even be a Scot!

Before making the call next morning, I checked with Don Pancho when I was needed the following week. "Not until Wednesday!" In a room off the courtyard that I didn't even know existed, after much clicking and humming, I was put through to the Consul.

"Come in on Monday first thing," he showed no surprise. "I will make an appointment with the Civil Guard. We'll renew your visa together."

"You see! Didn't I tell you?" Doña Lutgarda and the girls had been at my elbow throughout the conversation. I'd had to translate it for them word-by-word, after I'd hung up.

When I reached the British Consulate the following Monday morning, the Consul's smiling secretary opened the door. "The Consul apologises, Mr Mackay, urgent business has taken him away. However, he has made the appointment as promised and I will accompany you to the Civil Guard barracks in his place."

We couldn't have been received more graciously by the Coronel-in-Charge whose office she confidently led me into. The Coronel's minion, the miscreant who had initially attended me the previous Friday and then disappeared, was told to bring all his forms, stamps and coloured ink-pads into the Coronel's office, "¡Ahora mismo! – Right now!"

Surrounded by multiple portraits of Generalissimo Franco in various military uniforms but in the same haughty pose, he had his minion complete the paperwork. With a dramatic flourish, the lackey stamped a visa in red ink that took up an entire page in my passport. He then scattered powdered chalk liberally over the still-wet ink and blew it off in a great cloud of white dust that caused the Consul's secretary to retreat. The Coronel glowered at him; the minion withdrew, apologising profusely and taking his armful of bureaucratic paraphernalia with him.

"¡Senor!" The coronel soberly handed me my passport, offered a denture-white smile to the Consul's secretary and bowed stiffly from the waist. "It is always a great pleasure! May your return be soon." It was clear he wasn't referring to me.

"Will you accompany me back to the Consulate, Mr Mackay? Mr Foxe said that you left something after your last visit." Once back in her office, she handed me a small, lumpy object sealed in a brown envelope, too large for whatever it contained and so had been neatly folded several times and sealed. Puzzled, I stowed it in my shoulder bag. She accepted my thanks, offered me her hand and a smile as I took my leave.

When I returned on the guagua early that afternoon, Doña Lutgarda hurriedly washed and dried her hands before daring to touch my passport with my new visa stamped into it, still bearing traces of chalk-dust.

"You see, Orlando? In this world of ours, we have principally to count on God and on ourselves. But what we can't receive from Him or accomplish on our own, we can get done through other people. That's why it's important never to make enemies. You never know when you're going to need help and from whom!"

Her years and the many roles life demanded she play had brought her wisdom. I was glad to be one of the fortunate recipients.

When I went back up to my room, I remembered the envelope that I'd been given in the Consulate and searched for it in my bag. Inside, I found a compact cake of rough-textured pumice-stone. No longer need I appear in public with the Ganges Delta imprinted on my palms!

In 1797, Santa Cruz de Tenerife successfully fought off an assault by Rear-Admiral Horatio Nelson who lost his arm in the battle.

15. Those who Work within Plantations

Workers had to keep banana plantations weed-free and level, so that the irrigation water would flow to each of the hundreds of banana plants on which much of Buenavista's economy depended.

Burly plantation foremen, impeccable in their laundered khakis, animated their Sunday evening gatherings by bursting into song accompanied by a single, shared guitar. These jovial, but no-nonsense men had been friends their entire lives. Each had worked his way through the ranks by showing initiative, trustworthiness and leadership. They stood out from ordinary mortals by their self-assured carriage, the confident timbre to their voices, and the gallant way they doffed their battered bush-hats to Doña Lutgarda and the flattered girls when they arrived in the dining-room at sunset. They were the stout pegs on which much of the local economy depended.

Because I lived in the fonda, I was on nodding terms with all of them. Now that my duties at the packing station were unexpectedly expanding my world, I had the opportunity to meet and get to know them better, but only in the plantations they managed. Doña Lutgarda insisted that all residents eat early, leaving the dining-room for their exclusive use.

From early morning, the aroma of caramelised onions, peppers macerating in white wine and goat-meat browning in garlic would sweeten the courtyard. I knew that Doña Lutgarda would save a cogote – the neck portion of goat, considered a delicacy, for my Monday's dinner, tasting all the more delicious for having been allowed to marinate in its own juices overnight. For that reason alone, I welcomed the foremen.

Once I'd become a long-term resident of the fonda, I enjoyed a reduction in my weekly rate by accepting whatever meal was set before me. I was rarely served meat because it was expensive, but on Monday evenings, I could count on a tender and delicious cogote. Fortunately, out of necessity in post-War Scotland, we had been brought up to eat and enjoy everything that was put on the table in front of us. Pearl had even convinced us that carrots, which were often served with a handful of oats as the evening meal, would help us to see in the dark so that we could shoot down en-emy fighter-planes. I remember longing for the day when I would possess cat-like eyes and dispense with the candle that cast such dis-tressing shadows on the wall as we climbed the stairs to bed in my grandmother's house.

The plantation foremen were always courteous and well-be-haved, never overdid the wine, and talked, strummed, sang until no later than 10.30 p.m. Farmers, I'd learned from experience, are careful about who they exchange news with. In particular, they are careful when they might be expe-riencing challenges with labour, a disease, or an invasion of insects. They share such problems with the trusted few who can be relied on to suggest a solution while re-specting confidentiality.

El Llavero -- the Keyman would also irrigate small, out-of-the-way plantations. Water was valuable and every drop was made to count.

Through my work with the packing station that took us all over the locality, I was beginning to appreciate the skills a foreman needed to manage a banana plantation. There wasn't just the health and moisture content of the soil and the de-velopment of the fruit to take into consideration, there was also a large number of employees to manage. Some of these were casual labour who offered their specialised services to several different plantations in the area. Because bananas were produced all year round, these casual la-bourers would move from one plantation to another, weeding, hoeing, clearing channels, irrigating, cutting the piñas on time and removing the trunks on which they had grown. A trunk fruited once only and so a fresh trunk was always being encouraged to replace it immediately, so that a new banana stalk was permanently in the making.

Plantation foremen bore the full responsibility of understanding and then implementing the plantation owner's business strategy. The most common one in our region was to produce bananas for export. All of the plantations around Buenavista were relatively new and had been constructed with sound materials. They were well laid-out and planted with good quality corms, all at considerable expense. It was understandable that the owner was keen to get the best return on his investment and so the foreman was expected to manage the grove accordingly; and strictly within the allotted budget.

Every plantation was enclosed by a wall on all four sides. The main entrance would be of stone, like the one I'd helped el Maestro build, but the rest of the enclosure, which meant 95 percent of it, appeared to be made of breeze blocks. These were laid in such a way that there were narrow spaces, like random perforations, left in the wall. The breeze blocks I was familiar with in Scotland were large, grey, relatively light-weight rectangles made from a mixture of cement and ash left over from the ubiquitous plants that converted coal into gas.

At first, I had assumed that the purpose of the walls around plantations was to keep intruders out. With experience, I discovered that their principal use was to serve as windbreaks. Tenerife enjoyed constant breezes and even stronger winds from the Atlantic Ocean. Winds caused the wide leaves of the palms to flap and flutter and so chafe against the outer skin of the growing fruit. When the hands of bananas would eventually ripen to canary-yellow, even the mildest abrasions would show up as brown blemishes that shoppers find unattractive. These walls, with their entrances and gates, all had to be kept in good shape, to protect the fruit and optimise its value. The irregular spaces or perforations were created purposely in order to reduce the surface presented to the wind. By allowing some of the wind the pass through the holes in the walls, its force was reduced and the longevity of the wall better assured, while still offering adequate protection to the fruit. Currents of fresh also helped keep the banana plants free of disease.

One day, Don Salvador was preparing to return to Puerto la Cruz after one of his brief visits. "I'd like you to be at the empacadora tomorrow at eight o'clock, Orlando." We'd just completed a busy three days. We'd collected well over 2,000 kilos of banana-stalks from multiple plantations, packed them and sent Ángel off to the docks in Santa Cruz with a full load. Often, I accompanied Ángel because Don Salvador encouraged me to become familiar with everything happening at the docks, the final point of departure for all our efforts. So, in addition to long days at the empacadora, I'd spent an entire night and part of the next morning with Ángel, catching a few hours' sleep on the tailgate wrapped in a blanket. I'd been looking forward to having a day to myself.

"I'm available, Don Salvadór. What needs to be done?" We'd returned from the docks with a load of lime in 50-kilo bags. I imagined I was needed to help offload them into another warehouse owned by Don Pancho.

"Just turn up at eight and Epifanio will show you what to do. Bring something to eat because you'll be out all day. And wear something good and strong on your feet!" By the twinkle in his eye I could see that the duties were secret but that he knew I would enjoy them.

I found Epifanio, slim and agile, already working quietly in the packing station. On the table, he had laid out several light hammers with unusually-long handles.

"Carpentry work? Is that what we're going to do, Epifanio?"

"Take a closer look, Orlando!"

Hammers typically used by carpenters have a flat face on one side of the head and a claw on the other. Hammers used by metal-workers have one flat face and a rounded 'peen' on the other. The heads on the hammers on the table had two flat faces, one on either side of the head.

"Look closely!" he urged. I picked one up and examined it. Each face bore two parallel grooves. Epifanio handed me a slim, flat wedge of metal with letters on it that looked like a portion of type, as used by typesetters to lay out a page of a newspaper. "Try to attach it." I did as asked and the flat metal wedge slipped into the grooves, firmly fixed in place. "Slip this one into the other face." He handed me a second wedge and I did as asked.

"What does it look like?" He regarded me expectantly. I shook my head.

I examined the hammer with its metre-long shaft and the light, double-faced head. I looked at the letters that stood out prominently on the two metal wedges. Epifanio placed a flat banana leaf on the table. "Tap first one face of the hammer into the leaf and then the other." I did so. Bruised deep into the leaf were the dark, perfect impressions of the letters on each face of the hammer.

"These letters, AH," he pointed to the leaf, stand for Alhambra, Don Salvador and Don Pancho's export company." These others, he fingered the impression cut into the leaf by the other face, "stand for El Rincón". I knew that large plantation well. He showed me a small wooden box in which were arranged a tidy series of similar metal wedges, each bearing different combinations of letters. "These wedges represent the codes for the different plantations that Don Salvador buys piñas from. He paused. What do they look like to you, now?"

I thought hard. "They look like they might be branding irons for banana-stalks!"

"Exactly!" He was pleased. "They're branding irons for banana-stalks! You tap the face of the hammer onto a stalk and the letters are immediately imprinted into the flesh, The impression bleeds and doesn't heal, so each stalk permanently carries the plantation owner's brand as well as our Alhambra brand." Ingenious, I thought. I liked the idea that each piña carried an identifying mark, just as every sheep on a Scottish hillside carried an indelible blue or red 'keel mark' on its rump or shoulder so that the shepherds can easily distinguish members of one flock from another. "We're going to spend the day branding piñas in five different plantations. I hope you're wearing good alpargatas because we'll be walking for many, many kilometres!"

We prepared four hammers, two for Epifanio and two for me. We each had one hammer with AH for Alhambra on one face and the option of one of several plantations on the other, and a separate hammer with the brand E for Export on one face and P for Plaza, meaning internal market, on the other. Just before leaving, Epifanio attached a machete in a sheath to his belt and handed me another. "Inside a plantation we wear these. You never know when you might need it." Too overjoyed to ask why, I adjusted the weight of the unaccustomed blade. I'd fulfilled the ambition that had been sown the day I'd met the plantation manager on the road above Puerto la Cruz.

Proud as Punch, I walked on Epifanio's right so that anybody could see machete flapping on my right hip. Duly armed with branding irons and machetes, we were on our way to visit our first plantation of the day. A fresh breeze swept in from the Atlantic bringing puffy clouds that collided with the mountains high above our heads to the southeast. We strode along the footpath that took us past la Casa Blanca. The farm-girls were already about their chores and shouted greetings as we passed.

"What plantation are you working in today, Epifanio?"

"El Rincón's the first, but we have another four to finish before the day's over." He listed their names.

"And el Extranjero?"

"El Extranjero's learning to brand the piñas."

"Well, remember that we want E for Export at La Casa Blanca!" Everybody knew that the real profit margin was made in exports.

"Oh, never fear, el Extranjero has got the eye! He knows the difference between E and P!"

I straightened my back, striving to reach my full 5'7" to impress the laughing girls and gave them a casual wave. I'd been selected by Don Salvador to learn how to brand banana-stalks!

When we reached El Rincón, we were met not by the usual group of labourers who helped us load on those days when we came to collect the cut stalks, but by the Encargado – the foreman himself.

"¡Buenos días Epifanio!" They shook hands. "I hear that el Extranjero's going to help brand piñas for El Alhambra! I hope he'll be as good as you at the job!"

"He's going to be even better!" I loved Epifanio for his quiet confidence in me.

"Well, he has the best teacher!" The foreman gave me his hand and his Christian name, Jacinto and sized me up. I took his hand, "Orlando". His handshake was firm and he looked me straight in the eye, approving my addressing him as 'Don Jacinto'.

I'd moved into a different league. Labouring was one thing and not without its responsibilities. However, branding! Now, branding took responsibility to a higher level. It required a combination of knowledge and sound judgement. The visible brands I would give to each stalk, E or P, made me publicly accountable. Through the quality of my decisions, I would earn – or lose – the trust and the respect of the foreman on any plantation and eventually, of the entire village.

El Llavero -- the Key-man, always in a good mood. He controlled the irrigation water from the mountains to the arid plain. His work required him to walk for many, many kilometres each and every day.

A plantation foreman managed his plantation in order to produce the best possible quality of fruit. His ultimate performance would be judged by the ratio of fruit he sold for export over fruit destined for the do-

157

mestic market. A plantation's reputation depended on its producing export quality; and here I was, learning to bear sole responsibility for determining the standard of a foreman's work and the reputation of the plantation he managed.

Women would wash the family's clothes in communal troughs like this one in Guia de Isoria.

Before we started, Don Jacinto gave both Epifanio and me a brief run-down on the status of the entire plantation. He rattled off the total number of plants; their spacing; the frequency of irrigation and the date of the last delivery of precious water to the plants; any disease problems he'd run into and how these had been dealt with and when. Had he not mentioned such problems, we would have seen with our own eyes any desiccated plants, any tell-tale white insecticide dust. We would have reported our findings to Don Pancho or Don Salvador and they would have asked questions of the owner. It was, therefore, in a foreman's interest to be up-front about anything that might affect the quality of the fruit, so that the packing station could take the appropriate measures. Export regulations were strict about how many days a banana stalk had to be free of insecticide before it was eligible for export. Fortunately, the climate in the Canaries and the agricultural practices were such that there was little threat from pests in the plantations. The greatest challenge came from blemishes on the fruit caused by scratching, from leaves agitated by the wind.

The foreman bade us "Good branding!" and left us. I turned to follow Epifanio and walked straight into a spider's web half as big as my body. Panicked by clinging web all over my face, hair and upper body, I began swinging my arms to free myself. The spider responsible for the trap was not far from my face. It was as big as my fist and seemed to be heading boldly towards me down its torn web. I flailed wildly.

"Did I forget to tell you about the spiders, Orlando?" Epifanio was barely able to suppress a grin. "We'll run into lots of them. But don't worry! They may be as big as your fist and look fierce but they're quite harmless." He paused. "At least most of them are not dangerous!"

I shuddered and flailed more wildly. He poked the monster gingerly with the handle of his branding hammer; it fled up the remnants of its web and took refuge under a banana leaf, eyes peering from the gloom. I looked into the rows of banana plants that closed off the sky above my head. A shaft of light illuminated what looked like dozens of huge webs spun between plants blocking our progress. "Just hold your hammer like this!" Epifanio held his hammer erect like a mace. "The webs cave in and the spiders run away. Then you can proceed. It's no big deal." I was only just managing to keep my revulsion under control, unwilling to allow Epifanio to think I wasn't up to the job. I bore my upright mace into the next huge web and felt relieved as the spider glared at me for a moment, made a fake pass and then took off into the shadows.

The first crisis over, and satisfied that I'd emerged from it victorious, at least outwardly, Epifanio quietly began to explain the conditions necessary to judge a stalk as ready for branding and whether it merited an E or a P.

We had to bear many factors in mind. First was the relative maturity of the stalk. Only those sufficiently advanced to be cut within a few days could be branded, alerting the foreman that they were ready to be transported to the packing station, where the export process would begin. Each would be packed in straw-cushioned paper, then transported to the docks in Santa Cruz to be loaded aboard a cargo ship and sit in the hold for a week, before reaching the fruit importer in Stockholm or Helsinki. There, it would be sold on, first to wholesalers, then to retailers and finally would end up in the hands of the consumer. During that period, the fruit would continue to mature, fill out, and ripen from the hard, dark green of the plantation to the mellow, suave, canary-yellow crescent that shoppers favoured.

"The trick for us branders, Orlando, is to look at a piña and be able to see in your mind's eye, exactly what it will look like in ten days' time." I glanced at Epifanio to see how serious he was. He read my look. "It's not that difficult. Before we leave El Rincón I'll have shown you a thousand banana plants and by then you'll have mastered the knack. I'm here to teach you and I'm confident you can be as good at it as I am!" I felt myself swelling with pride but then Epifanio cut me down to size. "If, that is, you survive the next spider attack!"

Teach me he did. In the following few hours, Epifanio showed me banana-stalks in every possible stage of growth, from drooping stem with the bulbous purple male flower at the tip and the whitish-yellow female flowers circling the stem in symmetrical whorls, through the expansion of the green ovaries, to the point where they turn into recognisable hands of miniature bananas clustered around the central stalk. He focused most of all on the later stages of development, where the candelabra of green bananas are almost, but not quite fully, grown. He explained rates of growth and how to judge them. I was ready to be tested.

"This one?" He pointed his hammer at a beautifully curved stalk thick with curved rows of upward-pointing hands of green bananas but so thin that much of the central stalk was still visible.

"No!"

"Why not?"

"It's insufficiently well-filled out. It needs another five to ten days."

"Good! This one?"

"It's ready for branding, but it's domestic quality."

"Why?"

"It will weigh only 17 kilos or so. It's too short and too light for export."

"Correct!"

"This one?" It was long, well-formed that would weigh 22 or 23 kilos when cut.

"P. Plaza! Domestic market!"

"Why?"

"The individual bananas, even when they ripen, will be too short to meet export standards."

"Good! Now these are the piñas you need to be most careful with. A plantation foreman will question your judgement on a well-formed stalk that meets the weight requirements, so always be prepared to back up every decision you make with solid facts. This job has to be done right from everybody's point of view." I was beginning to enjoy the challenge of using my inner eye and my judgement, on many parameters at once, to arrive at a sound conclusion. I liked the idea of making an informed decision and being able to explain it to a third party, then have that third party examine the evidence and agree. So many countrymen's skills were founded on instinct born of experience.

"Brand it with your hammer." I reached my hammer up to the point just below where the plantation workers would cut the stalk with their machete and gave a light but firm single tap with my branding stick to leave a clear, dark, moist P for Plaza. Another tap with my second hammer left an equally clear AH for Alhambra.

"This one?"

"It's an E."

"Why?"

"Because the hands of bananas are almost but not quite fully developed. Each banana will be longer than 15 centimetres and the entire stalk will weigh close to 26 kilos."

"Good!"

In this way, Epifanio and I covered El Rincón and three smaller plantations. One small plantation of about 200 plants remained. "Right, Orlando, now you're on your own! Keep track of those branded the way I've showed you." Epifanio had begun the task of examining a plantation by cutting a single immature banana from a piña. A banana does not take its round shape until it's almost mature. When still immature, it is made up of four faces, each separated by a ridge that runs the length of the fruit. Every time I'd branded a stalk with a P, Epifanio had dug his thumb-nail into one of the ridges to create a clear shallow cut. When I branded a bunch with an E he made a similar cut with his nail on a separate ridge but deeper. By the time we'd finished examining a plantation, he had a long banana with finger nail indentations down at least two of the ridges. The E's always greatly outnumbered the Ps. All we had to do then was to count the number of P-cuts and E-cuts and enter the numbers on a prepared sheet of paper. These figures would be taken back to Don Pancho and he and Don Salvador would then know the exact number of piñas they could have available within a few days, in order to fulfil an export order.

"Oh, by the way," Epifanio added, "the foreman won't meet you in this last plantation. He's had to go to Orotava to buy lime. So you're on your own."

"Don't worry, Epifanio! I can handle this. Off you go!"

I entered the small side-door of this final plantation full of my own importance but still timid enough to hold my hammers up in front of me, to collapse the spider webs before they clung to my face and hair. The afternoon was getting on; it was cloudy and the gloom and the loneliness gave me a slightly spooky feeling. Nevertheless, I made up my mind to pace myself, put my new knowledge into practice and perform this task perfectly. I took a deep breath, that smelled of warm, decaying soil.

I took two steps off the concrete edge of the irrigation channel and immediately sank up to my knees in sucking, brown mud. It happened so quickly that I involuntarily called out in alarm, overbalanced, made a grab for the nearest banana plant, caught it and pulled it over on top of me! So now, I was sitting up to my waist in a deep bath of thick mud without any purchase to extract myself. There was nothing close enough to hold on to since I'd already felled the only trunk at hand. The plantation had been recently irrigated and the top half-metre of soil had turned into porridge the colour and texture of melted chocolate.

I felt my earlier confidence drain from mind and body. Panic swelled inside my chest. But then my life-saving training from the Dundee Swimming Baths kicked in: Rule #1: Don't panic. I did my best and fought it, partially. Rule #2: Take stock of the danger. I sat still in the clinging mud, looked around and took stock. I knew that the soil in a plantation wasn't very deep and the irrigation water was still sitting close to the surface. Looking behind me, I saw that I was within arm's distance of the concrete channel that delivered the irrigation water. I reached out and pulled myself back onto the concrete. There was a great sucking noise as I hauled and the mud reluctantly released its grip but swallowed both my alpargatas in the process. Fortunately, my precious machete was safe. There was still a dribble of water in the concrete channel and I did my best to wash most of the mud off my back, my rear end and my legs and feet. As I sloshed the mud from my feet, I tried to talk myself into simply abandoning my alpargatas and continuing barefoot.

Suddenly, I panicked. "My branding irons!" I'd left them in the mud in my anxiety to extract myself! There was nothing else for it! I had to step back into the glutinous cess-pool, reach down and scramble about blindly to locate the hammers. In the process, I trawled up my alpargatas but by now, not only were my feet and legs caked with mud again, so were my hands, my arms and my chest, after the sub-surface fishing expedition! Back to the now muddy water in the irrigation channel and I cleaned off the hammers, but how to get the thick coating off my clothes? Inspired, I drew the machete and used it like a razor, drawing it carefully my left arm and then both legs and manged to remove most of the mud. To my delight, it did a fine job on my alpargatas, allowing me to walk without slipping. I was sweating from exertion. Thank goodness neither Epifanio nor the plantation foreman was here to witness the humiliating use I'd been forced to put the machete to.

Now, I desperately wanted to go home. From head to toe, I was wet, filthy and scared. Epifanio had told me, I remembered too late, that if I ever entered a newly-irrigated plantation, I had to keep to the ridges of dry earth that stretched along every row of plants. "Never ever get too close to the wet plot around the bole of the plant. The hammer handles are long," explained Epifanio, "not just because sometimes the plant is tall, but also so that you can brand a stalk from a relatively safe distance." He'd given me fair warning but I'd failed to take the caution on-board. I felt defeated and more than ever wanted to return to the comfort of the fonda. Two things prevented me. Firstly, I was almost certain that Epifanio had known that this plantation had just been irrigated. Secondly, the work of branding had to be undertaken. He was likely to be sitting in the cafe in the plaza, with an audience, waiting for me to appear caked from head to toe in what looked like excrement. My work-mates loved practical jokes, especially ones that could be shared simultaneously by lots of exultant onlookers and at the expense of the victim!

"Well, I thought, I can handle being jeered at but I can't live down not having completed the job! Epifanio and his chums may laugh at my filth but at least I'll have the satisfaction of having fulfilled my duty!" And so, wet, miserable and uncomfortable, I set about branding the piñas in that plantation, taking great care to keep to the dry edges and taking full advantage of the long hammer handles. Warm air circulated about the plantation as I worked and the mud began to cake on me before I'd finished.

A woman makes use of the remnants of irrigation water to do the family laundry. In desert conditions like those of Buenavista, water was a scarce and valuable commodity.

Task completed, back to the village I trudged, feeling relatively pleased with myself but braced for whatever I might meet. Sure enough, by the time I was within sight of the plaza, I could see Epifanio with a group of villagers sitting in wait for the spectacle. I stepped into the square as nonchalantly as I could, feeling like the Black Knight in full armour.

"How did it go, Orlando?"

"No problem at all, I said casually. All done! Here's the tally." His friends laughed as Epifanio shrank from the mud-caked banana I thrust at him with the number of Ps an Es cut by my thumb nail. First point to me.

"What happened to you?"

"What happened to me? Nothing"! I said innocently.

"The mud!"

"Mud?" I pretended surprise. "Oh, this little drop of mud? I suppose I must have slipped or something. I didn't even notice it! Can I buy you a cortado, Epifanio? Your friends too?" His planned joke at my expense wasn't going quite the way he'd expected. "Let me buy you and your friends a cortado!" I insisted. "Six cortados!"

A proud plantation worker gets ready to harvest a good-sized banana stalk.

The barman brought them and Epifanio's friends thanked me. Epifanio looked disconcerted. I drank my cortado most gratefully, shook dirty hands with Epifanio and his friends and turned to head across the road to the fonda. "Oh, by the way, I accidentally knocked over a banana trunk. Let the plantation manager know that I'll pay for it out of my wages." Epifanio's eyes were wide. Second point to me.

"He's a quick learner, is el Extranjero!" I heard Epifanio praise me to his friends. "It didn't take him long to figure out the ins and outs of this branding business! I'll bet he's learned to keep away from freshly irrigated soil, though!" I heard quiet laughter behind me. I didn't mind; I'd got the job done, survived, and, when all was said and done, Epifanio was indeed, a fine instructor!

Unseen, I slipped upstairs and showered, using far more than my daily quota of rationed water.

Our team from the packing station often collected banana stalks using this 1930s lorry.

16. Out of the mouths of babes

Carmita and Toño (Angélica's children); Mario and Caya (Lu-la's children); Ronald's young friends at the fonda, la Pension Méndez in la Plaza de los Remedios.

The Pension Méndez, known in the village simply as 'la fonda', combined all of the very best elements of all the many pensions I'd stayed in since entering Spanish territory. It stood fair and square on the north side of the plaza. From the street, with its two-tone ochre walls and its wide balcony on the second floor, it breathed old-world dignity. Like all traditional houses in the village, it kept its real beauty and its warmth, hidden and protected for the comfort of those inside.

The matriarch, Doña Lutgarda owned the fonda and ran it with the help of 'las chicas' – the girls – as she called her three handsome, hard-working daughters, Pastora, Obdúlia and Angélica, and Lula, her equally hard-working niece. Although Doña Lutgarda was probably only in her late forties, and las chicas in their twenties, they acted more grown-up than I felt and so I tended to treat them all with a distant respect. Angélica, the eldest, was a full-time mother and wife. She and her husband, Alfonso, had two sons, Fónfon about six and Toño 4, and a daughter, Carmita not yet three. Obdúlia, the middle daughter, was haughtily courting a young man from Buenavista. They were planning to marry late the following year. The youngest, Pastora, earnest and good-natured, was perhaps a year or two my elder. Their cousin Lula, cheerfully in her late twenties, had two children. Caya was nine and Mario, six. Lula's husband was working in Maracaibo in Venezuela and saving to send for his wife and children. All of the girls, with the exception of Odúlia's fiancé, lived as one big family together, in the fonda.

Because I was younger than las chicas, a paying guest, a solitary foreigner who initially mastered neither their language nor their customs – and a Protestant to boot – I was, at first, treated with a certain benign aloofness. Their attitude made me feel a tiny bit like a harmless unfortunate, a fugitive afflicted by multiple infirmities some of which, given effort on my part, might be overcome.

Aware of some at least of these shortcomings – my inability to communicate with ease and clarity being the most obvious – I'd made the decision, as soon as I'd decided to stay in the village, that I would overcome the linguistic barrier by learning Spanish. By mastering their language, I would be able show them that even if I were not wholly redeemable because of my failure to follow Rome, I posed no threat and might be worthy of their trust and eventually of their respect.

This wasn't the first time I'd come face to face with a communication challenge. In 1946, after the War, we moved from my grandmother's house in Coupar Angus to a council house in Dundee. I'd immediately been faced with living in a city alongside unfamiliar neighbours and noises, sights and smells, for the first time. I arrived from the country with a Scots-saturated vocabulary pronounced with a rural accent, whereas the city, and especially

Carmita trying hard to spot me use my 'second tongue'!

the Morgan Academy, insisted on ways of talking that were not entirely familiar to me. From daily experiences as a five-year-old, I'd learned that if I watched and listened, was willing to invest time, make the effort and adjust, we'd meet on terms fair to all. It was a matter of time, and time I had aplenty in Buenavista.

As is so often the case, it was the children with their wide-eyed curiosity, their unsullied trust and artless candour, who provided me with the first, timid stepping-stones. Caya, at nine, was ring-leader. Direct and comely like her mother Lula, Caya also possessed Lula's broad, confident smile and her ability to command.

"What are you doing, Don Orlando?" Caya's voice interrupts my train of thought as I sit reading on the upper terrace. I look up to see her open face framed by short, fair hair peering at the pages of the book in my hands. Just behind her, Mario, Fónfon, Toño and Carmita's bright eyes are eager for my response.

"I'm learning Spanish."

Caya turns to them with grave authority. "The Foreigner says he's learning Spanish." Their dark eyes widen.

"Your Spanish is not very good, is it?" Even at nine, she has learned to be condescending to those who don't measure up.

"No." I admit my shortcoming apologetically.

"Carmita!" Petite, sweet, dark curls, Carmita responds by stepping timidly from behind Caya's back. She stands twisting in embarrassment on one small, sun-tanned leg. "Say something to el Extranjero in Spanish!" Carmita puts a hand

Caya, Lula's daughter. She was amused that her three-year-old cousin Carmita could speak better Spanish than I could. Atop the mountains behind her is Teno Alto. It was down the precipitous path on these cliffs that I ran home to Buenavista to escape the Civil Guard.

to her mouth and looks down at the tiles, shy. "Say Platero!" Carmita changes legs and swings. "Say Platero, Carmita!" Caya insists.

"Platero es pequeño..." Carmita begins and stops. "Platero is small..."

"Go on!" urges Caya. "Go on, Carmita!" Fónfon and Toño urge Carmita to recite.

Carmita raises timid eyes, looks at me as if for support. I smile and nod. "Platero es pequeño, peludo, suave – Platero is small, fuzzy, gentle." She pauses. I nod and she continues. "Platero is so soft that you might think he was made of mere cotton, as if he didn't have a single bone in his entire body!"

I clap my hands in applause but Caya steps forward, keen to make her point, seeing that I've failed to capture it. "Carmita's only two-and-a-half!"

"I'll soon be three!" Carmita insists.

"Carmita's not quite three! And she can recite Platero!" Caya pauses meaningfully. "How old are you?"

"Much older!" When I'd previously been asked my age by Doña Lutgarda, I'd countered with, "How old do you think I am?" And she and the girls had made guesses, 20, 22, 21. I'd left it at that, aware that if I told them I'd recently turned 18, it would make me a runaway in their eyes.

"Carmita's three. She can recite Platero. She can speak Spanish. So why can't you speak Spanish if you're so much older than she is?" Caya's logic is impeccable.

All too aware now, of the conclusion that Caya is formulating in her nine-year-old mind by insisting that her baby cousin recite the opening line from Juan Ramón Jiménez' children's tale about the little donkey called Platero, and duly chastened by how poor my linguistic performance is compared to that of a three-year-old, I'm lost for words. I pause, attempting to cobble together a credible defence. In Spanish, the word for language is 'lengua'. Lengua also means 'tongue'.

"In my country, we use a different lengua – a different language", I begin.

"You use a different tongue!" Five pairs of eyes enlarge.

"Yes. My first tongue is Inglés. Spanish will be my second tongue. When I manage to learn it, that is!"

Mario, Lula's son.

"The Extranjero has one tongue already and his second will be Spanish!" Caya, wide-eyed, makes the announcement to her followers. She holds up two fingers. Points to my mouth.

"A second tongue!" The children look from one to the other, impressed, then wander off to play.

Later, I'm sitting on the terrace studying my Hugo's 'Spanish in Three months'. Lula smiles to me and begins pegging sheets to the line. The children are playing hide-and-seek, using the sheets for concealment and threatening to pull the neat line of sheets into disarray. Despite Lula's repeated warnings to go and play elsewhere, the children continue their game. Finally, in desperation, she shouts, "Go and ask the Extranjero to teach you something in English!"

Aware from her exasperated tone that Lula has reached the end of her tether, they approach me. Remembering how Juan Ramón Jiménez' words to describe Platero held a huge attraction for the children, I'm put in mind of many instances when our grandfather had hypnotized and amused Vivian, Euan and I with children's rhymes in Scots.

"Carmita, come and sit here between my knees." I make room for her.

"What are you going to teach us?"

Lula is relieved and grateful to have them out from under her feet. Carmita wiggles herself into the space I make on the tile ledge. I can feel the excitement in her tiny body and the other four crowd round expectantly. I grip Carmita's wrists and gently clap her tiny hands together, indicating that the others should so likewise keeping time with me. Then, exaggerating the rhythm of the rhyme to encourage their clapping, I begin:

"Jock Mackay, wi horseshoes fine,
Wid ye shoe this cuddy o' mine?
Aye, indeed man, that I can,
I'll dae't as weel as ony man!"

The rhythm of the rhyme and the comfort of repetitive clapping delight them and make it unnecessary to understand the words. They laugh uproariously. "Now me! Now me!" The two smaller children try to take Carmita's place between my knees but Carmita isn't going to budge! Used to being the baby of the family, alone all day while the others go to school, finally, she's found a special niche and refuses to surrender it. In appeal, she turns her little face up to mine.

"This is my place, isn't it, Don Orlando?"

"Of course this is your place, Carmita!" I reassure her and insist the others stand in front of me. To their noisy delight, we go through the verse again and again until they are all repeating the magical Scots rhyme from memory. Lula finishes hanging out the clothes and comes over, smiling. She too, is soon clapping and repeating along with us.

"Now for the second verse!"

"A second verse!" Their faces glow and their eyes sparkle. Carmita's slim brown wrists are warm in my fingers and her dark curls tickle my chin. The children hold their collective breath as I start the second verse, beginning slowly and exaggerating the rhythm as before.

"Pit a nail upon the tae," I make the forefinger of Carmita's right hand touch the tip of the fingers of her left. She is Jock Mackay, the blacksmith, driving a nail into the fore-edge of the horse's upturned hoof.

"Tae mak the cuddy spiel the brae," I make the fingers of her left hand climb from her right elbow to her wrist in short, cumbersome, movements to imitate the slow, ponderous plod of a cart-horse struggling up a hill. I pause for effect; they are all waiting, watching, listening to discover what's coming.

"Then pit a brod upon the heel," I make the forefinger of Carmita's right hand touch the heel of her left palm as if driving a brad into the rear edge of the horse's hoof.

"Tae mak the cuddy gallop weel, gallop weel, gallop weel!" I take her elbows and shunt them rapidly to give the impression of a well-shod, horse at a confident gallop.

There are gales of laughter and every elbow shuttles back and forward as fast as they are able.

"Again! Again!" And we go through the verses again and again while the children, and now Lula, repeat the Scots words and imitate Carmita's gestures. We are making so much noise that Pastora comes up from the courtyard below to see what is going on. She joins in and calls excitedly over the balustrade, "Angélica! Obdúlia! Mamá! Venganse! – Come up! The Foreigner's teaching us songs in a foreign tongue!" And rushing breathless up the stairs, come her mother and her sisters. We go through the rhyme and the motions many more times. They are as merry as the Wives of Windsor with grins from ear to ear.

"¡Ai! La cocina!" Doña Lutgarda rushes off to attend to a pot she'd left cooking on the stove.

A few short weeks after that incident, I was making great progress with the language. I could understand most of what the women in the fonda, my friends and workmates said to me. I could even tell Doña Lutgarda and the girls anecdotes about my excursions and daily exploits with el Maestro, Juan-the-Foreman, and the work-gang. Occasionally, inevitably, I would completely misunderstand the import of a question and give a totally unrelated response. They, and even the children who were always around, would laugh uproariously and take delight in pointing out my errors, to help me improve. Misunderstandings became fewer and fewer as my comprehension and my powers of expression grew.

Soon, I was being complimented on coping so well with the Spanish language, which they were convinced was the most difficult language in the world because, in their eyes, it was the richest.

To prove, beyond any shadow of doubt, that Spanish was the richest, they would point to a nearby household object. "What's that in your language?" "Bucket," I'd say. They would exchange superior looks. "See! You have one word for that, but in our language, Spanish, we have lots of synonyms," and they would begin to recite, "cubo, balde, cubeño, cubeta." Then they'd wave their arms amply to give the impression that they could recite a further half-dozen synonyms if only they cared to. There was little point in my listing the several English synonyms for bucket. They had firmly made their minds up that Spanish was undoubtedly the richest language in the entire world. Anything I might say was not going to change their opinion.

One evening I came back from work, mounted the stairs that led from the interior courtyard to the upper level and heard childish laughter coming from my room, which stood permanently open. Surprised, I stepped inside and found all five children going through the many pockets in my well-worn, ex-army rucksack. They froze instantly, alarm on their faces, as if caught in the act of some grievous transgression.

"¡Hola!" I greeted them cheerfully but they shuffled their feet in guilty silence, eyes down-cast. "What are you up to?" I was curious.

"Nothing!"

"Are you looking for something?" I tried to sound reassuring. If I happened to be at home, they sometimes came to my room to play, especially if it was raining outside. Sometimes Carmita, Mario and Fónfon would rush in wanting to show me a lesson they'd completed that day in school. Or Carmita, from time to time, might bring me her coveted bottle top collection, to surprise me by how much it had grown since the previous showing. Dark eyes shining, she'd proudly present the most recent caps that the bus-driver and conductor had collected, from the bars in the small towns along their route from the capital to Buenavista.

It is evident from the children's uneasy silence that I'm not going to get an answer and so I pick my old, olive-green rucksack off the floor, web straps undone, dangling. "What would you like to see?" I have very little in the way of possessions and nothing at all of value, except my passport and a camera I use only occasionally because the cost of 35 mm film is exorbitant. But my question only serves to bring a tiny quiver to Carmita's lower lip and I realize that, if I am to avoid tears, I must persuade the children that I'm not angry.

"Don't worry! I'm not annoyed. I'm just curious." Relief floods their faces. "I've already shown you everything I have, but if you really want me to, I'll show it all to you again." I offer an encouraging smile.

They stand in line, silent, the younger children eyeing Caya. They're willing her to speak for them all. Caya's young face takes on an almost-adult seriousness.

"Do you remember that day you told us that you were going to get Spanish to be your second tongue?" I nod. "My grandmother says you've now acquired that second tongue." She pauses. I'm trying to follow her gist. I smile encouragement. "Well, now that you've got your second tongue, we're searching everywhere to find out where you keep your first one."

Four little heads nod, signalling sober agreement, eyes bright with contrition now that they've been assured my forgiveness. "We only want to look at it!" Fónfon's eyes are enormously large, dark. "We want to see what your first tongue looks like." Carmita's face glows with anticipation. Caya, at nine, is already more pragmatic. "You won't tell mamá, will you?" First things first.

Their literal interpretation of what they believe it takes to be bilingual leaves me in awe. Substitute tongues that can be slipped into place with a simple click to meet the linguistic demands of the moment. Oh, that it were so easy! But how to reveal to young minds that the fix doesn't lie with replaceable anatomy? I'm hopelessly lost for words. It's still well beyond my linguistic capacity to explain how the single Spanish word 'lengua' serves two completely different purposes. One refers to the system of sounds and words we use to communicate with family and friends; the other to the pliable muscle we use to taste, or mould, point, curve and infinitely flex to create the sounds that express what we feel and allow others to understand us.

"Of course I'm not going to tell your mamás!" It's all I can think to say. For now, it's all they want to hear. Off they troop, one after the other with grateful looks but without the understanding I would like to have shared with them. Their years are too tender to disappoint them with stark facts about how demanding some of life's many challenges will turn out to be.

"Before I leave," I make a solemn promise to myself and to them. "I will learn enough Spanish to explain clearly what it means to possess a first and to master a second language."

17. Eight arms are better than two

Juan and the author are beneath the wave, battling the octopus!

"Today, we're going to hunt octopus!" Juan-the-Foreman, wearing his usual worried look, came striding into the courtyard of the fonda just as I was finishing breakfast, early one Saturday morning. "You'll need one of these!" He showed me a knife with a foot-long blade, protected in a sheath woven from dried banana leaves. I wondered if I too, should be worried.

Doña Lutgarda, smiling, popped her grey head through the opening in the wall that separated the kitchen from the court-yard, "¡Buenos días, Juan! I'll lend Orlando one of my kitchen knives!" A moment later, she reappeared, brandishing an even larger knife than Juan's. "Be sure to bring enough octopus back so I can fill the large cauldron!" To cook octopus, she liked to use a huge black cast-iron kettle that I had christened 'the cauldron'. At home, in Coupar Angus, my grandmother had both kettle and cauldron just like it. She used to hang these on the 'swey', a moveable iron bar with a hook and chain that allowed the kitchen fire, called the 'range', to be used for cooking. Doña Lutgarda handed me the blade wrapped in a kitchen towel. "Bring it back in good condition!"

Since building the plantation and setting dynamite charges under Juan's direction, he and I had remained friends. On days when neither of us was working, we'd go on excursions together. He lived near Los Silos, but came to Buenavista regularly to visit his fiancée. I gathered that his future father-in-law was planning to build a banana plantation and Juan was gaining a broad range of work experience so that, in due course, he could take over its management.

I'd become used to the pattern that the friendships I was making were all one-to-one. Being the friend of someone did not result in being introduced to their friends or their families or even learning where they lived or being invited to their home. A friendship was conducted in public, at least with el Extranjero, and centred around the plaza or on walking excursions to show me something the friend thought I would find interesting. I'd gained a reputation for being inquisitive about the region, interested in everything, and a tireless walker. That last quality was important because virtually all excursions, at least those on land, involved walking, often for very long distances and usually over rough terrain. Hunting octopus, however, struck me as a new adventure; and one conducted at sea.

"Won't all the fishermen have already left?" I knew from experience that on days they went to sea, the local fishermen invariably left the village around 4 a.m. to walk together to the cove. Nobody in the village, it seemed, enjoyed walking alone past the Campo Santo, the isolated graveyard that lay half-way to the coast.

Juan and Doña Lutgarda both laughed. "You don't use a boat to go after octopus! Octopus in the ocean are too big to tackle. The ones you will hunt are about this size," she held her hands about two feet apart. "But even these are powerful enough to be dangerous, so take great care!"

Although I had no clear idea about how we were going to tackle octopus two feet long, especially with knives almost as long as the prey, I felt that I was going to enjoy this escapade. Like all of my village friends, Juan had a wide range of skills and knew exactly how to employ them so as to reduce the risk of danger to life or limb. Experience told me that I could have confidence in virtually anything Juan, or any of my friends, suggested and my role was to listen and learn from their expertise.

As we walked through the lower village towards the dry plain that separated it from the ocean, Juan explained our tactics. "When you go hunting octopus, Orlando, you must go in pairs for safety's sake." I nodded even though I couldn't quite imagine the nature of the danger presented by a mere two-foot-long predatory mollusc. "When we get to the beach, the tide will be out."

"The beach? I'd no idea there was a beach!"

"There is, but it's only used in summer. Nobody goes swimming in the sea except during the school holidays. For one thing, the water's too cold, and for another, the sand only arrives in summer."

"Sand arrives in summer?" I had visions of el Bachillér carting loads of white sand in his lorry.

"When the sea gets rough before winter, the tides strip the sand off the beach. In spring, the tides change and wash the sand back again, so that during the summer holidays we have a beautiful black beach!" I looked sideways at Juan to see if he was pulling my leg, but his face was serious. I decided to leave to one side the existence of a beach, the vagaries of the tides, the black sand, its odd behaviour throughout the year, and focus for the moment on the task at hand – hunting octopus.

"So we have to hunt together?"

"Right! What we'll do is strip off our shirts and trousers and leave them safely on dry land. We keep our rope-soled sandals on so our feet can have a firm grip on the basalt. Then we'll wade out to the rocks that are underwater even at low tide and search for octopus in the crannies."

"We'll be able to see them?"

"Oh, we'll see them alright! They'll be hunting prey. As soon as they see us they'll take refuge in the cracks among the rocks. We don't want to go in deeper than our chests because we mustn't lose our balance in the backwash, which can be quite strong." I was beginning to appreciate that hunting octopus might just be a challenge!

Juan continued. "You put your head into the water and when you see an octopus hiding in a crevice, you extend your left hand towards it. The beast will immediately take hold of your left hand and arm with two or three of its tentacles. Then you give a sharp tug so as to dislodge it from its cranny." In my mind, I was now fighting this under-water battle. "With your knife in your right hand, you stab the octopus in the head while it's clinging to your left arm." Juan was miming each act in sequence, face serious.

"And the octopus will die right away?"

"Only if you manage to get the blade of the knife through one of its eyes and out the back of its head! Wriggling the knife about inside its head can also help to makes sure it dies quickly."

"What if it doesn't die?"

"Ah! Then you have a problem!" Juan looked at me seriously. I was beginning to feel uneasy. "That's why we have to work as a pair. You see, if the octopus gets angry – "

"If? It's sure to get angry if you poke a kitchen knife through its eye!"

"Of course!" Juan agreed. "It will get very angry and try to grab your right hand too, with its remaining tentacles."

"So now it has both my arms in its eight?"

"That's a possibility!"

"So it's as if I had a pair of handcuffs around my wrists? And I'm up to my chest in seething backwash?"

"Right! And the harder you try to free yourself, the tighter the octopus grips you."

"I'm getting the picture, Juan!"

"If you panic and lose your balance, you'll topple over into the water and drown!" Juan's face took on a super-serious look.

"That's where you come to my rescue?"

"Exactly! Or you come to mine! If the octopus gets both my arms, then you take your knife, put it between my arms and draw it steadily towards my hands severing its tentacles as you go. Simple!"

It sounded far from simple. "I'm glad that Doña Lutgarda gave me her sharpest knife!" Seldom was I successful in expressing irony in Spanish. Juan simply nodded to acknowledge that the knife had to be sharp, otherwise...!

"Here's the beach!" Juan gestured to a rock-strewn foreshore that possessed none of the qualities that I associated with a beach. It was low-tide. Great shelves of crenelated rock could be seen above the surface of the sea. Waves broke over these and the backwash seethed ferociously. It would take me all my time to keep my balance even in my rope-soled sandals.

We stripped off and, with knives in our right hands, waded into the sea, wincing at the chill. The first wave hit my chest and left me breathless. Juan got to the first shelf of rock that looked for all the world like liquorice toffee that had been incinerated into a lump of porous cinder. "The good thing about the coastal lava-rocks here," I thought to myself, "is that their porosity makes them easy to grip onto, not at all like the slippery rocks I'm used to in Carnoustie or East Haven on the white-capped, forbidding North Sea." My rope-soled alpargatas gave me a reassuringly firm grip.

We were in above our waists now. Juan crouched down, head under water. He withdrew his dripping head. "I see one!" I put my head under the surface. There was a sizeable octopus glaring at us from enormous eyes, backing itself into a crevice in the lava. Octopus, Juan had explained to me, have no bones in their bodies and so can squeeze themselves into incredibly narrow spaces. As I watched, Juan offered it his left hand. As soon as it grabbed his arm with three of its tentacles, he tugged and straightened up at the same time so the upper half of his body was above the surface so he could breathe again. The octopus, two feet long, was clinging to his left hand and arm, its remaining five tentacles searching wildly for purchase on any part of Juan's anatomy.

"Now watch!" He drew the knife in his right hand towards its head and, avoiding the free tentacles, deftly rammed the blade deep into its eye and twisted. The octopus's free tentacles cartwheeled in frenzy and then went limp. He returned into shallower water and prized the tentacles off his left arm with difficulty. The suckers left red weals around his forearm. He grinned at me. "See? That's how it's done! Easy! Now it's your turn!"

How could I refuse?

I approached a shelf of rock where the backwash appeared to suck with least malevolence. At less than 140 lbs, it wouldn't take much to unbalance me. Much as I trusted Juan, I didn't fancy his brandishing a sharp, two-foot blade close to my body while the sea and an eight-armed monster did their best to drown me.

I copied Juan's technique, wading in above my waist, inclining my face into the water to find a suitable victim. Even without a face-mask, the sea was perfectly transparent and I could see all sorts of fish and crabs going about their business, seemingly oblivious to me. Then I spotted a purple-red octopus swimming away from me towards the rocks. Juan had warned me to wait until it settled in a crevice and was at rest. "If you grasp a swimming octopus, it allows the beast too much freedom. It can turn on you and grasp whatever parts of you it wants!" As soon as this one settled and was staring at me with malevolent black eyes, I stretched my left arm out. Without warning, the beast grabbed my hand and arm tightly with several tentacles. I'd entered the battle. It crossed my mind that this is how Beowulf must have felt as he pursued Grendel!

I tugged but couldn't dislodge the beast. I tugged harder, still without success. Then I had to come up for air, my left arm still captive beneath the surface. Juan nodded encouragement. A deep breath and down I went again. The creature had wedged itself deeper into the crevice and now managed to add another tentacle to my arm. I could feel the tide surging in and came up for air once more. The water was now up to my chin. I had to kill this monster before the tide rose any higher. I could try to release myself by slashing its tentacles but that would put my right arm in danger of being seized. My life would be in Juan's, or worse, in the monster's, hands.

Juan had, however, anticipated the danger and was right beside me. He moved quickly and stuck his knife deep into the crevice where the octopus was wedged. There was a powerful tug on my arm and the tentacles tightened their grip. The backwash now threatened to pull me off balance. I raised my head, managed another watery breath and sank back down to see what was happening. The octopus had one long tentacle around Juan's right arm that held the knife. Quickly he snatched the knife with his left hand and cut that tentacle off. Then he switched hands again and twisted the blade deep into the crevice. Fearful now, I tugged. My head searched for air. The entire creature, minus the severed tentacle, came free. It dangled lifeless from my arms like some malignant homunculus. I lurched into shallower water, the backwash sucking at my heels.

"That's a big one! Juan helped me prise the suckers of its remaining seven tentacles off my arms. "It's over three feet! I told you to go for the ones under two!"

"It looked smaller in the water," I gasped. The monster's head was like a big, wet, leather bag; its beak, vicious, predatory.

We placed this prize, minus a couple of feet of its eighth tentacle, onto the rock alongside the first one. "Have you had enough?" Juan asked me, worried.

"We don't have enough yet to fill the cauldron! Doña Lutgarda is counting on us." I didn't want our first hunt to end just because I'd lacked the experience to make sure my prey was of a size I could manage easily. I didn't want that to be part of the story. Also, I needed to come to terms with the panic I'd felt by learning the technique of the hunt better. So we continued for another hour and this turned out to be the right decision. My heart stopped pounding and we managed to catch and kill another half-dozen smaller octopus. We learned to work comfortably and confidently together, developing a firm bond of trust, each in the other.

Later, when we reached the narrow, walled streets of the village, we were constantly stopped. "What have you got there?" We'd open our sacks and display the purply mass of heads, huge eyes and thick, suckered tentacles. "¡Hombre! There's a good catch!" Juan and I nodded soberly, conscious of the distinctive, red sucker marks that tattooed our arms.

The women were thrilled. "So many!" Doña Lutgarda set about cleaning the strangely beautiful beasts, using coarse sea-salt to remove the slippery gel that coated them.

"Look at this one!" The girls crowded round their mother to admire the creature that had given me so much trouble. "It's huge! It's going to need a cook-pot all to itself! But it only has seven tentacles!"

"Juan!" Doña Lutgarda addressed him accusingly. "It's dangerous to hunt after a beast as big and strong as this one! Where's your common sense?" Juan looked appropriately guilty. "I'm glad to know that even if you don't, at least Orlando has the good sense to hunt the smaller ones! You always were a wild one Juan! You're going to be a married man soon. You must take care of yourself! What if you'd drowned?" She shook her head in despair.

"I told Juan the very same thing, Doña Lutgarda! He has to be more prudent" Juan avoided my eye.

Word quickly circulated around the village that Doña Lutgarda had made a cauldron of delicious stewed octopus. That evening, a message arrived from the spokesman of the plantation foremen who gathered on Sundays. "Please reserve 10 large portions of octopus stew for our dinner tomorrow."

The following evening, I watched discreetly from behind the flowers on the gallery overlooking the courtyard as the contented plantation foremen swabbed their empty plates with bread, scraped back their chairs, tuned their guitars and called for more white wine. "Doña Lutgarda, that's the best octopus you've ever made! Tell whoever brought you this lot to make sure and bring you more. And soon!"

I was lulled to sleep by their music and cordial conversation.

Buenavista's streets were made for more liesurely travel.

18. The Deserted Village of Teno Bajo

Francisco-el-Diablo and his first hand. They could handle their coble in the worst of seas. They always rowed standing up for better control in the huge waves.

Since the day Pepe Mendibles had pointed across the waves to the blur of red desert, that lay cut off by sea and mountains from the rest of the island, I'd been determined to visit the ghost-village of Teno Bajo. However, when the subject of my making that visit came up in the court-yard of the fonda, Pastora and Lula tried to dissuade me.

"Why would you want to go there, Orlando? There's nothing there except smelly goats and cactus and desert!"

Doña Lutgarda, however, was more encouraging. "You like to see strange places and meet unusual people, Orlando. There are few places like Teno Bajo and fewer folks like Daniel and María. The easiest way to get there is by falúa with Sebastian from Los Silos. He could take you to the lighthouse. Teno Bajo is just a few kilometres' walk across the desert from there."

"I'd thought of that," I told her, "but Sebastian-de-la-Falúa tells me he'll only be making the trip to the lighthouse on Sunday – there and back the same day. I want to visit Teno Bajo next Wednesday, walk from there to the lighthouse and then stay there three nights with the keeper and his family. I plan to return on Sunday."

"Then you're out of luck!" Pastora and Lula looked relieved.

"I've heard that there's a path over the mountains." Three appalled faces looked at me.

"It's hardly a path. You could easily get yourself lost up there. Especially if the clouds roll in from the ocean!" Pastora and Lula were determined to discourage me.

181

Doña Lutgarda's reaction was more measured. "Over the tops of the mountains?" She shook her head. "That's a route you should first try with someone from up there who knows it well. It's dangerous. The people who live up on the tops know their way about, but folks like us from the village have neither their eyes nor their sure-footedness." I was flattered to be included in 'folks like us from the village'.

"There's still another way to get to Teno Bajo," Doña Lutgarda continued. "Have one of the fishermen row you to El Callao de Márquez and put you off at the great flat rock there. When the tide's right it can be done."

So I made inquiries. The only fisherman willing to land me at El Callao de Márquez was Francisco el Diablo – Francisco the Devil, so called for his fearless risk-taking. He dared to put to sea on days when more cautious fishermen preferred to cast their cane rods from the safety of the rocks. "Meet me at the cove before dawn on Wednesday!"

It was past dawn now, but the black vertical cliffs filled the sky, shutting out all trace of the sun as Francisco-the-Devil rowed south-west. I was paying Francisco and his first-hand for their services. A modest sum, but as a consequence, they felt obliged to give me the grand tour.

"Look! La Punta del Fraile – the Friar's Point!" I turned and followed Francisco's eyes to the highest point on the massive cliff wall perhaps 1,000 feet above us. "At night, la Dama Blanca – the White Lady – tries to lure boatmen to her but they never make the shore alive. They get sucked onto las Rocas del Fraile – the jagged Friar's Rocks – before they know what's happening." We were approaching ragged fangs of lava that reared like sharks' snouts to snatch great watery bites from the wind-whipped waves that ploughed relentlessly into them.

My eyes shifted from the top of the cliffs where I imagined I could make out, against the sky, the figure of the solitary, pale-robed Lady, seducing hapless victims onto the Friar's spellbinding rocks. As a wall of water approached, the Friar's Rocks slowly submerged as if of their own accord and then equally slowly re-emerged, wild foam spuming from their cracked teeth. Like loose hair in a hurricane, the backwash flowed off them to reveal their hypnotic savagery. I clutched the prow thwart with nothing at all to hamper my view. The constantly repeated sight thrilled me as we drew closer and closer.

Suddenly, Francis the Devil let out a great shriek that bolted me upright. He rowed standing up, facing the direction we were heading in. I could see the flashing whites of his eyes and a look of utter rapture on his dark, stubbled face. For a brief stomach-turning moment, I felt panic; he was taking us straight into the maw of those ravenous fangs. I glanced at his first-hand. He was sitting in the stern with a tight smile on his face, judging the wave that was carrying us to the rocks and measuring every calculated movement of Francisco's long oars. This told me all I needed to know. He'd seen this joust with death more than once and had survived. Francisco let out another maniacal cry and at the very instant before the wave would upturn us onto the serried teeth to be ripped apart, his oars, like wands, created magic. They swung us into the backwash and away to seaward. Down, down, down, then up-and-over a 15-foot wave leaving the Friar and his ravenous rocks cheated and furious.

"What do you think, Foreigner?" Francisco screamed maniacally over the roar of the crashing waves. "Mess yourself, did you?" I forced a grin. Now I understood why he was reputed to have difficulty finding a partner to fish with. The odd thing was that I had not been truly frightened. The massive form and sheer power of these living, moving walls of green water swallowing and regurgitating the rapacious bayonet-like rocks truly awed me but I'd seen enough Canarios in action, in many and varied settings and knew the consummate skills they possessed. I knew too, that they valued life too much to cast it all away on the Friar's Rocks for fun.

Francisco el Diablo was Tamburlaine, and his primal howl was the expression of a feeling he lacked the talent to put into words:

"I hold the Fates fast-bound in iron chains
And with my hand turn Fortune's wheel about!"

"Sooner shall the sun fall from his sphere," I considered as he mightily pulled us through the waves towards el Callao de Márquez, "than a combatant like Francisco the Devil be overcome!"

There was only a single spot on el Callao de Márquez – the Beach of Boulders – where Francisco could put me off, and although it was a hazardous undertaking, it was child's play compared to Francisco's dance of death in the arms of the Friar's Rocks. I made the leap with split-second timing from the boat to the flat bench of rock. Francisco and his first-hand, well-pleased with themselves – and with me too presumably since I hadn't fouled the thwart – dragged themselves back into the unending green waves to repeatedly disappear. Each reappearance took them further and further away.

With care, I made my way from the shelf of rock I'd leaped onto, along a narrow lava catwalk and eventually to the boulder-strewn beach, grateful for the secure grip that my tight-fitting, rope-sold alpargatas afforded me. As I passed one spot on the beach, I noticed that the rocks had been cleared to one side and the black sand heaped in long, low banks – a sure sign that someone was living in this barren region. I looked at the patterns that whoever it was had taken such time and care to create, trying to figure out why and for what. By now, the sun was hot and the air heavy with the sharp, briny smell of iodine. It brought to mind the long, golden-brown ribbons of leathery seaweed, 'dulse' we called it, that as children, we happily dragged from the sea at East Haven to see whose was longest.

Daniel and Maria's son-in-law with one of their herds of goats. They made cheese and traded that, and goat meat, to residents of Teno Alto who passed them on for sale in Buenavista del Norte.

There's always something disconcerting, even slightly menacing, about finding traces of human enterprise in unexpected places and whose purpose you are unable to fathom. It's as if we possess an instinct for suspicion until, with a flash of insight, the uncertainty is banished and we experience the comfort of understanding. I sniffed again and examined the banks and the pools of seawater behind them, in different stages of evaporation. "Someone's using the power of the sun to crystallise salt!"

Instantly reassured, I now recognized the patterns of years of work. Shallow trenches dug to allow sea water into slight depressions in the sand at high-tide. Simple banks to prevent the water from draining back out. The sun and the process of evaporation would do the rest. Yes! Here was a pool now dried-up and full of blinding-white frost. I put one delicate shard on my tongue. The antiseptic gratification signalled its life-sustaining authority. Where but here could sea-salt be more pristine? I took care not to breach the simple technology, and with my back

184

to the sea, set out into the red slice of desert closely hemmed in by a crescent of blue mountains with deep, dark, crevasses, permanently sunless.

With each step, my rope-soled sandals sent up puffy coils of red dust as if I trod an elevated carpet of smoke. There was no path, no sign that any foot before mine had trodden the red ground. When I breathed deeply I could smell brine, the astringent aroma of cactus in flower and the warm, acrid stench of goats. Soon I could hear them. The hollow tinkle of the lead-billy that kept the flock together; the pathetic bleating of the herd. When I suddenly appeared through the scrub and cactus they stopped, silent but assured, regarding me with inquiring eyes. "You are the interloper," they seemed to accuse, "and we'll stand here eye-to-eye until you give us a full and satisfactory explanation for your presence!" The penetrating look of a bearded billy-goat with its head cocked slightly to one side is as eloquent and as intimidating as that of a pretentious maître d' in an upscale restaurant.

"I'm here to visit Daniel at the ghost village of Teno Bajo. Which way should I go?" The billy, with his curling, ribbed horns and uncanny Satanic eyes, didn't deign to respond. Nor would any of his followers dare to speak out of turn. "Fine! If you don't feel it's your duty to help a weary traveller, I'm simply going to go in the direction I see you're coming from. You've probably just been freed from your corral and surely that can't be far from Daniel's house." Silently, they turned heads to watch me follow their tell-tale compact prints, delicate as almonds in the dust. Soon I'd left the hollow rattle of Satan's tin clapper behind.

The stench of goat became stronger and, sure enough, I came on an extensive collection of corrals made of driftwood, dried branches and tubes of dried cactus piled to form prickly walls. They were roofed with branches and thatched with dried leaves to give dappled shade. I stopped and looked around. Red desert; the muted greens of different kinds of cactus; the constant rasping of contented crickets. The sun now beat down fiercely. The shade within the maze of corrals looked inviting. I stepped gratefully into its coolness. Hanging on rails under the thatch were dozens of goat skins, all scraped clean but in different stages of curing. There were sets of mule harness that looked as desiccated as old skeleton bones. I was puzzled by a set of small, kid-shaped pouches from which the outer hairs had been shaved and the holes at what had been the neck and the fore-legs tightly tied and plugged with wooden dowels, to leave but a single opening at the rear end. Strips of hide from the back legs were pleated together to make the rudimentary loop by which these bag-like objects hung from a pole in the shade.

Wondering if they might be the makings of a primitive bagpipe,

I took a step closer to examine them. The Gallegos, in the north-west of the Peninsula, still played a single-drone bagpipe. Some sixth sense told me I was being watched and I turned to see a young man in his mid-twenties standing no more than a metre from me. He had an easy, open smile on his dark, tanned face. I flinched involuntarily. His arrival had been unheralded. Moreover, I'd expected to see a much older man.

"Daniel?"

"Soy Manolo. Daniel's son-in-law." We shook hands. I'd been led to believe that Daniel and María were the only inhabitants of the ghost village.

"What is that object?" I pointed to the bag made from a goatskin.

"It's a zurrón." Daniel unhooked one and handed it to me. "Feel it!" It felt like the chamois leather we used to clean windows in Scotland. Dry, it was like thin cardboard; wet, it turned into a slippery mass from which most of the water could be wrung and then used to polish window-glass.

"What's it for?"

Manolo looked puzzled. "It's a zurrón!" As if the word explained its use.

"A zurrón?"

"We make them. Small zurrónes from day-old kids, useful for a single person, but sometimes larger ones, big enough for a family." I was at a total loss. I had absolutely no idea what a single person, let alone a family would do with a little empty bag made from the skin of a baby goat.

"And what does a person do with a zurrón?"

"¡Amasar, por supeusto!" He gave me a pained look that suggested I was being intentionally obtuse. "Amasar, of course!" I had never heard the verb 'amasar' before and so was none the wiser. To take an interest in his goats would be more productive, I decided; the meaning of 'amasar' could wait. He and his wife, Daniel and Maria's daughter, kept several flocks, he told me. Each had its own billy-goat and each flock had been so managed over the years that it kept faithfully to its own distinct area. No only did the practice avoid fighting among the billies, it made fences unnecessary. I'd seen Scottish shepherds in the Highlands manage their flocks in the same way. They called the practice 'hefting' and the area grazed by a single flock, its 'heft'.

"You already introduced yourself to the billy of our northern flock." So Manolo had been silently observing me ever since I landed! In such an isolated place, even a rowing boat out at sea was an event with human overtones. "Another flock grazes closer to the foot of the mountains and the southern flock wanders as far as the lighthouse." He pointed first south-east and then south-west.

"What do you do with so many goats?" I gestured to the desert plain, not a habitation in sight.

His eyes were telling me that my questions puzzled. "We sell them, of course!"

I looked around meaningfully, "Sell them?" He nodded. My silent appeal for an explanation, was lost on Manolo so I was forced to be explicit. "Who do you sell them to?"

"To our neighbours in Teno Alto." He gestured upwards in the direction of the mountains. White clouds were massaging their tops, trickling into their ravines. "There's better grazing up on top, so the people can keep sheep and even the occasional cow. Now goats!" His tone suggested he loved them. "Goats are not so fussy. So, down here in the desert, we breed our nannies, wean the kids, milk the lactating nannies and make cheese. When those from up there," he jerked his thumb back up towards the clouds, "come down here, we kill the billy-kids. Our neighbours can then go back to Teno Alto with fresh goat meat and kebbucks of cheese." His tone said that my request for such self-evident facts put my mental powers in question.

"Is it far to Teno Alto?"

"It's not far but the track up this side of the mountains is tricky. It's far trickier than the more frequently used track down to Buenavista on the other side." I was interested in knowing more. Manolo obliged. "From here to the foot of the mountains, it's easy going, but the rock up this side, all the way to the top is soft in places, like sand. If your foot slips, it's a long way down into one of the ravines. There's nothing to break your fall except prickly cactus full of long spines. Get these broken off into your body and they're impossible to get out." I shuddered at the thought. Manolo, seeing my reaction, warmed to his tale. "A broken spine can circulate round and round in your body. Then one day, it goes through your heart!" Dramatically, he clutched his chest in mock pain, closed his eyes and let his head sink slowly onto his breast. Though I doubted the accuracy of his explanation, I got his point: At all costs, avoid falling onto the spines of a cactus plant!

A young woman appeared silently and inexplicably at Manolo's side and clutched his hand. She was dressed identically to her husband, dark from the sun, and if it hadn't been for her impressively comely looks, she might have been his brother. "My wife, Carmen." She offered me a hand that was as broad and calloused as her husband's. She stood there looking at me as if expecting an announcement from the outside world. I began to explain who I was but they stopped me. They knew all about me, how long I'd lived in the village, the jobs I'd held, and how I had recently helped Pepe Mendibles install windows in the lighthouse. I was at a loss to know what to tell them that they didn't already know.

"Tell us about where you come from!" And so, I summarised the similarities and differences between what it was like to live in the village of Coupar Angus in east-central Scotland and Buenavista del Norte in Las Canarias. They listened intently to the similarities in modest rural conditions and on the farms where I'd harvested oats and barley and fresh green peas. How the entire pea-plant, roots, stalks, leaves pods and all were tumbled whole into one end of a mechanical viner, and shaken about. How then, from one spout at the other end of the machine, came a shower of shiny, sweet, green peas and, quite separately from an adjoining spout, a continuous belt of bruised waste that included the empty pods, the 'shuch' in Scots, much sought after by farmers to feed to pigs. Both wanted to know the details of how the separation was accomplished. Fortunately, I'd often watched mechanics repair pea-viners right there in the farm-yard and was able to give them a graphic, if not an accurate explanation. They listened, enthralled.

Manolo and Carmen walked me round the goat pens. They showed me the harnesses and explained that they were from an earlier time when the village had been populated and the plain irrigated for crops. They were a happy, friendly couple, delighted to have their casual routine interrupted by a visitor whose experiences were so different from and yet so similar to their own.

"There's Teno Bajo!" I followed Manolo's finger and saw old, low adobe houses with ochre walls and broken tiled roofs the same red colour as the surrounding desert. The houses were scattered like desiccated crab shells on a beach. In places, the large adobe blocks had cracked and yielded to searing sun and occasional showers of rain to expose the mixture of animal manure and straw they'd been formed from. I pulled a yellow straw from one and it came away easily in my hand with a puff of smoke-like dust that smelled of hard work, human devotion and baked history. I stood in silence, trying to imagine what Teno Bajo must have looked like, what it sounded like, when it was a thriving community.

"What happened?" Manolo and Carmen looked at each other and shrugged. Another of el Extranjero's odd questions! "People moved away. The aquifer at the foot of the mountains went dry. There was work for wages in other parts of the island, in Cuba, and in Mexico. People here had little. They wanted more." They looked at each other and shrugged again.

"And you?"

"Us? We live here!" They looked at me as if waiting for an explanation that might tell them why I asked such an obvious question. When I could think of nothing because their simple answer had said it all, I nodded. "You live here!" They looked at each other and smiled. It was obvious that they were happy together. They couldn't imagine more than they already had.

One house stood out from the compact cluster. It was grand, two stories with a red-tiled roof. It looked as if it had been built on a corner because its two wings met at an oblique angle. Set in the intersection was a nail-studded, wooden door and above it an equally-weathered wooden balcony with double French-doors. On the balcony's wide balustrade stood a series of unmatched earthenware pots and from them tumbled geraniums so scarlet that the desert itself was outdone. I stared in amazement. The green leaves and glorious blossoms told of care and love and water.

"My father and mother live there!" As if on cue, the double doors were thrown open and a smiling man and woman stepped onto the balcony. If they had broken into the courtly duet from Federico Torroba's popular operetta 'Luisa Fernanda', it wouldn't have surprised me in the least.

CAROLINA
Caballero del alto plumero,
¿Dónde camina tan pinturero?
Los caminos que van a la gloria
son para andarlos con parsimonia.
JAVIER
Señorita que riega la albahaca,
¿Cuántas hojitas tiene la mata?.
Me parece que pasan de ciento,
como las plumas de mi plumero.
CAROLINA
Sir! You with the fine cockatoo in your hat,
Where are you off to, so gallantly dressed?
All roads to glory
must be ridden with care.
JAVIER
You, fine lady, who waters the geraniums,
How many leaves are there on your plant?
More than a hundred, I'd guess,
like the plumes in my cockatoo.

"¡El Extranjero! ¡Bienvenido! – Welcome!" That Daniel and María, neither of whom I had ever seen and neither of whom could have known I was coming that day, recognised who I was, came as no surprise to me. I was constantly being surprised that there were no surprises! Although I liked to imagine I'd learned a great deal about the life of my adopted village and its surroundings and flattered myself that I might be becoming one of them, there were dimensions to their lives and how they related to and communicated with one another that I couldn't even begin to imagine. Because I floated comfortably on the surface, I was encouraging myself to believe that I was swimming with equals, but in reality, I was still bobbing about in the shallow end, blissfully unaware of the hidden depths within the life of Buenavista and its surroundings.

Daniel, the guardian of the abandoned village of Teno Bajo.
Behind him are the mountains I had to run across to escape from
the Civil Guard after we used dynamite to 'catch' fish!

Daniel, a good-looking, weather-beaten man in his fifties, wearing khaki trousers and a French-blue shirt, now emerged from the lower front door, cramming a time-worn straw hat onto his head. He shook my hand warmly.

"José el Farolero told me you would come to visit." Daniel for one, I noticed, had taken José's suggestion about his nick-name seriously. He used that preferred by José – 'José-the-lighthouse-keeper'. "María will make us coffee. While the water boils, let me show you my salt-pans. Manolo told me that he'd seen you examining them." So I was right! Manolo had been watching me since the moment Francisco rowed the coble into sight round Friar's Point!

Daniel traced with his outstretched hand the maze of salt-pans he'd created. He'd been working them for many years. He regularly sent bags of salt up into the mountains as well as to Los Silos with the falúa. He loved the isolated desert plain of Teno and knew intimately every

190

square inch of the red land and everything that lived on it, flora and fauna. He pointed out different kinds of cactus to me.

Not long after I'd arrived in Buenavista, Juan-the-Foreman had shown me how to eat 'tunas' – prickly-pears. He'd taken me to see el Cardón, the giant cardón cactus that had grown since time immemorial in El Rincón and the Drago Milenario, – the Dragon Tree, – in the village of Icod de los Vinos. Now Manolo was able to give me additional information even about these types of plants. While Juan had taught me to open prickly-pears by selecting a long spine from the leaves of purple variety, Daniel told me that neither of these 'nopáles' – prickly-pear cacti – were native to Tenerife. After the sugar-cane industry collapsed on the island, they'd been brought from Mexico so that cochineal insects for the dye industry could be bred by the millions on their leaves. "Each flat, prickly leaf of the nopal offers grazing to a prairie of 'cochinillas'!" Daniel was able to conjure up a picture of each plant being a veritable mini-cattle-ranch! Teno Bajo had gone into the business of making 'ácido carmínico' from the dried bodies of millions of 'cochinilla' insects.

He warned me to steer clear of the cholla cactus. "Watch this!" He brushed his shirt-sleeve lightly against a single spine. The spine hooked into the cloth and immediately a piece of the plant broke off with other, smaller spines attached to it. He held his sleeve up with the clinging chunk of spiny cholla for my inspection. "These little spines work their way into seams of your shirt, your pantalones and then, when María washes them, into her flesh they go! In so far that you have to use a razor blade to cut deep into the flesh to get them out. Even then...!" He gave a discouraging shrug to suggest the person washing might have the tip and shaft of a fine spine in her flesh forever. With great care, he detached the piece of cholla from his shirtsleeve.

Daniel's favourite cactus was the cardón, as it was mine. Its multiple trunks are pale green and from a distance appear round and tubular. Up close, however, you appreciate that the trunk is created from four or five distinct surfaces with spines along the edge where each surface meets, like well-pressed seams up a trouser-leg. "Look at this one!" It must have been ten feet high, a single trunk at ground level, but a couple of feet from the desert floor two great arms, almost as thick as the main trunk, curved and then rose vertically to form a symmetrical triptych. From the entire length of the multiple edges of each of the three trunks sprang rows of triangular, cinnamon-coloured pods, all identical, like plump buttons on a military uniform. "These are the flowers. They open only at night to attract moths."

We both stood in admiration of the symmetrical beauty of the cardón and its nocturnal ingenuity. Daniel repeated the warning that Juan had given me, "If you scratch the outer bark of a cardón it bleeds thick, white milk. Even a single drop of that milk on your skin will give you a very painful burn that takes weeks to heal. But look over here," he pointed to a shrub with a smooth grey stem that branched into handfuls of long, spiky, green leaves. "That's the beród! Juice from the leaves of the beród is the antidote for the cardón's searing burn."

For a moment, I was back in Coupar Angus, sounds of war still raging in faraway Europe. My sister Vivian, not yet five, held onto my Grampa's left hand and I, still short of three, clutched his right. Down past the 'big hoose' at Inverdale, just short of the 'stony-brig', I accidentally brushed my bare leg against a bank of nettles. Sympathetic with my sobs, Grampa showed me how to spit on a docken leaf, a variety of sorrel, and rub it on the red rash. Immediately, as if by magic, it eased the scalding pain. "For every hurt," he smiled at us reassuringly beneath his bristly, grey moustache and bare, round wire spectacles, "God has made a cure that grows close by! You just have to make the effort to find it!"

Together, Daniel and I walked back to the opera set on the stage that he and María shared, each thinking our own thoughts.

María had set a ceramic porrón and four spoons on a solid table made of wooden boards in the shade of the north wall of their home. Daniel and I sat down on two of the chairs. He gestured to the porrón, where droplets were sweating from the cool water inside. I stood up, took its handle in my left hand and holding its cool, plump body at arms' length from my face, let a stream of sweet, cold water flow into my mouth. I drank, swallowing with my mouth open. When I'd had enough, I lowered the heavy ceramic vessel to the table without having lost a single drop and pushed it towards Daniel. He did the same. Manolo joined us. We could hear María and Carmen's quiet voices inside. I smelled goat stewing in coriander.

After we'd eaten, María brought out a jar of gofio and a pot of honey. Manolo produced a small zurrón no larger than a woman's handbag. "We're going to show you how to use a zurrón to 'amasar gofio con miel'," explained Daniel. I understood that now I was going to be treated to a practical lesson in the art of the verb I hadn't understood earlier, 'amasar'. Clearly the zurrón was the technology, gofio and honey, 'miel', the raw ingredients.

Holding the tiny goat-skin upright, Carmen spooned dry gofio into the open hind-end and poured in a viscous glob of amber honey on top of it. Then, holding the hind-end almost closed with one hand, she gently let out the air. She began to massage the goat-skin with the other, kneading the gofio and honey inside until it turned into a thick, almost dry paste. She released the end so that I could look inside. I saw a ball of brown dough that smelled of toasted corn and syrup. She added another handful of dry gofio and kneaded the dough some more to pick up any trace of liquid honey left on the inside surface of the zurrón. When she was satisfied, she turned the zurrón upside down and let the ball of sweet-smelling dough fall onto the table top. Then she plucked small handfuls from the dough and rolled each under her palm until they were perfectly round and firm.

"Try one!" I popped a little ball into my mouth and enjoyed the musky flavours of warm toast and earthy honey. Immediately it came to me, 'amasar' means 'to knead!' Right here, in a dozen small balls of protein, carbohydrate, glucose and fructose, were well-kneaded nutrients sufficient to keep a working man going for an entire day.

Daniel and Maria on the balcony of their home in the abandoned village of Teno Bajo. They lived happily in the desert raising goats and working their salt pans along the coast. The village was accessible only by fishing boat or a long, dangerous trek over the mountains.

Daniel expanded. "The villagers in the mountains carry a zurrón with them when they're grazing animals far from home. Inside the skin they store handfuls of gofio, sugar and crushed almonds. When they feel hungry, they add a little squirt from their 'bota', the leather bag they use for carrying water or wine, and hay presto, an instant meal!"

"The zurrón is an all-in-one, kid-leather lunch-box!" Maria took the empty skin and shook the crumbs from it. Satisfied, we sat back and reflected on the simple life.

Daniel deflected all my indirect, and not-so-indirect, questions as to how he and María came to be at Teno Bajo, at first a couple alone and now with a grown daughter and son-in-law. He briefly mentioned 'complica-

193

tions' at the beginning of the Civil War in '36, when Franco took possession of the Canary Islands, suppressing with unimaginable brutality all opposition from outraged republicans. "The bodies of those who showed the slightest opposition were hung by wire from the iron bridge! They were left to rot!" Having taken Las Canarias, Franco invaded the Peninsula via Spanish Morocco, where he held his military command in the Spanish Legion and had his troops armed and waiting in readiness.

Daniel referred to himself and his wife as the 'guardianes' of Teno Bajo, the 'custodians' of the isolated desert and the remnants of the village. But on whose behalf they performed custodial duties was left vague. A 'duque' – a hereditary titled peer – was mentioned, the owner of great estates in La Peninsula. Much earlier, I'd heard that an aging aristocrat lived in exile with his mistress in an ancient house buried behind trees on a small estate on the edge of Buenavista, and so I asked, "Is your 'duque' the same duke who lives on the edge of Buenavista?"

"Let me show you the route you have to take to get to the lighthouse!" Daniel rose from the table without answering my question and stuck his battered straw hat back on his head. María was clearing up. Manolo and Carmen had disappeared earlier to attend to goats.

As Daniel left me facing in the direction of the little peninsula where the squat, dark tower of the lighthouse could just be seen, he shook my hand. "You are welcome here anytime. We're always at home! Go with God!"

I threaded my way between cactus. Now I knew which was the poison and which the antidote. I knew from the colour of their flowers alone, which nopal would offer purple prickly-pears when ripe and which would offer green. The only sounds were the relentless rasp of crickets and the random dry scuttle of lizards. I passed a couple of beehives in ceramic pipes shaded by overhanging rocks and knew who would harvest the honey and how some of it would be used. I knew too, that I'd been right not to probe too insistently into Daniel and María's circumstances. Without asking me, they knew I had enough common sense not to gossip about them to others but precautions had to be taken, nevertheless.

A lesson from one of our English classes at school came to mind. The topic was the Romantic poets and Keats in particular. Keats encouraged the cultivation of 'negative capability'. Negative capability was that human capacity which allows us to take pleasure in beauty without demanding a full, factual explanation of how that beauty arises. There are times when reverence holds a deeper truth than certainty. I would, I decided, allow myself to cherish my memory of the compact huddle of desiccated, crumbling adobe, the enigma deep within the heart of this red desert, and the mysteries safeguarded by Daniel, María and their family, without fully understanding them. I kept walking, watched intently by bright-eyed lizards large and small.

José-el-Farolero, lighthouse-keeper at el Punto e Teno, waved to me from the wall of his quarters. "¡Bienvenido, Orlando! – Welcome back!"

Daniel was proud of the salt he made in his evaporation pools.

19. Pepe-of-the-Pneumatic-Drill

Pepe-de-la Perforadora's brother working in a quarry. The rock is used for building walls.

A few kilometres to the north-west of our compact village, past the grey-walled banana plantations and beyond the scattering of tomato fields, to where the desert was still largely untouched by human hand, rose a single, perfectly-rounded hill that covered an area the size of a dozen football fields. Because it was the one and only feature of any altitude in the otherwise flat plain between the mountains and the pounding sea, it had constantly drawn my attention. Tall, limb-like cardón cactus stood out on the hill like angry hackles on a farm-dog's neck. Despite my asking, I'd learned nothing about the hill, not even if it had a name. One day, when I had nothing better to do, I decided to walk across the plain and climb it, simply because it was there. By leaving just as day broke, around 7.30, I reckoned, I could be back in time for lunch.

It was Pastora's turn to walk to the edge of the village where the family was fattening a pig. She was happy for me to carry the heavy buckets full of kitchen waste as far as the rancid sty that used mounds of dried cactus to pen the animal in. As soon as it heard the rattle of the buckets, the beast grew excited and its expectant grunts joined the roosters' confidence in the dawn. I'd worked on a small-holding near Tealing in Angus where I had learned to respect pigs as well as to keep out of their way when they were hungry, which appeared to be always. The pen had been dug out below the level of the surrounding land for increased security and to make it easier to deposit the contents of the buckets into the trough. I could see a beautiful white barrow-castrate with the characteristic black markings that told me it was a Gloucester Spot. Sure enough, Pastora knew it as a 'glowsester espo', the Spanish phonetic equivalent of its name, complete with the extra syllable in Gloucester, the intrusive 'e' before the initial 's' in spot, and the suppression of the final 't'.

"In another month or so," she told me, in the matter-of-fact way of rural people who wisely refuse to anthropomorphise their meat while it still lives, "we'll have him butchered. Then we'll have lots of morcilla." She smiled at the thought of it. 'Morcilla' was the Tenerife equivalent of what we, in Scotland, call black pudding, a favourite fried with bread for Sunday morning breakfasts. It was made from fresh pig's blood, oatmeal, pork fat, onions and milk and liberally flavoured with freshly-ground, aromatic allspice and seasoned with salt. Typically, in Dundee, we bought it ready-made, but because we had a distant relative, a traditional butcher who cut his own meat and prepared his own haggis, white-puddings and black-puddings, we'd often watched it being made from scratch. Tom Gray and his wife Annie were always happy to have Euan and me stand in the back shop and watch, while he and his wife mixed the lightly-cooked ingredients and finally passed them through the sausage machine that extruded the dark, savoury, mass into paper-thin casings.

"It's going to rain!" Pastora, ever thoughtful, handed me an empty potato sack. Most of the rain fell high up on the mountainsides as the warm, moist air blown in off the Atlantic was driven upwards and met the higher, cooler air that forced it to shed its moisture. Nevertheless, as often as two or three times a day, the village and the surrounding desert plain would get what the natives called 'lluvia', rain but I would simply dismiss as 'drizzle'. Eskimos, I'd heard, were supposed to have many different words for snow but in the north-east of Scotland we had many, many more names for atmospheric moisture in all its different states and variations. We had also learned to cope with every single one of them. Villagers in Buenavista didn't enjoy any kind of precipitation and so it was a common sight to see working men and women wearing a sack as a hood to protect their heads, shoulders and backs from even the most inoffensive of glistening mist. Nevertheless, I accepted the sack to acknowledge her thoughtfulness. Before I was half-way to my destination, I was wearing it over my shoulders, enjoying the familiar earthy scent of potatoes and jute.

As the sun rose over the mountains behind me, light swept in over the ocean. The fast-moving wave of sunlight converted the sea into a vast expanse of stippled green and transformed the spume sent up by the breakers on the distant rocks into downy dandelion tufts. It rushed over the plain, turning the muted morning shades into vibrant reds and ochres; it sprang long shadows from the cactus and brought welcome

life and warmth to the morning. Great puffy clouds with dark under-
sides chased one another in disciplined teams across their sky-blue playing field and I walked now in warm sunlight, now in refreshing shade.

Although occasional tracks made by the odd vehicle snaked
through the cactus and the spiny shrubs to isolated areas marked out
for the future development of tomato fields or banana plantations, none
led in the direction of the hill I was making for. Undaunted, I took
a north-west bearing from the highest cactus on the mound and held
to my course as best I could, given the constant need to give a wide
berth to the cardónes and the prickly-pears that spread their catcher's
mitts wide to trap the unwary. I had no need to worry about snakes, for
there are none in the Canary Islands, and the lizards, though many, are
harmless. Lizards no longer than my hand would stretch out on a rock
in full sun and perform their morning press-ups, ignoring me unless I
went too close for their comfort.

On one of my frequent stops to get my bearings and just enjoy the
freshness of the morning, I noticed a roiling plume of moving yellow
dust about a kilometre from where I stood. A vehicle was weaving its
way across the dry land towards the same rounded hill that was also
my destination. Eventually, the dust-plume disappeared; the vehicle
had stopped. When I was close enough to identify it, I recognized the
green lorry belonging to El Bachillér. He was a man who seemed to get
everywhere.

His lorry was parked at the base of the mound near to an excavation or quarry of some sort, its dark red-brown interior exposed like
a flesh wound. As I drew closer, I could make out two men loading
blocks onto the bed of the truck. El Bachillér was watching and talking
without fear of competition from the sweating labourers. A lorry-driver,
whether in Scotland or in Tenerife, was just that, a lorry-driver. His job
was to supervise the loading and the unloading of his vehicle, to make
sure the load was safely distributed between the axles, and to travel
from point A to point B. In general, his job was not to toil when his
lorry was parked.

"¡El Extranjero! Welcome!" El Bachillér shredded his cigarette
butt and shook my hand. "The Foreigner follows me about all over the
island – even to the most godforsaken of places!" He introduced me
to his two companions. I had already seen both of them under other
circumstances. The elder of the two, small and slight and in his late
thirties, was Pepe-de-la-Perforadóra – Pepe who ran the pneumatic
drill. The younger, Ramón, a reserved, genial man in his mid-to-late-
twenties, was Pepe's antithesis. He was several inches taller, built like
a professional body-builder and gave the impression that work of any

kind demanded no effort whatsoever. Often, I'd see him at the end of the working day heading for the bar in the plaza. He had showered and changed and smelled of aftershave. He would lean casually against the bar, order an aperitif – invariably a Licor 43 – and talk in a low, measured voice with anybody who happened to be around. He'd spoken briefly to me several times and told me that he was saving for his fare to Venezuela. "There, a man who works hard, takes care of his earnings and keeps his eyes open for opportunities, can do well!" I'd no doubt whatsoever that Ramón would do well. Behind his relaxed, casual manner, I could detect a shrewd ambition and the willingness to work however hard it took to succeed.

"What are you loading, Bachillér?" I gestured to the dark, rectangular slabs that looked vaguely familiar.

"Wall-blocks!" As soon as he said it, I recognized these slabs as the porous blocks used to build walls around plantations to protect the fruit from the wind.

"What are wall-blocks doing down here?"

"Here is where they come from!" Pepe called over his shoulder.

"Pepe cuts them out of this very quarry." El Bachillér jerked his thumb towards the quarry I'd seen from the distance. "When Pepe and his brother have finished loading, they'll show you."

Pepe was more than happy to oblige. All three of us followed him into the shallow quarry. The entire surface, including the cactus plants, had been scraped off a small portion of the hill to expose what lay underneath. It looked like one huge, porous cinder merging in colour from ochre and umber through purple and pink, into blood-red, sienna and dark grey.

"It's compressed ash from the volcano," Pepe explained. "The whole hill is made from one huge cinder. It's a ready-made building block. All I have to do is cut it into blocks the right size." He showed me the tools he used, mainly saws of different lengths and breadths, some with handles offset so that he wouldn't graze his knuckles while cutting. I'd never have imagined that the walls of the plantations were cinder-blocks cut directly out of the earth's crust!

"This is what I do when I'm not operating the generator and the pneumatic drill." Pepe was very matter-of-fact.

I reflected on how often I was amazed to come across trades and skills that I'd never even imagined existed. Recognizing how little I really knew about Tenerife gave me the same feeling I used to experience when I examined the open stacks in the Dundee Reference Library. At the age of nine or ten, when it was raining and we three children were at a loose end, Pearl would tell us, "Off you go to the museum or the reference library!" We would walk the mile and a half to the centre of the city and quietly marvel at the amount and range of knowledge on the shelves.

"There's so much to know, isn't there!" Pepe and Ramón nodded in agreement with me, even if they weren't privy to my memories. El Bachillér lit another cigarette. He struck me as someone who was convinced that he'd already mastered most of what was important to him in life.

"The three of us are going back to the far side of the village to unload the slabs. Are you coming with us, Orlando?" Feeling pressure to go with them and consolidate our friendship, I abandoned my idea of climbing to the top of the

When Pepe wasn't working with his pneumatic drill, he helped cut solid blocks of ash from a mountainside. The blocks were used to build windbreaks on top of the stone walls that surrounded plantations. They were easier and faster to work with than volcanic stone.

Great Cinder Block. That was a solitary task that could easily be accomplished another day.

After that, I became good friends with Pepe and his brother Ramón, but principally with Pepe. It turned out that he lived with his wife, his baby, his mother-in-law and Ramón in a modest house immediately behind the fonda. Like most houses in the village when viewed from the street, nothing could be seen except a high stucco wall with a wooden door in it. The beauty of a home lay in the private space reserved exclusively for the enjoyment of the family who lived in it. It was hidden from the eyes of the casual man-in-the-street. Pepe's home was built in a long, narrow lot surrounded by high walls. The rooms were a series of separate chambers along the foot of the high wall and their doors all opened onto the common patio. The patio itself was scattered with bright geraniums growing in a surprising array of chipped terracotta pots of different sizes, old coffee cans and even cooking utensils that lacked a handle or were so beat up as to be no longer fit for cooking. At the extreme end of the patio was the kitchen with the tiny, open charcoal fire permanently tended by the women.

Over the following weeks, I enjoyed several simple meals with them. Pepe's was the first house I'd been granted entry into in the village. All visiting and socialising seemed to be undertaken either in the plaza or in one or other of the shops, cafés or bars whose doors were open from early morning until late at night. For the honour of having been admitted into Pepe's family, I wanted to show my appreciation.

"What can I do to show your wife and your mother-in-law how much I appreciate your hospitality, Pepe?" I'd thought of inviting them to the fonda for an evening meal but needed to be sure.

"The only thing you need to do is come to our home again!" Pepe's response was generous, even predictable, but it did nothing to solve my dilemma, and so one evening, I asked Doña Lutgarda. She was common-sense personified and I relied a great deal on her judgement, when it came to questions of how I should behave in the village.

"The very best thing you could do, Orlando, would be to buy an unweaned goat-kid and take it to the family on a Sunday morning after they return from mass."

"But they'll have the trouble of killing it, cutting it up, cooking it, and they'll probably feel obliged to invite me to eat it with them!"

"Nevertheless, that's what I suggest. Presenting a live goat-kid as a gift is something very special. Killing, cleaning and cooking it is a task that every woman in the village is happy to undertake as a matter of course. They'll cook the meat exactly as they like it. Then they'll have the head, the bones and the entrails to make soup for the rest of the week and they'll use the contents of the stomach to start cheese. A goat-kid is the finest of gifts!"

And so I arranged with Pepe that early the following Sunday, he and I would walk up to El Palmar. "If we go early enough, we'll find an unweaned goat for sale at one of the farms," he assured me.

What I called the Pilgrim's Way, the centuries-old, stone lane that wended its way up from the plain to the mountain village of El Palmar, a distance of several kilometres, was one of my favourite walks. To undertake that journey was to comfortably slip back into the Middle Ages with every step. On either side of the cobbled lane, narrow terraced fields crept up the mountainside revealing the patient labour of countless generations. On weekdays, men and women, girls and boys

I christened the trail from Buenavista to El Palmar 'Pilgrim's Way'.
Cultivated terraces graced both sides of the path. Villagers grew
alfalfa to feed domestic rabbits, a delicacy in the village.

would be tending, hoeing, weeding, harvesting a wide range of vegetables, exactly as their parents and grandparents had done before them. They'd straighten their backs, their faces would relax in that timeworn grimace of temporary relief, they'd rest on spade or their hoe and call a greeting as I passed, grateful for a fellow voice, before turning back to their solitary labours.

Always, I would see the same ploughman and stop to talk to him. He was a tallish, well-built young man in his early thirties. He carried out his tasks with the quiet confidence of someone whose services are in constant demand and who knows exactly what he's doing and why. He operated with a beautiful, massive, docile, dun-coloured ox and a simple, wooden plough. The handle and the beam of the plough were made of thick, naturally-bent branches shaped by an adze and jointed together with stout wooden pins. The shoe, also wooden, was fitted with a steel share, and on the landside of the frog he'd fitted a steel bar. He was the one and only ploughman I'd come across in the area. I'd seen a few small farmers use tine-driven, mechanical cultivators, but the majority relied on their short-handled, wide-blade hoes for most cultivation tasks and, once a season, on the ploughman to turn the soil for a new crop.

We started off shortly after daybreak under a clear sky. "It smells like rain!" Pepe was right. Once we'd left the village behind us and began the ascent up the winding path, it began to drizzle but the clouds soon blew over and drifted up the mountainside and over the tops as if being sucked from above. The sky then took on the colour of a robin's egg and we breathed in the smell of fresh, damp soil and the promise of strawberries. Occasionally a child would be parked on a boulder above the lane, with small bundles of bright green alfalfa; boxes of purple and green figs, dazzling orange carrots with the green tops still attached, a dozen eggs, a large grey rabbit with floppy ears.

"Who's got an unweaned kid for sale?" A little girl pointed eagerly to the curve in the lane above us, "There! My uncle has one."

"How much?" Pepe called up to the uncle as we approached.

"¡Viente duros, nama! – Only 20 duros!" A duro was five pesetas, so the price was 100 pesetas, about two days' wages.

"¡Quince! – Fifteen!" Pepe bargained. The farmer laughed. I could see that Pepe wasn't used to buying unweaned kids. The going price was 20 duros but Pepe waved him away and we climbed higher up the lane. We were approaching El Palmar and hadn't come across a single other kid for sale.

"Let's go back and buy the one we saw before it gets sold," I suggested.

"Right," said Pepe. "Now, if he still has it, he'll sell it to us for 15 duros for fear of losing the sale!"

We strode back down the sunken lane between the terraced fields letting the weight of our bodies carry us down rapidly.

"See! He's still there and still with his kid on a rope! Oyez, amigo! We'll take the kid off your hands for 15 duros!"

The farmer descended from the edge of the field where he was standing; the kid, a tiny, beautifully marked billy-goat, black lines down the head and back and a body of rusted ivory, came skipping down enthusiastically behind him.

"It's only ever suckled?" Pepe felt the little animal all over.

"It's only ever suckled," the farmer nodded.

"He's a real skinny little fellow." The farmer said nothing. Pepe hefted the kid in his arms. "Light as a feather!" The farmer made no indication that he'd heard the insults. "So, what do you say," pressed Pepe, "fifteen duros? I'll be doing you a favour!" The farmer laughed again. "How many kids have you seen since you passed me the first time?" Now it was Pepe's turn to remain silent. The farmer smiled triumphantly.

"How much for the kid?" The question came up the hill from a group of four adults and a troupe of children all dressed like city-dwellers out for a day in the country. They were still a hundred steep meters below us.

"Twenty-four duros!" Answered the farmer.

"Hold it there, we're coming to see it!"

The farmer grinned at Pepe, "See?"

Figuring that the canny farmer well knew that a bird in the hand is worth two in the bush, I took the fresh 100-peseta note I'd brought with me for the purchase from my pocket and held it up before him. He looked at the clean note and then back down at the group of city-slickers. They'd stopped to haggle with two little boys over the price of a box of figs. The man doing the negotiating was browbeating the kids, trying to get the price down to a lower figure. The farmer looked back at the crisp, blue 100-peseta bill, uncertain. I held the bill steady, right in front of his eyes. He grabbed it and handed the string lead to Pepe. "You've got yourself a good bargain today, Señor," he said to me and scrambled back up the slope to his cottage.

As we passed the group still haggling over the figs, one of the adults asked us, "Is that the kid we wanted to look at?"

"That's it," nodded Pepe, holding the string tightly. There was no way he was going to part with the only kid on sale that Sunday from Buenavista to El Palmar.

"And it cost 24 duros?"

Pepe nodded. "That's the going price these days. No use bargaining!"

"We really wanted it!"

"Well there are more further up!" Pepe gestured up the lane towards El Palmar.

The adults looked crestfallen. "Further up?" They'd driven from Puerta la Cruz, reluctantly parked their car at the foot of the lane because there was no way it could take the grade or the uneven stones. They were unused to strenuous walking and already looked dead beat.

"Lots of them! Twenty-four duros!" The exhausted group slowly turned their faces upwards and we swung down the hill with our little billy tripping along merrily behind us.

"Why did you tell them that, Pepe? There are no more kids for sale."

"I wanted to teach these city people from Puerto la Cruz a lesson. They can't just come out here in their motor-cars and exploit the poor mountain people at will. They think they're better than the poor ignorant peasants who don't even know the value of a good unweaned billy-goat!" Better I keep my mouth shut, I decided.

We reached the bottom of Pilgrim's Way and were about to enter the village. I picked up the little billy and slung him gently across my shoulders, holding his forefeet in my left hand and his rear feet in my right. He bleated in protest and immediately unleashed a flood of urine down my back followed by a shower of aromatic droppings. A massive discharge for such a tiny creature. Pepe roared with laughter. Since there was absolutely nothing else I could do, I plunged on soaked with a great patch of warm, pungent goat's urine and faeces from my shoulders to the backs of my legs.

"It's just as well I didn't bother to splash my face with after-shave lotion before I left," I thought to myself. Pepe suffered spells of uncontrollable laughter as I led the way to his house with the prize of the day. However, his wife and mother-in-law brushed off the indignity I'd suffered as a minor mishap.

"Take your shirt off and I'll wash it." Stripped to the waist, I sat in the sun in the courtyard bright with flowers, while my shirt dried alongside the tiny goatskin pinned to the clothesline. Pepe and I savoured the mouth-watering aroma of kid simmering in a sauce made with green peppercorns sprinkled with fresh cilantro. Mother-in-law was gently warming a pan of milk to which she added the rennet from the goat's stomach to start fresh cheese. The happy, expectant faces of the entire family were evidence that the present had indeed been well received and my embarrassment insignificant in comparison with their pleasure.

The colourful courtyards of houses in Buenavista were invisble from the street.

205

20. Dynamite!

"Sebastian and some friends from Los Silos are taking the falúa to La Punta de Teno this Sunday. Want to come?" Since Pepe Mendibles introduced me to the lighthouse-keeper and his family some months ago, we'd become friends and I seldom missed an opportunity to visit. So, Sunday found eight or nine of us heading down the coast in Sebastian's falúa, taking each massive green wave at an oblique angle, to keep our southerly course and prevent us from being forced onto the rocks. The coast would disappear as we plunged down into a trough only to reappear minutes later as we crested the next wall of water. The morning smelled of brine, tar, and the dried fish scales that still clung like silver transfers to the gunwales, evidence of the success of the previous day's fishing.

Pepe had told each passenger what he must bring. Protocol demanded that guests to the lighthouse took all their provisions with them so as not to put a burden on the limited stores the family kept at the lighthouse. All their supplies came by boat. Now Pepe went through his list. Each responded as our name was called. Mine came last. "Orlando?" I raised my voice above the slapping of the prow, "Gofio! Two kilos! Pepe relaxed. "That's everything, then. Oh! Luis! You have the fish, of course?" Luis, who fished out of Garachico a little further north, didn't answer. "Luis?"

"We'll get them en route!" Luis pointed to a canvas satchel that he'd laid carefully on the bottom boards close to his feet. It looked far too small to carry fish to feed more than a dozen people, but I didn't think any more about it. Miracles happen. I was more concerned about why the helmsman was on a heading different from the one I knew took us directly to the lighthouse, one that was taking us further out into the ocean. Probably to avoid the turbulence where the two contrary tides meet, since we have so many in the launch, I decided.

When we were a good six or seven kilometres from the shore and well to the north of the lighthouse, Sebastian cut the throttle and scanned the depths beneath the launch with his glass-bottomed tin. "Perfect!" He indicated the port-side. Luis drew two sticks of dynamite from his satchel, gingerly primed one with a blasting cap, lit the fuse and waited. When the sparkling fuse had almost reached the cap, Luis threw the stick of dynamite into the water as if it was a dart and he was going for a-the bull's eye. The stick fast disappeared below the surface. There was a breath-taking pause and then a sound like a larger-than-life, circus strong-man tearing a gigantic telephone directory in half with a single jerk. The surface of the sea roiled and flattened like a cauldron of molten glass. A moment later, two 'bonitos' – a variety of tuna, each weighing about three or four kilos and several smaller viejas floated to the surface and lay on their sides as if asleep. Sebastian touched the throttle and steered towards them. Eager hands scooped up the still fish and laid them down on the boards. Two men drew sharp knives and began scaling and cleaning with swift, confident movements. I watched, intrigued, having heard of, but never before seen, poachers dynamiting fish.

"Show el Extranjero what happens when you dynamite tuna!" One of those gutting handed me a cleaned fish split open with his knife. The guts had been removed but the bones were still in place. However, instead of a single, solid spine with comb-like ribs running vertically from behind the head to just short of the tail, each vertebra had come apart like an explanatory picture from an anatomy book and the normally white flesh was tinted red with diffused blood.

"When the dynamite explodes under the water," Sebastian explained, "it sends out shock-waves that kill everything in the vicinity. It doesn't affect the taste but you can see from the bulge of the eyes and the shattered vertebrae that they weren't caught legally."

"So you could fillet them and nobody would know?"

He shook his head. "If it were as easy as that, fishermen would use dynamite more than they do. Look at the colour of the flesh. The blood vessels shatter and red flecks are spread throughout the meat. These can't be washed away, so that's the tell-tale sign!"

"So we could be in trouble!"

"Only if the Civil Guard catches us!"

"Fortunately, we're so isolated up here that we can get away with the odd explosion on a quiet Sunday morning." Having procured all the tuna we'd need and more, Sebastian was now steering a course for La Punta de Teno and the lighthouse.

When we landed, it was to a noisy, smiling welcome from José, Mary Carmen and their children. Within the hour, we were all sitting down together at their long table with plates of fried tuna steaks and salty wrinkled potatoes in front of us. We were just finishing the last of the potatoes when José, who had gone up into the lantern room to make one of his regular, obligatory meteorological observations, rushed back in, breathless.

"I spotted the Civil Guard motor-launch leave Santa Catalina!

207

Judging by the huge wake it's throwing, it's on its way over here at full throttle!"

Santa Catalina was the closest port on the neighbouring island of La Gomera more than 30 kilometres away. Immediately, Sebastian was on his feet. He made his living from the falúa and couldn't afford to have it confiscated by the Beneméritos.

"Let's go! Right now! We'll try to outrun them back to Los Silos!" Suddenly, everybody was in frantic motion. José scraped the bowlful of tell-tale-shattered fishbones over the wall where the gulls fought over them before they reached the water. The bones were followed by three or four viejas that María had kept back for the following day. "We can't afford to leave a single trace!"

Two of the passengers were diesel mechanics who had come to service the generator that provided electricity for the lighthouse-keeper's accommodation. They weren't returning and Pepe Mendibles decided to remain at the lighthouse as well. He began gathering up what tools José had in his workshop to make it look like he was there to service the windows. The rest of us rushed to the landing and were soon heading at full throttle back up the coast towards Los Silos. The tidal current was against us and the going was heavy. Sebastian and his first-hand were discussing in loud voices so as to be heard against the wind and the wave-slap, how best to make it back before the much faster launch might catch us. They seemed to agree. Sebastian addressed me.

"Orlando, it's likely we'll make it back before the Beneméritos can catch us. But if they do overtake us, it won't be pleasant. And it will be worse for us to be caught with a foreigner!" Now my excitement was tinged with concern. I remembered how the Civil Guard had been on the point of accusing us of espionage when a friendly crewmember of a trawler in El Ferrol had tried to use his short-wave radio to communicate with a Scottish fishing boat just to please me. Spain was run by a single-minded dictator who brutally crushed all opposition and I'd no desire to experience the inside of a Spanish jail. I looked at Sebastian and his first-hand, fearing for a split-second that they might be planning to toss me overboard!

"We'll drop you off at El Callao de Márquez. You can make a run for it over the mountains. If you get home to Buenavista, lie low and claim you've been there all day! We'll take our own chances." I noticed the 'if you get home'!

We cruised on a tall wave up towards the great, flat rock at El Callao de Márques. I stood on the board that covered the bow-storage area and leaped just a split-second before the backwash sucked the falúa three metres back down into the trough. Fortunately, I'd done it once before. "Good luck!" Sebastian shouted and without even a pause, his first-hand swung the falúa back to sea and gave the engine full throttle.

I took off running across the black rocks and then into the red cactus-strewn desert. I was in good shape from work and had run cross-country in my last years at the Morgan Academy. My virtue lay in stamina and after about 10 minutes, when my body had overcome the thrill of being left entirely to my own devices to escape from the clutches of the Civil Guard, I settled down to a steady trot that I knew I could keep up for hours if necessary. On my first visit to Teno Bajo, Daniel had pointed to a crack in the base of the mountains: "That's where the path up to Upper Teno begins." I made a bee-line for that.

I knew enough to give the abandoned village and Daniel's house a wide berth. If Sebastian and his fishing companions felt I might be a liability to them, it would be no better for Daniel who was, apparently, carrying delicate political baggage from the Civil War.

In the blue shade at the base of the mountains, I stopped to get my bearings and check out what I could see of the path. If I hadn't done so much walking in the dry deserts around Buenavista, I would never have been able to identify the track. Red soil, slightly more compacted than that around it was the only give-away. It began in cool shade, appeared to go straight up the exposed ridge to one side of a bright yellow canyon and then disappear into the ragged cactus. The surface of the ground was dry and granular like polished barley. Despite the good grip my rope-soled sandals usually afforded me, I occasionally slipped, especially on the steeper parts. Lizards watched me, unconcerned. The path suddenly left the ridge and I found myself jogging along the wall of a canyon with a near-sheer drop of several hundred feet to my right. One false step and I'd have nothing but hungry cactus spines to break my fall all the way to the bottom.

I paused, wondering if I should have stuck to the ridge. The only way to make certain was to go back and see if there was another way. I retraced my steps and found there was no alternative route; I was on the right track. Then I noticed gashes that someone had made in the cactus with a machete. These confirmed I was right. It was clear that this route wasn't used more than a few times a year and even then, the traveller had to be desperate. Clouds blew in off the ocean as I climbed and I felt a few spots of rain on my arms. Just as suddenly as the steep path had begun at the foot of the mountain, it levelled off, but at that very same moment, a massive grey wall of mist enveloped everything. I could see nothing at all except tiny droplets carried like shining white pearls in the fog that told me somewhere far above, the sun was still shining.

Fortunately, the cactus had given way to a short, stubbly growth like green heather. It grew in patches leaving whorls of bare ground that made it impossible to distinguish the path, even if there still was one. Terrified to move too quickly in case I might plunge to my death, I cast about slowly, first to left and then to right to see if there was any clue at all that might help me. My forays came up with nothing and a sickening panic began to rise in the pit of my stomach. Here I was, lost on the alps of the mountains split by steep canyons in impenetrable fog that had robbed me of my most valuable asset, my sense of direction.

The little shepherd-girl who led me through the mist to safety when I was running from the Civil Guard. I returned to Teno Alto to thank her and her grandfather -- and also met her mother, by chance.

Suddenly, right in front of me I saw a sheep standing stock-still. It was looking at me as if surprised, its wool a mass of water droplets. Just behind it, also stock-still, stood a little girl of about seven or eight. She was barefoot and wore a white dress. Over the dress hung a shapeless, yellow woollen cardigan, buttoned from her waist to her throat against the chill. On one arm, she carried a woven basket and a sheathed knife hung from the other. She smiled expectantly at me out of a weather-beaten face. My fear evaporated. If a child was up here grazing her sheep, I couldn't be far from some kind of habitation.

"¡Buenos días!" I offered; she repeated the greeting and then stood in expectant silence. "I'm el Extranjero from Buenavista. I'm lost. Can you tell me how to get back to the village?" Continuing to smile and without a word, she pointed into the drifting mist. "But where's the path?" She continued to point. "Isn't there a path?" She frowned as if she didn't understand me, turned slightly and called, "¡Abuelito! – Grandpa!" Immediately, out of the fog, an old man appeared, silent, smiling. He wore a battered black hat, a shirt without a collar and carried a crook longer than himself We shook hands. Yes, he'd heard of me. I lived in the fonda in Buenavista.

"I'm lost. I want to get back to the village. Fast! Can you help me?" He frowned in the same way that the little girl had frowned. I repeated myself, injecting greater urgency into my voice.

"Just follow the path!" He gestured confidently into the impenetrable mist.

One of life's greatest challenges is to try to put ourselves into others' shoes. From the comfort of our own footwear, we tend to assume that others know what we know, believe what we believe and see the world as we see it. Having spent their entire lives in the mountains grazing their sheep and cattle, likely never venturing down even to Buenavista more than once a year if that, neither the girl nor Grandpa imagined that I might be lost in such a familiar place.

Identifying a problem is half way to resolving it. "Señor," I said, "this is the first time I've been up here. I'm not familiar with Teno Alto nor its paths. Could you take me to the point at which the steep path descends down into the valley where the farm known as El Rincón is?"

He turned to his granddaughter. "The Foreigner has managed to get himself lost." She regarded me in wonder. "Take him to the edge of the cliff. I'll keep my eyes on the sheep." I could see more wet, woolly shapes behind him.

"Wouldn't it be better if you both came with me?" I was concerned. "Your granddaughter might not be able to find her way back to you." Both grandpa and child laughed at my unfounded fear. Meekly, I followed the child through the blinding mist until suddenly we were in warm sunshine again, as if we'd emerged from an enclosed elevator into the upper floor of a department store.

The mountain fell abruptly away in eroded, yellow canyons and rough, rocky ridges. A thousand feet below me I could see Buenavista crouched on the plain like a lone crab. The only distinguishable feature was the bell-tower of Nuestra Señora de los Remedios and the green thatch of palms waving above the plaza. The village was surrounded by fields of tomatoes, walled banana plantations and terraces of vegetables that crept up the hills for a short distance like green steps, narrowing successively the higher they rose until they gave way to sheer mountainside. I felt acutely embarrassed for my earlier panic and my unashamed plea to a little girl and then an old man for assistance. It had taken a seven-year-old child, who may never have gone to school for even a single a day in her life, mere minutes to resolve my problem. I turned to thank her but she'd already withdrawn into the silent mist.

The path down the mountainside was exceptionally steep. In some places, it was more of a stone staircase than a trail. Judging by the smoothness of the steps, it was used frequently. I took my time going down. It was so steep that any slip could take me tumbling into an abyss from which there would be no survival. My body might never be found. Once on the valley bottom, I ran again, trotting through El Rincón, past la Casa Blanca, and into the maze of close, compact houses that made up my village.

The shepherd near Teno Alto who directed his granddaughter to guide the author through the mist to safety. This photograph was taken some weeks later when Ronald returned to thank him.

No sooner had I entered the fonda than Doña Lutgarda ushered me into the dining room and sat me down at my regular table. It had already been set for me. Breathlessly, she told me that Sebastian de la Falúa had called on the telephone. His companions had made it back to Los Silos before the Civil Guard. He and his first-hand had hurriedly used a derrick to lower an old diesel engine on top of the closed engine housing of his launch. When the Beneméritos arrived, they were told that Sebastian hadn't been to sea in his falúa for a couple of days because he'd had to pull the engine for routine maintenance. The old engine and all its parts strewn haphazardly on the boards were stone cold. Everybody in the tiny harbour confirmed his story. Lula washed the tell-tale red dust of Teno off my alpargatas.

The Civil Guard launch didn't have enough fuel to make the return trip to La Gomera and the owner of the only petrol station in Los Silos, which was normally closed on Sundays, had been hunted down and persuaded to refill their tank. Thankful they hadn't had to wait until the following day to buy fuel, they were already on their way back to Santa Catalina, puzzled, frustrated and empty handed.

21. Down the well and up again

Camels used as draft-animals were not uncommon, especially in the south of Tenerife.

"**M**amá, the well caved in! Mamá!" Doña Lutgarda and the girls flew to the door of the fonda where Pastora stood in distress. I looked down into the street from the open terrace above. Faces set, Pata Cabra and some of his work-crew were marching determinedly across the plaza, a growing group of sombre followers in their wake, stage-whispering: "Have you heard? The well caved in!"

Several days previously, Juan-the-Foreman had invited me to join his crew charged with digging a well on the outskirts of the village. It wasn't a common practice to dig wells in or around Buenavista. Water for use in homes was collected daily at the strategically-located, communal taps by the women from each household and carried home in cans balanced on their heads. Their elegant bearing attested to the beneficial effects of this chore. To tomato fields and banana plantations irrigation water was channelled from the base of the mountains through a complicated set of open, concrete channels. These were managed by el Llavero – the Keyman – who was able to direct the water to its exact destination at the exact time and for the required number of hours. This new well that Juan was about to dig was intended, apparently, to service an expanding corner of the village. It would provide a communal tap and so reduce the drudgery for women who lived there by shortening the distance they had to carry the heavy cans on their heads. Because I now worked unpredictable hours at the banana packing station, I had to refuse Juan's invitation to join his work-crew.

Later that week, however, a couple of days after the well-digging project had begun, I bumped into Juan in the plaza. It was mid-afternoon. I'd finished work early. "You should come and see our progress, Orlando. We've hit a tricky patch. Almost three metres down. I'm going to find el Loco."

"El Loco?"

"He's utterly fearless. Any time we're in a bind, el Loco takes over. He'll sort it out in no time."

More than once, friends had pointed el Loco out to me in the street. Tall, strong, slim, he was in his late twenties. He strolled in the square, mostly alone, but sometimes with his mother. Everybody greeted him. A handicap had limited his intellectual development and his ability to speak coherently. It was said his father had left the village years ago to work in the oil refineries near Maracaibo and although he regularly sent money home to his wife and son, he appeared to want neither to return to Buenavista nor to have them join him in Venezuela.

"How can el Loco help you?" I was puzzled.

"He keeps his head when we hit sand." Juan's response was matter-of-fact.

"Sand? You mean there's the chance of a cave-in?"

"It's unlikely. But me, I can't stand it when dribbles of loose cinders and sand start trickling down on top of me. It gives me the willies! The others are the same."

"So you ask el Loco to take the risk instead?" The words came out with a force stronger than I'd intended.

Juan's sincere, concerned face took on a puzzled look. "It's what he's good at, Orlando." He nodded to stress his point. "Some men are good at heights. I'm good at blasting rock with dynamite. You too! It doesn't frighten us. El Loco's good at digging in tricky wells. They don't frighten him. He actually enjoys it down there." I still looked askance but Juan persisted. "It's what he's best at, Orlando!"

Within a couple of minutes, Juan came striding back into the square, el Loco at his side. They looked for all the world like a couple of Midwestern gun-slingers on their way to deliver an ultimatum to an undesirable band of outlaws. All they lacked were silver stars on their breasts.

"¡El Loco!" a few excited voices shouted. El Loco couldn't keep up the gravity. His face broke into a broad grin and he smiled to left and right. "¡Vamos a excavar el pozo!" Juan explained to all. "We've run into a tricky patch three metres down but el Loco will sort things out!" Any novelty, any event which was even the tiniest bit out of the ordinary, drew an eager audience in the plaza. Further encouraged by the excitement of the growing group, el Loco grinned all the wider, clasped his hands above his head and exaggerated the swagger in his shoulders. Not without misgivings, I decided to join those who had nothing better to do than see for themselves how el Loco was going to sort things out down in the bottom of the unfinished well.

Operated by two men, a double-handed windlass set into a stout wooden frame spanned the hole. The operators lowered a short-handled shovel, a crowbar and a couple of empty tin buckets into the well. Then Juan gestured to el Loco, "Your turn!" Like royalty, el Loco waved to the crowd who cheered in response. Pata Cabra tied the rope round the celebrity's waist, the windlass-operators cranked the handles and el Loco, clinging to the rope with both hands, disappeared into the dry well. It was about four meters deep but a bare, claustrophobic meter-and-a-half in diameter. Sufficient light filtered down so we could watch el Loco untie himself and for him to see what had to be done in the damp floor of the pit.

"Stand back!" Juan spread his arms forcing us to retreat from the edge. "Be careful not to kick any stones down into the well. We don't want any accidents." We could hear the dull clang of shovel against soft aggregate. El Loco wasn't wasting any time. As soon as he filled one bucket, he shouted: "Up!" and started filling the spare. The windlass operators cranked the full bucket up, emptied it, lowered it once more, and so on it went. The rest of the work-crew and the band of supporters stood around the perimeter shouting encouragement with each raising and lowering of the bucket.

I felt slightly uncomfortable. "If men capable of assessing the risk had refused the challenge," I asked myself, "was it fair to ask el Loco to stand in for them?" Juan must have read my discomfort. He put his arm around my shoulders. "There's nothing to worry about, Orlando! El Loco's done this many times before. He's good at it. He loves being called on to do this kind of thing. It's what he lives for! It's his thing!"

With one hand on the windlass for support, I peered down into the pit. El Loco was standing at the bottom, face upwards grinning delightedly at grave, respectful faces looking back down at him. "That's the way, hombre!" "Don't fill them too full, you don't want a pebble tumbling down onto your head!" "Maybe that's just exactly what he needs!" Laughter. "Look how fast he can fill those buckets!" "He'll save the day!" El Loco's lopsided grin proclaimed he was revelling in the attention. Now the second bucket, already full, stood at his feet, and he upbraided the operators demanding they crank faster. The crowd laughed and cheered. El Loco was out-pacing those who only had to wind the handle and empty the bucket. "Faster! Faster!" His muffled urging raised another cheer at the expense of the sweating windlass operators.

I looked at the bystanders and listened to what they were saying to one another. There was admiration and wonder in their eyes for el Loco. I detected no mockery, no ridicule. Their affection and their cheers were genuine. "See el Loco? He's a fearless hombre!" "See when the sand trickles out of the sides of the dry well, he pays no attention to it." "He's a brave hombre, there's no doubt about it!" They continued to applaud each full bucket brought up out of the dark depths.

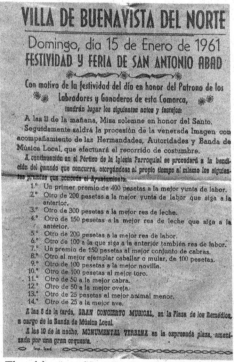

The celebration of San Antonio Abad, patron saint of farm-animals, was an important annual event in Buenavista del Norte.

Although I was seeing the truth of what Juan had confided in me about el Loco with my own eyes and hearing it with my own ears, I couldn't shake off a gnawing disquiet. With a final glance into the depths of the pit, a glance that confirmed the joyful glow on El Loco's face, I offered a final encouraging wave and made my way back to the fonda.

The following day, wearing my machete, I walked beyond El Rincón to identify and mark the stalks of bananas that showed the promise of reaching the standards demanded for export. I enjoyed the silent, solitary work, that took me through the sun-dappled plantations smelling of warm soil and decaying leaves. I'd become inured to the curtains of cobwebs that raked my face and the huge spiders that seemed to swell with fury at my intrusions into their private domain. They would make an initial, false charge at me, stop an arm's-length away, and then retreat up into the banana fronds. I'd also learned, from bitter experience, to avoid newly-irrigated soil and to keep to the higher, firmer edges.

As I did on any afternoon I finished early, I delivered my clipboard, the branding hammers and sheathed machete back to the warehouse and returned to the fonda. There, I showered off the cobwebs using the minimum of water, and went to a shady corner of the terrace, to study my Hugo's *Spanish in Three Months* and search my dictionary for any new words I needed. But my studies were rudely interrupted.

"Mamá, the well has caved in! Mamá!"

Casting my books to one side, I looked over into the plaza and then rushed down the wide steps to the ground floor, through the cool, tiled entrance hall and out into the street. Pata Cabra, at an unusually brisk trot for a man of his years, was just disappearing up the alley where el Loco lived with his mother. A member of the work-crew remained in the plaza and was gesticulating to onlookers. "Just like that!" He clapped his hands dramatically. "The sandy side of the well collapsed! No warning!" Reluctant to quit centre-stage, he clapped his hands again and expanded his story with more dramatic gestures. The dazed onlookers flinched every time he clapped his hands. "Just like that! Smack!"

"Just like that?"

"One minute things were fine and the next…! Smack!"

"El Loco?"

"Buried!" He raised both hands above his head to show how deep.

"Smothered?"

"Juan's down there in the pit now, trying to dig the poor fellow out. But there isn't much room to work! Juan was struggling to reach him when we left!"

Pata Cabra reappeared with el Loco's mother, grave, purposeful, numb to the hot sunshine, blind to the symmetrical golden flowerbeds that divided the plaza into separate paths for the leisurely after-dinner promenade.

In a single still-frame, the scene is forever engraved on my mind's eye. The impression is not in sepia nor black-and-while, neither is it in colour. It's simply, silently and everlastingly, 'there'.

Pata Cabra extends a broad, supportive forearm uselessly to a mother who is beyond all needs save one. Neighbours, bystanders are out of focus. She is in clear, sharp mid-stride. Erect, proud, utterly alone, eyes fixed in a mother's unceasing vigil, she registers neither the offered forearm nor the murmured consolations. Her right arm and cupped hand reach forward, protecting, the accustomed gesture of duty, affection, love. In this moment, she is not present in the plaza among the bright marigolds peppered by bees. This mother exists on the furthest edge of creation looking at a point just beyond the horizon, a point occupied by the only person left in her world and without whom her universe is void. Amidst the desolation and the doubt, beyond the love and the veiled hope, lies resignation, a calm acceptance of the anguish that will overwhelm, if not today, tomorrow, or the next day. A grief borne from that moment when she first held her son, looked into his perplexed eyes and knew. Without the midwife having to tell her, she simply knew. She had gripped him fiercely, then, conscious that she and she alone, now bore sole charge of two lives. But after hers, what then? The permanent heartache through which a mother pays for love.

All of that and more is revealed in the single, freeze-framed image before the reel catches again, jerking legs and arms and bodies back into motion, pouring colour into the marigolds, murmur into the bees. Silent now, in the mother's wake, even Pata Cabra, the self-made, general contractor used to action, authority, cedes leadership, grants ownership over this moment, to her. The sober throng follows; mute mourners.

Beside the windlass, on an upturned bucket with the loose rope still knotted to its handle, as if he were a living statue painstakingly put together cinder by cinder, grain by grain of sand, pale hair dusted, caked eyelashes, sits Rodin's crumbling Penseur, spitting grit.

"¡Hijo mío! ¡Hijo mío! Son, son! What has it done to you?" The tenderness of a woman who loves more than she dares. El Loco slowly raising bloodshot eyes, lips curving into a wet apology: "¡Mamá! ¡Se me cayó encima! – It caved in on me, Mamá!" For one brief, still moment, her face deeper, far deeper, than any dug well, Mother looks at Son. Reverently, she begins to wipe the sand from her uplifted child's face with her gentle apron. The air carries the damp smell of cool gravel that has grown old, hidden from sunlight for lifetimes, beneath the surface of this earth.

That moment in the plaza, those long-dreaded, lonely paces to the well-site, and now the tender, slow reclamation of a living face that can never lose its innocence, a face that will forever trust in the protection claimed by the privilege of eternal childhood – all that and more – instantaneously and fundamentally changed me. It restructured my universe in the same, sudden, inexplicable way that the slightest, inadvertent nudge to a kaleidoscope causes the multifaceted symmetry of colour and shape at the end where the soft light is polarized and echoed into mirrors, to re-pattern itself. No matter how hard you strive and struggle to recapture the original, the former order is forever past and gone.

As I watch, I'm fully aware that this sudden change in me and in my world has nothing whatsoever to do with my earlier discomfort inadvertently shared with Juan. I know, beyond any fraction of doubt, that my instinctive unease was malapropos. It surged, quite inappropriately, from another, entirely different place, from ill-fitting assumptions and quite another, alien set of rules. Now, I understand what Juan has always known, what the mother has always accepted as her life's truth. Being part of a community means each doing the thing he is good at, performing the task he is fitted to perform, making the just contribution. Such are the dues levied for membership, the contributions that guarantee belonging, the sources of recognition, respect and public approval. Unconditional acceptance is the obligation of attachment.

A self-contained hamlet depends on the willing, even the unquestioning participation and accord of all of its members. They must perform what they are best equipped to perform, accomplish what is expected of them. This is how the common good is served. It matters that members strive, using whatever gifts they are born with no matter how aberrant: el Loco, by plying his with enthusiasm; his mother, by enduring while aware of the odds. Both earn their apportioned place among all the others, from baptism to grave. So thrives a close-knit community from generation to generation. Where individuals claim rights to reluctance, aversion or raise self over community, there is freedom to quit, respect for honours won elsewhere. The price, however, is loss of membership.

No, the change I experienced related not to the village but to myself. It fundamentally altered how I perceived myself, what I was doing with my life, and what I needed to be doing in the future. Essentially, my activities throughout this year – working, travelling, working even harder, exploring – were undertaken to block out a previous life in the hope that the part of it that I least liked would simply go away. Now I knew categorically that it would not. That look on the mother's face when first she stepped into the plaza accompanied by Pata Cabra showed me, with the miracle of flicking a light switch, that none of us can choose to live just those bits of life that we prefer. Life comes as a package. We relish the good but unless we can change it, we must also put up with the ugly. Escape is an option, but always temporary. By choosing flight, I had won the right to gather insights and skills, I'd been granted the time to acquire a deeper perspective on life. Now, it was time to return. Now, I knew I could do so better equipped to handle circumstances I'd previously found paralyzing. I'd learned the mother's lesson about adversity: "This is one moment, but know that another shall pierce you with a sudden painful joy!" Thomas Becket's way of putting it.

Somehow, in that profound, unguarded expression on a mother's face, I knew that I would return home to Scotland to play a willing and an integral part within my own family or that portion of it that

219

we – Pearl, Vivian and Euan and I together – chose to hold onto. Now I understood how fitting it had been for me to go my own separate way so that we might come together again in a new pattern, a fresh birth.

Shortly, Euan would complete his education at the Morgan Academy. There would be nothing to prevent us from leaving George to the shrivelled existence he preferred. We need be no part of it. By amputating the decayed, we would free ourselves to sprout afresh wherever we chose. Together we would recreate, and blossom, disencumbered for the first time since Coupar Angus days.

Pearl and Vivian – both well qualified, one as a book-keeper the other as a dental nurse – could escape to the anonymity afforded by London and the opportunities it offered. The Royal Air Force had already selected Euan for officer-training school to serve as aircrew. My role, my duty as I see it now, is not simply to give these developments my moral support by weekly letter as I've done for almost a year; but to be close and present so as to lend a practical hand at the decisive moment that has been many long years in the making.

Occasionally camels would be uncooperative with their owners.

22. Up and down Teide

Juan-the-Foreman (Juan Gonzáles) and the author descending into the ice-cave close to the summit of Teide, the 3,718-metre volcano that dominates Tenerife. It last erupted in 1909.

Now that, in the secret recesses of my mind, I'd made the decision to return to the UK, it struck me how little I knew of Tenerife other than the region around Buenavista, to say nothing of the other six islands. The year before, I had stepped off the *Ciudad de Cádiz* in Las Palmas in Gran Canaria, I had admired the distant outlines of La Gomera and La Palma from the lighthouse at Teno, but never had I even set eyes on Fuerteventura, Lanzarote or El Hierro. Since I'd neither the money nor the inclination for simple tourism, I didn't feel deprived. I couldn't leave, however, before climbing to the top of Teide, the 3,700-metre dozing volcano that gave birth to Tenerife and whose distant, perfect cone I admired, sun-flushed, every morning from the plaza.

My plan to climb to El Pico del Teide, the very summit of the cone,

221

attracted lots of interest. Although, on any clear day, we could look in a north-easterly direction towards the centre of the island and see the conical, yellow peak sometimes with a dusting of dazzling snow, nobody I knew had ever made the ascent. Many said they'd love to come with me but couldn't spare the time. Juan-the-Foreman and Pepe-of-the-Pneumatic-Drill both swore they would accompany me.

The evening before the planned Teide trip, we three met on the corner outside the fonda to make last-minute plans. Pepe arrived crestfallen.

"My patrón," he was referring to the owner of the pneumatic drill who employed him, "just told me that we have a job on tomorrow. I can't come."

"You're working on a Sunday?"

"The job's urgent. It came up at the last moment."

Juan and I both were disappointed. Pepe was a wiry, indefatigable little fellow with a great sense of humour and lots of common sense. He had been looking forward to the excursion.

"Oh, well," I reasoned, "at least you'll earn double time."

"My patrón doesn't pay me extra for working on a Sunday! It's not because of the money I'm not going. It's so as not to let him down."

Much as I admired the enterprise of locals who took the risk to invest in projects that gave work to others and acknowledged that they deserved a good return on what they invested in time, I was often surprised at how unwilling they were to allow those they employed to help them realise and make their investment viable, to share, even in simple ways, like paying overtime, in their success. It was as if the personal sacrifices that they were forced to make justified their adopting a harsh attitude to their one-time peers. Perhaps the struggle for success curdled any milk of human kindness they started out with.

Pepe was truly crestfallen not to be coming with us. He was the kind of man who'd always worked for somebody else, who had neither the enterprise nor the capital to go it alone. He would always be dependent on employers. The tougher might exercise what they saw as their prerogative to remind him that the little he had could be taken away. His job, operating a pneumatic drill, was a responsible one and he earned a higher wage than a mere labourer; but to it he was shackled.

"We're sorry too, Pepe!" Juan and I commiserated. Pepe hunched his bony shoulders and retreated round the corner to his home.

"I'll bring all the food we'll need in my duffle-bag, Juan. A loaf of bread, a kebbuck of hard goat-cheese. And I'll pack gofio and honey into my zurrón." I'd become adept at surviving on 'gofio amasado con miel' – gofio and honey kneaded together to form a sweet, nutritious dough, using the chamois-like kid-skin Daniel had given me at Teno Bajo. The bread and cheese had been Doña Lutgarda's idea.

"I know you, Orlando, you can survive on the absolute minimum, but Juan, he's twice your size and has the appetite of a horse! He'll need more than a few handfuls of gofio to get him to El Pico del Teide and back in one day!" With Juan's needs in mind, she had bought an extra cheese from the vendor who regularly came down by donkey from El Palmar, and had kept back a whole loaf of bread from dinner. She'd wrapped it in a moist cloth to prevent it from drying out.

The following morning, Juan came up to my room and woke me at 5.30 a.m. Together, we went to the bar in the plaza for coffee. I'd succeeded in persuading Doña Lutgarda not to rise and make breakfast for us. Before we boarded the 6 a.m. bus for Orotava, Juan had the barman fill a small thermos-flask of coffee sweetened with condensed milk.

The little town of Orotava, in the centre of a productive agricultural valley four or five kilometres inland from Puerto la Cruz, was stretching itself awake when we arrived. There, feeling every inch adventurers, we changed buses. Among the few people who boarded was a young man in his mid-20s dressed for walking. Seeing the bulky bag, he came and sat in the seat in front of us: "Are you climbing to the top of Teide?" We told him we were. He was from La Laguna, a village close to Santa Cruz, where he worked in a bank. His hobby was hiking. Every Sunday he would choose an interesting area on the island, take the bus as close as he could, and walk for the greater part of the day. He'd reached Teide's peak several times. Today he planned to reach the old, extinguished volcanic cone called El Teide Viejo – Old Teide in las Cañadas. He explained landscape we were driving through.

We started off passing field after field of leafy, green vegetables. "The valley surrounding Orotava has some of the richest volcanic soil on the island. These are the market gardens where vegetables to feed Santa Cruz are grown." The extensive vegetable-gardens came to an abrupt end and we started to grind our way up steeply out of the valley on the traffic-free, zig-zag road to Las Cañadas. The slopes were young pine forests. The trees looked like a more delicate version of our Scots pine. "These are unique to Tenerife and just one or two of our other islands. They can thrive even without rainfall." Juan looked sceptical. "Look!" Our companion pointed. Rags of white mist were drifting through the pines and then enveloped us completely. The bus-driver switched on his windscreen-wipers. "These Canary Island pines use their needles to condense water from the clouds that drift in from the Atlantic. That way, despite growing in what is technically a desert, they comb enough moisture from the mist to survive!"

Higher up, we ran into taller, more mature trees. They were as stately as any I'd seen in the Rothiemurchus forest when I'd stayed at Aviemore youth hostel a few summers earlier. I sensed a distinctly Scottish character to the landscape. The driver turned the engine off and told us, now the only passengers, that he'd wait till he could see where he was going. None of us objected to his prudence. We shivered in the damp air and drank coffee until the mist cleared and the bus began climbing again. Shortly, we were in yet a different world. Now it was a wide valley of red and black rocks scattered over yellow cinders that looked as if they'd been raked, still glowing, from an enormous blast-furnace. The bus stopped, let Juan, the bank clerk from La Laguna and me out, turned around, and disappeared back downhill into the glistening mist.

We looked around. There was almost no vegetation whatsoever. Below, a carpet of billowing white clouds swirled around the slopes cutting off our view of the island. Above, scorched red and black, rose the rim of Teide's volcanic cone. The thin air was fresh and the breeze chill, but the sun beat down warmly on our skin. No sign of life at all save a rusted metal post bearing a rusted metal arrow bearing the remnants of a stylised painted car pointing upwards. Apparently, car drivers could continue further up the track and park, before having to make the final ascent to the cone, on foot, a distance of several kilometres.

At the end of the track we came on a space devoid of vehicles, but three locals, each with a saddled horse and two mules stood smoking in the thin air. They were waiting for a group of tourists from Puerto la Cruz. The animals were to carry guests and food up to the Refugio for the night. The price was 200 pesetas per person.

We ate some bread and cheese and talked to the guides before braving the foot-path. Dotted about were low bushes of white sweet-smelling flowers. "These are flowering plants unique to Tenerife. They're called retama," our companion from the bus told us. I examined one. It looked like a dwarf version of the yellow-flowering broom that gilded the lower parts of the Scottish hills every spring. The plant was literally growing directly out of the red cinders. Here and there we could even see occasional cedar trees whose lush green contrasted with the red or black or yellow rock they sprang from. We made our way upwards through plains of coloured rock chips strewn with enormous black boulders. Teide had spewed these out of its maw in some earlier, ferocious eruption. As we walked, the loose cinders and chards of rocks slid under our feet sliding us back. Occasionally we'd lose our balance altogether. Fortunately, the slope wasn't so steep that we might cause an avalanche.

After an hour or so we reached the Refugio – the Refuge – and stopped for a rest. The Refugio was an uninviting, stone house offering beds for walkers to spend the night. Our companion left us there.

Juan and I continued on to the next point of interest on the track, la Cueva de Hielo – the Ice Cave. This was a cavern on the side of the cone which became packed with blown snow in winter. The snow compacted into ice, hence the name, Ice Cave. This had been much talked about in Buenavista. Nobody in the village had ever seen ice save in the form of the blocks made in the bar on the plaza and sold to households in summer for their ice-boxes. The idea of 'natural' ice intrigued Canarios. Unfortunately, it had snowed little this past winter and we had to scour the cave to find even the slightest trace. Eventually we discovered some on the floor in the deepest recess. Despite its being well mixed with black lava-dust that was constantly hurled round the mountain by ferocious winds, we dug up some chips, sucked on them and spat out the tiny cinders. We had to boast to our friends about the taste of the ice on our return home!

The day was now getting on and so we sped up the final pitch towards the volcanic cone. En route, we met a group of German tourists descending. They'd spent the previous night at the Refugio and climbed to the peak before dawn to witness the sun rise over the African continent to the east. They spoke no English, Juan and I no German. After exchanging a few comical gesticulations, we continued our ascent.

We passed many cracks in the surface of the cone. They spouted continuous jets of sulphurous fumes that caked the edges of the fissures bright yellow. The rocks around them were hot to the touch. Our erstwhile companion from La Laguna had warned us about these. "You'll see solfitaras – volcanic vents," he'd told us, "the fumes are very dangerous, highly toxic! You must make sure you don't breathe in these gases." At first, we found the solfitaras eerie as well as foul. The very idea of fissures connected directly to the molten interior of Teide was disconcerting. However, there were so many and of so many different sizes, that we became used to them and vied with each other to find the one with the greatest amount of lemony sulphur dusting its edges. We held our breaths a lot!

The yellow cone we'd been climbing for an hour began to narrow and seemed to take on a more severe incline as if to discourage us from attempting to ascend any higher. We were already at 3,700 metres – well over 12,000 feet. The air was thin and the black and yellow summit contrasted sharply with the flawlessly clear-blue sky. The scree was so loose in places that we slid backwards. The only solution was to lie down full-length on the slope and let the increased friction act as a brake. Laughing uproariously at how foolish we felt – and looked – to each other, we struggled upwards. "We haven't come this far to go back without seeing what's inside the caldera – inside the crater itself! Juan was as determined as I was.

Finally, we reached the rim. We stopped, panting for breath in the thin air, and looked down inside. The sudden brightness of the sun reflecting off the caldera's concave, yellow interior forced us to cover our eyes until they grew accustomed to the assault. The crater was maybe two hundred yards or more across, mostly yellow, but there were great red and white rocks littering the crumbly surface. Choking, stinking vapour spewed from menacing solfitaras many times bigger and more threatening than those we'd passed on the way up. Generations of visitors had made paths that criss-crossed the crater and focussed on the largest cracks belching out the most aggressive plumes of murky yellow reek.

Juan and I looked at each other. We were both thinking the same thing. Despite the warning about the toxicity of the fumes, we wanted to get down into that crater and examine some of the most active solfitaras.

"It looks like lots of people have done it before us – what can go wrong?"

And so down into the stinking fumes of the caldera we went, gingerly at first and then with increasing confidence. We poked our fingers into the lemon dusting of sulphur crystals that encrusted the gaping cracks. We even put our ears to some of the larger solfitaras and listened, hoping we might hear the molten fury deep within the mountain; noises that had convinced the Guanches, the original natives of the islands, that Teide – 'Echeide' in their language – was the source of all the evil that beset their world. They had engaged in rituals, and no doubt in human sacrifice, to appease Echeide's unpredictable rage.

The rocks surrounding these larger vents and fissures were scalding to the touch and the putrid, foul gases made us gasp for breath. I began to feel slightly sick. Juan didn't look great either.

I began thinking: We're completely alone inside the crater. If I'm overcome with fumes, Juan will have to drag me up the concave interior and somehow get me over the top to fresh air and safety. On the other hand, I don't stand a chance of dragging Juan out of here. And if we're both overcome...I couldn't bear the thought.

"What do you say we leave now, Juan?" Discretion would definitely be the better part of valour.

"¡Vámonos! – Let's go! I don't feel well." His face was now pale green. Before the situation could get out of hand, we began climbing back up to the black rim. On reaching it, we sat down, faced into the wind that came unimpeded all the way from the Americas and gasped in great lungfuls of fresh air. We admired the awe-inspiring 360-degree view contained entirely within a horizon of water. Nothing moved except the waves rolling in from the Atlantic, long, blue and uniform. To the south, we could see the black-lipped crater of Old Teide, the previous crater before it was overtaken by this, higher one in a cataclysmic eruption. A little to the west and much further away, we could see green banana plantations merge into the blue haze and imagine Buenavista del Norte cradled there.

Juan, one eye closed, a wan smile on his pallid face, pointed dramatically into the blur. "Look! There's Pepe rattling away with his hydraulic drill!" We laughed, drunk with the triumph of victory.

"Everybody in the village is going to be jealous of what we've done," he crowed. "Just imagine! I've lived in Buenavista all my life. I've raised my eyes to Teide every day, and never even once imagined I'd climb the volcano! He gave an ear-splitting roar of joy and immediately vomited up everything he'd eaten since we'd alighted from the bus a couple of hours earlier.

The wind blew chill as we sat on the very summit of Teide at 3,718 metres. Juan gulped air in an effort to recover. I felt like Keats' stout Cortez, eagle-eyed, 'silent upon a peak in Darien'. Much of the island was under cloud cover. To the south, I imagined I could make out smudges that might be El Hierro, La Palma and La Gomera; to the north similar smudges that might be Lanzarote, Fuerteventura and Gran Canaria.

I hadn't mentioned to anybody that I might leave. I was still coming to grips with the conviction that I should return to Scotland and I needed to digest the implications of leaving relative tranquillity in Tenerife for certain vexations at home. As soon as I felt ready, found the moment and the words, I would tell Doña Lutgarda first. She was the person I owed the greatest debt to. In the family warmth of her fonda, the Pension Méndez on la Plaza de los Remedios, I had found the conditions I needed to evolve and grow. To the sound of Juan's deep breathing and the keen wind ringing in my ears, I sat in quiet reflection.

My departure would not be a rejection of the village, its people or their way of life, nor would it reflect an inability on my part to accommodate. I wasn't being drawn by nostalgia. I would return home because I was beginning to appreciate that living life cannot be an easy task; the heartaches and disappointments it brings do not simply evaporate because you decide to ignore them or flee to some distant haven. A turned page merely hides the previous which nevertheless remains forever there despite having been folded out of sight. I was learning that life is not under our control the way building a wall is, drilling a blast-hole to set an explosive charge, or branding banana stalks within a plantation. Life is essentially something uncontrollable that must be engaged in with others whom we love and trust; more like hunting octopus with a dependable partner – a perilous undertaking where you hone your skills, calculate the risks and undertake the task with prudence without ever being absolutely certain of the outcome.

The author on the very peak of Teide, overlooking Las Cañadas, the desert plateau that surrounds the volcano. It is now a national park.

I had imagined that I was becoming part of a new society in Buenavista. Perhaps I was, but only in part. El Loco's near-disaster showed me how intricate, complex and involved true relationships are inescapably interwoven within family and community. My relationship in Buenavista, on the other hand, was relatively simple – so simple that it could be encapsulated in a single phrase; el Extranjero – the Foreigner – exotic, truly welcome, but since bereft of the generation-old ties that bind, essentially lacking. The outsider who must constantly prove himself. Although I lived in the very heart of the village, I sat on its spiritual periphery, a place without competition, a uniquely privileged seat that required little of me save that I not to tread on toes. Or tread so very lightly, apologize, and be forgiven as the clumsy other.

To be sure, I felt that Buenavista was a place from which I could make many new starts. I'd confirmed that I was developing what it took to be self-reliant, that I was an independent being who could choose to negotiate his own route through the world, face options, reflect, select wisely, and not shirk responsibility for having chosen. I could fit in without feeling or causing undue discomfort.

I'd arrived on Tenerife, embraced my village of Buenavista del Norte, in an unconscious search of the experience of home as lived with my grandmother and my family in Coupar Angus. That idyll had been confiscated the year after the War ended, when we moved from the country into the urban anomaly of Dundee, when war-damaged George intruded. In the fonda with Doña Lutgarda, with Pastora, Obdúlia, Angélica and Lula, and with her grandchildren Carmelita, Fónfon, Mariao and Caya, who believed I possessed two tongues, I'd found a temporary haven. I'd thrived on the camaraderie of work-mates on land and on sea; I flourished at the empacadora, branding the export seal into curved green stalks in cool plantations, ably accepted increasing responsibilities entrusted to me by Don Salvador. Now, as I reflected on these matters, I found myself more fit to return to my own. I'd climbed Teide; I felt almost ready to scale my own mountain.

Juan's voice interrupted my reverie. "What time is it?" He'd regained some of his colour.

Because, by now, we were late, we bounded joyfully down the cone, sliding extravagantly in the scree, competing with each other to see just how far a single slide could take us. We stopped to catch our breath outside the Ice Cave but didn't enter, the hellish mystery of the caldera was still in our minds and we didn't want anything to disturb it. At the Refugio, we sat down at an outside table. The exertion had whetted Juan's appetite. He nibbled some cheese and then we sped off down the track again to the road.

We arrived 15 minutes before the bus that would take us back to Orotava was due. I'd eaten very little all day, only gofio amasado from my zurrón. Juan had eaten more, but had left most of it on Teide's cone after reacting badly to the noxious gases and so we used the time to replenish the energy we'd burned in the previous ten hours, and wolfed what was left of our supplies.

We reached Icod shortly before the last guagua to Buenavista was due to leave. Juan stretched out on a bench and slept. I had an expresso with a blob of condensed milk added to it. Nothing ever tasted sweeter.

For the entire week that followed, Juan and I were celebrities. We were stopped in the plaza, on the street and asked all sorts of questions about our trip. Even Pepe-de-la-Perforadora was mollified when Juan insisted to everybody that we had been able to see and hear him quite clearly, rattling away with his pneumatic drill, from the very peak of Teide!

Teide's volcanic cone dominates the entire Island of Tenerife.

23. *Scaling my own Mountain*

Days passed and I still made no mention that I was planning to leave. However, one evening after dinner, as I sat with my map of Tenerife spread out on the table in front of me thinking of all the places I'd been but the many that I'd never explored, I looked up to discover I was alone in the darkening courtyard. Doña Lutgarda was tidying her solitary kitchen. Pastora, Lula and Obdúlia had quietly hung up their pinafores, and left for the camaraderie of the venta in the front room. Here was the perfect opportunity, if I didn't want word of my departure turned into a performance. In all things, Doña Lutgarda was thoughtful and moderate and I was grateful to have the moment to speak to her alone.

"Doña Lutgarda!" She turned at my voice. She too had been absorbed in her own thoughts. "On my next day off, I'm taking the early guagua into Santa Cruz." She was used to my keeping her informed of my movements so she could plan food accordingly. I also did so because, like Pearl, she was genuinely interested.

"Not your passport again, Orlando?"

"No." I paused, grappling for words. "I've decided to inquire about a passage back to Cadiz." Now I'd said it, aloud! Until that moment, it had been an idea, a feeling that sooner or later it would be the right thing to do. Now, the full significance of what I'd uttered hit me with the finality of a stick of dynamite exploding in a blast-hole. Words, once spoken, are irretrievable.

Doña Lutgarda finished wiping the pot in her work-red hands. She turned her grey head and looked into my eyes. Along with kindness, I recognized the hard-won wisdom of a mother and a grandmother. I saw the foresight and the understanding of one who had lived and struggled and still bravely bore the sole responsibility for holding an entire family together, for creating harmony and happiness for those closest and dearest. We shared the moment in silence.

"So, you're leaving us, Orlando." Doña Lutgarda's choice of words were confirming: 'leaving us'. Intuitively, she seemed to understand that I still needed encouragement. She was offering me help by giving substance to my words, reassuring me of their rightness.

"Yes." I said it and it didn't sound wrong.

"And when you get off the boat in Cadiz?" She was supporting me,

saving me from stumbling. I'd confided no details of my family circumstances. In Scotland, we held our grimmest secrets fast.

"From there," I was kneading shape from raw clay, "I'll hitch-hike
to Scotland." She nodded.

Her eyes, warm, held mine. "Your mamá will be pleased." She
turned back to her kitchen. Unnecessarily, she rearranged her cooking
pots from largest to smallest. I sat watching.

Doña Lutgarda had drawn me gently to where she knew I needed
to be. She cast a final glance at the perfect row of pots, turned, and
smiled. Her smile said, "Job well done!" She wiped her hands and
placed them on my shoulders. She had never touched me before. It was
an intimate moment, a sacred baptism of approval, an intricate passage
safely negotiated between friends.

Doña Lutgarda was a mother who bore her own history and was
now the matriarch and breadwinner for a large family, overseeing the
growing up-and-away of her own daughters, the raising of the first of
her grandchildren. She well understood the ties that bind and the ties
that beleaguer. Just as I knew nothing of her background or of the husband she must, at one time have had, she knew nothing in detail about
my family. It was as if each of us, the older woman and the young man,
recognised that life held private heartaches for which words were inadequate. The way to respect these secrets was to take care not to chafe
them. Only silent respect had the potential to ease heartache the way
that a warm poultice of aromatic herbs draws the pain from a bruise too
deep for the eye to see.

Doña Lutgarda was right. Pearl would be gratified. Faithfully,
I'd written to Pearl every Friday evening, knowing that she eagerly
shared my welcome news with Vivian and Euan. She had brought us
up to communicate with both her and with each other. George was the
anomaly. He lived in his own private world of fighting fires, delving in a
half-hearted vegetable garden, driving a solitary golf-ball and tinkering
with whichever much-used car he happened to be fixing. He'd disguise
what he couldn't repair, sell it at a modest profit, then feign ignorance
when the vehicle irrecoverably expired on the unwitting purchaser.
That was all he had, all he wanted.

His cars were never for enjoyment, never for family. Once, when
Pearl in a fit of homesickness had asked if he might drive us all out to
Coupar Angus the village where her mother had lived and died and
where her fondest memories still lingered – a distance of less than 14
miles – his barren response had been: "Aye, if you pay for the petrol!"
George had the Midas' touch in reverse; everything he laid his hands on
turned to detritus. He took pride in his singular talent.

From the time I was able, at 12 years old, to go off camping with the Scouts or cycling for two or three weeks around Scotland in summer, Pearl expected a news-filled letter every week. Telephones, besides being beyond our budget, were few and far between. However, the Royal Mail delivered a posted letter the very next day for tuppence. From that beginning, regular communication became habitual, never a chore. Verbal at home, written if away, honest exchange was simply the keyway that drove the joys and the expectations of our everyday lives – routine, clear and sufficient. I'd kept Pearl abreast of my desire to re-apply to Aberdeen University, to work again in Lockwoods' canning factory in Monifieth and to save. The City of Dundee would, on evidence of my having been admitted into a degree course at any Scottish university, pay my fees. I would have to cover the cost of my living expenses, books and clothing myself. I had every confidence that, in addition to summers, I could work winter and spring vacations to earn, save and live frugally during term-time.

My friends were stunned when I quietly told them I was planning to return to Scotland. Pepe Mendibles, Juan-the-Foreman, and Pepe-of-the-Pneumatic-Drill, all tried to dissuade me. They had somehow imagined that I would remain in the village, find a job with long-term prospects, seek out a girl to marry and settle down to family life. El Bachillér resolutely refused to hear of any departure. "Buy yourself a lorry like mine, Orlando. Every day, more and more entrepreneurs are constructing plantations. They'll need reliable carriers. Besides, Tenerife, especially in and around Buenavista, is the best place in the world!"

I tended to agree with El Bachillér that Tenerife, and the region around our village, were unique, but at 18 and with no family history of business enterprise to draw on, I couldn't even begin to envision how to lay my hands on the money to buy a lorry, let alone reinvent myself as an entrepreneur. The idea was beyond my untutored, teenage imagination. Pearl had brought us up to aspire and our teachers at the Morgan had encouraged us to strive. That meant either entering the workforce directly as a trainee or studying at university.

Thoughts of settling, perhaps building a career in Don Salvador's banana business had entered my mind. Epifanio had taught me much about the selection and management of banana stalks, Don Salvador the commercial side of the business. I was aware however, that I knew nothing of the internal structure of the Alhambra brand, neither the nature of the partnership between Don Salvador and Don Pancho nor what the planned line of succession might be.

H' aníbal, Don Pancho's younger son, had taken, occasionally, to assuming duties that usually fell to me. That made me wonder if I was over-stepping myself. Loath to raise the matter with Don Salvador, I went with the current, surrendering any illusion of working my way deeper into Alhambra.

To my surprise, these realities didn't altogether disappoint me. One day, I imagined, I would attend university in Scotland. I'd work directly in some branch of agriculture somewhere in the world. The epiphany I'd experienced, watching El Loco's mother respond to the accident that almost led to his demise, had prized open a primal chamber in my mind. In some inexplicable way, it had given me a deeper appreciation of family and the ties that bind but for which words or reason did not suffice. I would return to Pearl, to Vivian and to Euan. I'd be a source of strength when, together, we made the final break for freedom. No competing primal ties bound me to the village, despite my deep affection and unreserved respect for its people and their way of life.

A proud family shows off its most valued possession -- a well-fed milk-goat.

234

24. Who says you can't go home?

The shipping company that operated the cargo-ferry from Las Palmas, Gran Canaria, to Cadiz on the Iberian Peninsula, had an office in a venerable old building near the docks. These same premises also housed other businesses that offered a broad range of marine services. Each boasted its own, polished brass plate.

"¡Buenos días! How can I help you, Señor?"

"¡Buenos días! I need a one-way passage from Las Palmas to the Peninsula." I searched for the Spanish equivalent of 'steerage' but the best I could do was: "The cheapest passage available."

"Of course, Señor. In Spain as in Scotland, poverty was more common than abundance. When were you thinking of travelling?" The clerk's matter of fact tone took me aback. For me, this wasn't just 'thinking about travelling', it was a was a monumental decision that would separate me from the only world I had known for the better part of a year. The three-day voyage would transport me back to all that I had intentionally left behind a century-like twelve months ago.

But of course! A shipping-clerk's, query about a clients' travel plans, was a mundane task. His practised questions had, for him, no more significance than the polite, "What brand?" had for a tobacconist when asked for a packet of cigarettes. It occurred to me how little we know, or even want to know about the private, inner lives of the vast majority of those we come into contact with, about their secret, inner hopes and fears, as separately yet together we all go about our daily chores.

"As soon as possible." The neutral tone belied my inner tumult.

He consulted a schedule. "We have a third-class berth on...let me see...*La Ciudad de Cádiz* scheduled to leave Las Palmas on the 10th of June. Might that suit?"

"Perfectly!" The symmetry pleased me. There was something fitting about returning on the very same boat that had brought me to the Canary Islands a lifetime ago. The clerk made out my receipt; I passed over the fare; the matter was settled. I was going home! The thought both excited me and caused me apprehension. I found it difficult to sort out, even identify, all the reasons why this should be so. At least, I thought, I'm going back a different person from the one who bought the passage in the opposite direction last year. My return meant that I was in charge; coping, not defeated.

I was aware now, and had come to accept in a way that I hadn't a year earlier, that life might be the hand fate dealt, but how I played those cards was entirely up to me. The rules even allowed me the freedom to select a card off the top of the deck and discard any of those I held, the one that fitted least.

"Here!" On a sketch-plan of the ship, the clerk pointed to a tiny space deep in the bows below the water-line. "You will be sharing with 12 others. An upper or lower berth?"

"Upper!" I wanted to be elevated. Many passengers would be seasick even if the weather cooperated which, in that part of the Atlantic, was unlikely. He inked a cross on the plan and wrote the number of the berth on my receipt.

"Where would you prefer to disembark?"

"I have an option?"

"You can disembark in Cadiz, Señor, but the voyage terminates in Seville."

Surprised, I hesitated. "Most passengers disembark in Cadiz, Señor."

"Why?"

"After leaving Cadiz, the boat takes almost an entire day to get to Seville. It's not far, only 100 kilometres or so, but traffic on the Guadalquivir is limited to just a few knots, so the voyage up the river is very slow." Pen poised, he raised his eyebrows.

Slow appealed to me; very slow, even more so. "Seville!" The idea of floating unhurriedly in an ocean-going ship up the Guadalquivir captured my imagination. 'Guadalquivir!' I savoured the four syllables. They represented music and mystery. Scotland's rushing rivers were monosyllabic, the Tay, Forth, Clyde, Spey, the Esk, the Isla. From our economic geography classes in the Morgan, I recalled that Magellan had begun his circumnavigation of the world from Seville and that cork, the bark harvested from live oak trees, was still exported in dry bundles from its quays.

Almost as soon as we'd cast-off and headed north, we ran headlong into scouring winds and massive, green waves. As had happened the year before, when I was making my south from the Peninsula in the same ship, the captain felt it necessary to take refuge close into the relative shelter afforded by the Moroccan coast. We poised there, bow to the wind, engine-power reduced.

I spent most of my time clinging to a rail on the forecastle, revelling in the spectacle of man's persistence in the face of nature. I left my spot only to eat in the empty dining-room and to sleep during darkness, in my berth down below in steerage. I thought of Tenerife dominated by the majestic Teide; of Buenavista, the fonda, Doña Lutgarda and her extended family. I gave thanks for how they and the many whom I had befriended, had given me more than they could ever know, more than I could ever repay, in my search for understanding.

The gale blew itself out and the ship resumed its voyage towards the Peninsula. "We'll arrive in Cadiz on the 15th," a deckhand told me. And when I rose before dawn to watch the coast of Spain emerge on the horizon, I whispered aloud to myself:

"Today is the 15th of June, 1961. Happy 19th birthday, Orlando!"

Doña Lutgarda and the author, Ronald Mackay in 1995.

Honourable Aurelio Abreu Expósito, Mayor of Buenavista del Norte, on behalf of all the villagers who had so warmly embraced me and taught me so much all those years ago, welcomed me back in 1995. This story is my way of saying: "¡Gracias, Buenavista! ¡Gracias Tenerife! ¡Con un gran afecto para todos!"

The End

CPSIA information can be obtained
at www.ICGtesting.com
Printed in the USA
LVOW03s0028251017

553657LV00003B/3/P